D0264027

Psychological perspectives on sexual problems

Sexuality has always been conceptualised as a potential problem. The regulation of sexuality and the distinction between normality (healthy sexuality) and abnormality (sexual problem) have a long history, in which psychologists have been deeply involved. Yet all attempts to develop a single psychology of sexual problems are fraught with difficulties. There has also been much criticism of the idea of a psychology of sexuality, and of dysfunction, particularly from authorities in psychoanalysis and feminism.

In *Psychological Perspectives on Sexual Problems* these controversies and debates are critically examined, while also addressing the need for individuals with difficulties associated with sexuality to receive help.

Psychological theories associated with sexuality and sexual problems are examined, along with examples of positive and empowering practice with groups of individuals whose sexuality is often marginalised by psychologists. These include people with learning difficulties or physical disabilities, sex offenders, injecting drug users, gay men with AIDS and women with eating disorders.

Psychological Perspectives on Sexual Problems is the first book to integrate critical theory and current clinical practice. It offers a radical new approach to the psychology of sexuality.

Jane M. Ussher is Lecturer in Psychology at University College London, and **Christine D. Baker** is Clinical Psychologist in the Psychology Department at the General Hospital in Jersey.

Also available from Routledge:

Gender Issues in Clinical Psychology
Jane M. Ussher and Paula Nicolson

The Psychology of the Female Body
Jane M. Ussher

The Psychological Treatment of Depression, Second Edition
J. Mark G. Williams

Psychological perspectives on sexual problems

New directions in theory and practice

Edited by
Jane M. Ussher and
Christine D. Baker

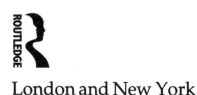

London and New York

First published in 1993 by
Routledge
11 New Fetter Lane, London EC4P 4EE

Simultaneously published in the USA and Canada by
Routledge
a division of Routledge, Chapman and Hall Inc.
29 West 35th Street, New York, NY 10001

© 1993 Jane M. Ussher and Christine D. Baker, the collection as a whole;
individual chapters, the contributors

Typeset in 10/12pt Palatino by LaserScript Limited, Mitcham, Surrey
Printed and bound in Great Britain by
Mackays of Chatham plc, Chatham, Kent

All rights reserved. No part of this book may be reprinted or reproduced or
utilized in any form or by any electronic, mechanical, or other means, now
known or hereafter invented, including photocopying and recording, or in any
information storage or retrieval system, without permission in writing from the
publishers.

British Library Cataloguing in Publication Data

A catalogue record for this book is available from the British Library.

Library of Congress Cataloging in Publication Data

Psychological perspectives on sexual problems: new directions in theory and
    practice/edited by Jane M. Ussher and Christine D. Baker.
    p. cm.
    Includes bibliographical references and index.
    1. Sex therapy – Philosophy.   2. Psychosexual disorders.
    3. Sex (Psychology) I. Ussher, Jane M., 1961– . II. Baker, Christine D.
    [DNLM: 1. Sex Disorders – Psychology.   WM 611 P9738]
    RC557.P78   1992
    616.85'83'0019 – dc20
    DNLM/DLC
    for Library of Congress   92-13346
                                                                          CIP

ISBN 0–415–05508–3 (hbk)
ISBN 0–415–05509–1 (pbk)

Contents

Figures and tables

Contributors

Christine D. Baker is a Clinical Psychologist currently working in Jersey. She has an interest in adult mental health and particularly the sexual problems of adults.

Jan Burns is a Clinical Psychologist, presently both teaching on the Leeds MSc in Clinical Psychology and carrying out research for Bradford Health Authority. Her interests include services for people with learning difficulties, service evaluation, and issues concerning women in forensic services.

Stephen Frosh is Senior Lecturer in Psychology at Birkbeck College, University of London, and Consultant Child Psychologist in the Child and Family Department of the Tavistock Clinic, London. He is author or co-author of several books, including *Identity Crisis: Modernity Psychoanalysis and the Self* (1991), *Psychoanalysis and Psychology* (1989), and *The Politics of Psychoanalysis* (1987).

Heather George is Top Grade Clinical Psychologist for Brighton Health Authority HIV/AIDS Services and Honorary Secretary of the Division of Clinical Psychology AIDS/HIV Psychology Special Interest Group. Since 1985 she has specialised in the practice of clinical psychology as applied to AIDS/HIV, psychosexual and relationship difficulties, and terminal care and bereavement.

Geraldine Mulleady is a Clinical Psychologist who worked for six and a half years at St Mary's Hospital Drug Dependency Unit, specialising in drug use and HIV. She is currently working for Bromley Health Authority in HIV and AIDS. She has written a number of publications, including *Counselling Drug Users about HIV and AIDS* (1991).

Paula Nicolson is a Lecturer in Psychology in the Department of Academic Psychiatry, Sheffield University. Her research interests include female reproduction, sexual harassment and female sexuality. Her publications include (with Jane Ussher) *Gender Issues in Clinical Psychology* (1992) and *The Psychology of Women's Health and Health Care* (1992).

Derek Perkins is Head of the Clinical Psychology Services at Broadmoor Hospital. He has published extensively in the area of forensic psychology, and has a special interest in work with sex offenders.

Padmal de Silva is Senior Lecturer in Psychology at the Institute of Psychiatry, University of London, and Consultant Psychologist for the Bethlem Royal and Maudsley Special Health Authority. His clinical and research interests include obsessive-compulsive disorder, sexual and marital problems, and eating disorders. He is the author of many papers in these areas.

Jane M. Ussher is a Lecturer in Psychology at University College London, and is a qualified Clinical Psychologist. Her interests include female reproduction, gender issues in mental health, and sexuality. Her publications include *The Psychology of the Female Body* (1989) and *Women's Madness: Misogyny or Mental Illness* (1991).

Chris Williams is Director of Psychology Services for Exeter and District Community Health Services Trust and Honorary Lecturer in Psychology at the University of Exeter. He is actively involved in aspects of sexuality and disability focusing on service delivery. He has also published in learning disability and sensory impairment.

Introduction

Sexuality: whose problem?

Sexuality has always been conceptualised as a potential problem. The regulation of sexuality and the careful distinction between normality (healthy sexuality) and abnormality (problem) has a long and chequered history. Yet throughout history, and across different cultures, the definition of exactly *what* is problematic about sex is clearly not invariant. Nor is the identity of the multitude of experts who pronounce and proclaim on the rights and wrongs of sex. For, whilst psychologists may now have confidently adopted the mantle of authority, attempting to understand the significance of sex, uncover the aetiology of problems, and prescribe appropriate cures, this is a relatively recent phenomenon. Prior to the 'psychiatrisation of sex' (Foucault, 1979) in the eighteenth century, and the subsequent development of sexology in the early twentieth century, the notion of psychological explanation or intervention in the private arena of sex was unheard of. If considered at all, sex was simply a biological drive; or, in theological doctrine, a licentious lust stimulated by the devil. That which crossed the boundaries of the current orthodoxy, be it manifestations of homosexual desire in a heterosexually orientated culture, women manifesting desire for men outside the bounds of wedlock, sex during menstruation, during old age, or within families, would undoubtedly have been contained and controlled, but certainly not 'cured'.

Today we don't punish, or segregate, or enforce abstinence upon those who stray from the path of sexual normality (except in the case of sex offenders, who are chastised most severely for their crime). Instead we offer understanding, scientifically validated explanations, and a wide range of medical and psychological interventions for sexual distress, dysfunction, or deviancy. We are careful what we 'treat': for example, homosexuality is no longer framed as illness.[1] We may even go as far as to contest the very notion of a sexual problem as deviation from normality, with our reams of statistics which show sexual difficulties to be the norm. The era of psychologist[2] as sex expert appears to have arrived.

Yet any attempt to identify a simple and unitary 'psychology of sexual problems', to evolve *one* successful paradigm applicable to all, is doomed to failure. There is no one view. Any serious scholar attempting to un-earth common threads of argument between the many theorists, re-searchers, and clinicians may be forgiven for concluding that there is little agreement between protagonists in this debate about definitions of sexuality (never mind what constitutes a sexual problem), about causes of difficulty, and about the right of professionals to intervene. Psychological textbooks on sexuality may appear to belie this fact, presenting sex, sexual problems, and psychological intervention in a straightforward and un-problematic way. In these texts, the problems of men and women are conveniently separated, their common dysfunctions listed, epidemio-logical statistics cited, and the current theories and therapies clearly elucidated. This is not that type of book. The contradictions and incon-sistencies within the psychology of sexual problems are tackled head on, with no flinching, and any notion of an anodyne analysis rejected out of hand.

Yet to cast an eye over what is the current *Zeitgeist* in this field is to reach the inevitable conclusion that the psychology of sexual problems, whatever that is, is in the doldrums. Even a leading expert in the field, a proponent of the psychological approach, has said as much (Bancroft, 1989). Practices evolved many decades ago (e.g. Kinsey; Masters and Johnson) appear to be still adopted unproblematically, as if the difference between the sexual climate of the 1960s and that of the 1990s had little bearing on sexuality or on intervention; as if the nature of relationships, and the demands made upon them, had not changed over the decades, to the extent that there is no longer a clear blue-print mapping out our expectations and behaviour; as if the stimulus–response view of sex, however enlightened it appeared at the time (particularly in the insistence on the existence of female desire and orgasm), could not be improved upon; as if sexuality, and therefore sexual problems, could be framed in an unproblematic way, without reference to culture, to history, to the dominant (and often oppressive) discourses of sexuality which permeate our society; as if the critiques and reformulations of sexuality which have taken place over the last three decades did not exist. If we still rigidly adopted Kraepelin's[3] taxonomies in psychiatry, there would be cause for complaint. Is this not what will be happening in the field of sexuality if we do not re-evaluate our current practices?

Yet outside psychology the debate on sexuality has been raging for many years, untouched by lack of interest and disavowal on the part of the sex experts. How can this be? How can the debates raging in fields such as philosophy, history, literary theory, psychoanalysis, or feminism fail to touch the very people who offer direct analysis and solace to those who find their sexuality problematic, those who have turned to the experts for help? Is there any common ground to be found between those who pronounce, for example, on the efficacy of the Masters and Johnson 'stop/start' technique for treating male premature ejaculation, or the need to introduce vaginal dilators gradually to treat female vaginismus, and, alternatively, those who focus on the belief that the penis signifies the phallus, the all-powerful, condemning women (the penis-less) to a secondary sexuality, an eternal lack, and men to grandiose and mistaken beliefs that the phallus is theirs – when it is not? Is there any common ground between those who advocate rational clinical treatments for sexual problems, and those who would deconstruct the whole notion of dysfunction, seeing it as yet another strand in regulation of the body, the pathologization of normality, or part of the discourse which maintains the pre-eminence of patriarchal heterosexuality? We think that there is.

The aim of this book is to provoke. Equally, we want to promote a glasnost between those whose work directly involves research and intervention in the arena of sexuality and those who would deconstruct, criticise, and reframe any understanding of sexuality outside the dominant discourse of psychology. These are not traditionally happy bedfellows (sic). The debates tend to occupy separate spheres: two circles which never meet, two worlds apparently without a common thread. This is wrong. There is common ground, yet also need for debate, so that integration can occur, and progress be made in both theory and practice. The post-structuralist deconstructions, the psychoanalytic accounts, the feminist or social constructionist analysis could be said to have had little or no impact outside the hallowed walls of academia, and certainly appear to have had little impact on clinical practice as yet. The applicability of these analyses to the reality of sexuality for individual men and women, often in severe distress, is unclear. Yet conversely, sexuality and sexual problems appear to be framed in an uncritical, decontextualised way within the psychology of human sexuality. Can a meeting of the two create a catalyst which will create fusion?

A MEETING OF TWO MINDS

The genesis of this book is in a meeting of two minds wherein very different perspectives and beliefs dwell. Yet reconciliation of views was reached. One is a practising clinician, daily dealing with the reality of sexual difficulty in women and men, using a range of clinical tools to provide amelioration of distress, and finding much success. The other is a lapsed clinician, research and critical theory having been adopted as a means of understanding sexuality, in the face of disenchantment with clinical practice, critiques of the psychology of sexuality being adopted in its stead.

What became clear was that despite appearances, there was much common ground. On the one hand, whilst tried and tested interventions for sexual difficulties were clearly efficacious for the clinician, underlying each therapeutic encounter was a basic questioning of the dominant discourses of sexuality current in our culture: a questioning of the association of sex with penetrative heterosexual intercourse; of the belief that anything else is secondary, or deviant; that failure to achieve penetration is evidence of dysfunction. Premises at the centre of the apparently contradictory critiques had permeated clinical practice.

For example, a woman presented with vaginismus. She had been referred by her GP, having been married for a number of years without ever having achieved penetrative sex with her husband. Perhaps clearly a case for intervention. But the marriage was a success, the couple having adopted a wide sexual repertoire, and both were sexually satisfied. It was only because the woman was unable to perform the 'normal' female function of accepting the erect male member into her vagina and thereby achieving pleasure that therapy was sought. After much discussion it became clear that neither partner was greatly dissatisfied, and a description of the accepted treatment for such 'dysfunction' was greeted with horror. No therapy was carried out. The woman was reassured that she should continue to enjoy her sexuality, her relationship, and not worry about the absence of intercourse, for, as she did not want children and both parties were happy, she did not have a problem.[4]

This is certainly not the oppressive model of sex therapy represented in many critiques (see Jeffreys, 1990). It is positive practice, acknowledging that sexuality is a complex, multifaceted phenomenon, wherein sexual intercourse is neither necessary nor sufficient for satisfaction; where sensuality is as important as genital sexuality, and where the cultural definitions of what it is to be 'normally' sexual are integrated into clinical practice. At the same time, the lapsed clinician recognised that theoretical critiques on their own are not enough; that the reality of distress, despair, and disenchantment in the realm of sexuality must be recognised, and then addressed. Deconstruction is only the first step; on its own it is not enough.

What we need is a new psychology of sexuality, which does not operate within narrow parameters, defining its modus operandi at the outset, without reference to the needs of individuals or the multiplicity of sexuality in its many forms. We need to acknowledge that sexuality is not a unitary entity, something to be pinned down, categorised, and analysed, or something which can be experienced in an unproblematic way. The very contradictions inherent within sexuality affect us all: the impossibility of desire,[5] the negative construction of both female and male sexuality in our cultural discourse, the all-pervasive representation of the all-sexual person in popular discourse, which contrasts sharply with the reality of many people's lives.[6] Sexuality cannot be separated from the self, it cannot be conceived of in a vacuum. To understand sexuality we must understand relationships, individual identity, and the pressures which impact upon the individual, be they conscious or unconscious: the pressure to perform, the pressure to be normal, the pressure to be sexual, as well as the difficulty in resolving unconscious desire and conflict. We must also address the question of who has the right to be sexual (or the right *not* to be sexual), and in what way, and who has the right to help, should they so desire. People with disabilities, those who are lesbian or gay, those who commit sexual crimes, may be seen as being outside the psychologist's remit, their sexuality something which is inherently private, because positioned as different or deviant. We do not agree.

This book attempts to address many of these issues and illustrate the influence of these different discourses on individuals with very different experiences. We want to present the critiques, for they have uncovered much that is wrong with current theory and practice. Yet it is important not merely to pay lip service to a progressive discourse, and so we also acknowledge the need for psychology to help those in distress, to attempt to uncover practices which will be ameliorative and empowering. So we have chosen to include contributions from clinicians working in disparate fields in order to illustrate the ways in which progressive practice can evolve. Work with women and men, both heterosexual and homosexual, work with those who have a physical disability, a learning difficulty, those affected by AIDS or drug use, women with eating disorders, those who are sex offenders: analyses of discourses of sexuality associated with each group uncover many common themes, yet each uniquely offers an insight into sexuality. Other areas of work could have been included, but short of producing an encyclopaedia, we have had to limit ourselves to these examples.[7] Some of the contributions may appear contradictory, but as this reflects the current psychological discourse on sexuality, it is important to allow these different voices to be heard. We may not both agree with every contributor in this volume, but we are here not to censor, but to provoke and promote discussion, and to strive for the beginnings of a revolutionary approach to the psychology of sexuality that moves out of the doldrums and into the twenty-first century.

NOTES

1 This applies to the official psychological discourse in Great Britain. In many countries homosexuality is still deemed an illness, and lesbians and gay men subjected to aversion therapy. One might also argue that many individual practitioners in Britain still regard homosexuality as illness.

2 Or psychiatrist: much of the research and theory in the field of sexuality has been developed by psychiatrists. In this instance, as we are discussing the psychology of sexual problems, we are looking at the psychological approach, rather than the specific professional background of the expert.

3 The nineteenth-century German psychiatrist who first classified schizophrenia.
4 A man referred for therapy because he could not sustain an erection for an extended period, yet could satisfy himself and his partner through other means, could be seen to be equally oppressed by a repressive and outmoded model of sexualiy.
5 In the psychoanalytic view desire is always impossible because unconscious and because sexuality is split, so the object of desire can never be achieved. See Frosh in this volume; Mitchell and Rose 1982.
6 For example, the image of the all-orgasmic man or woman in magazines and newspapers. See Nicolson in this volume.
7 What we most regret not including is a contribution on working with individuals from different ethnic or cultural backgrounds. Is it a reflection of the paucity of work in this area or of the pressures impinging on those who carry out clinical practice in this field that our efforts were in vain?

REFERENCES

Bancroft, J. (1989) *Human Sexuality and its Problems*, 2nd edition, London: Churchill Livingstone,
Foucault, M. (1979) *History of Sexuality*, Vol. I, London: Allen Lane.
Jeffreys, S. (1990) *Anticlimax: A Feminist Perspective on the Sexual Revolution*, London: The Women's Press.
Mitchell, J. and Rose, J. (1982) *Feminine Sexuality: Jacques Lacan and the Ecole Freudienne*, London: Macmillan.

Part I

Theory: deconstructing sexology, reconstructing sexuality

The three chapters in this first section represent a critical perspective, taking issue with traditional psychological conceptualisations of female and male sexuality. Whilst the approach of the early twentieth-century sexologists has been consigned to history by modern sex therapists, it is seen as having laid the foundations for a reductionist view of sexuality and sexual problems, which still exists today. Thus, by deconstructing sexology, by refusing to conceive of sexuality as an unproblematic pre-given entity, the flaws in much of our current theories and therapies can be exposed. However, this is only the first step in reconstructing a positive and empowering psychology of sexuality, and these three authors lay the theoretical foundations for the clinical considerations later in this volume.

The first chapter, by Jane Ussher, takes the notion of a sexual problem, and places it in historical context, whilst critically evaluating the current research and theory on female sexual problems. Ussher argues that current psychological therapies and practices potentially act to oppress women, through conceiving of sexuality in a reductionist manner, either as a dysfunction or as an easily manipulated experimental variable. The second chapter, by Stephen Frosh, examines masculine sexuality, whilst addressing the question 'why do men sexually abuse children?'. From a psychoanalytic perspective, Frosh argues that masculine sexuality, as it is presently constructed, is an almost impossible conundrum. The third chapter, by Paula Nicolson, examines the infiltration of sexology into popular discourse, whilst asking the question 'why do women refer themselves for sex therapy?'. Women's sexual passivity is seen as being reified within dominant psychological discourses associated with sexuality, then internalised by women, who see and believe.

Chapter 1

The construction of female sexual problems
Regulating sex, regulating woman

Jane M. Ussher

INTRODUCTION

To be woman[1] is to be sexual. Yet, paradoxically, woman is also asexual, her sexuality a lack, invisible, a liability, defined always in relation to men, conceived of within a patriarchal prism which confines and distorts experience. The construction of femininity is closely tied to the construction of sexuality, and as sexuality is regulated so are women.

Psychological discourse[2] on the subject of women's sexuality reflects this conundrum. Women are defined by their sexuality within psychology as other, as labile, as unequal to men,[3] often completely absent from the psychological agenda, for fear that they might contaminate the results of experimental research.[4] Yet, at the same time, women's sexuality is ignored or marginalised within psychology or conceived of only as problem. For, in stark contrast to disciplines such as history (Foucault, 1979; Weeks, 1990), psychoanalysis (Freud, 1895; Klein, 1952; Lacan, 1977; Irigaray, 1986), literary theory, or film theory (Rose, 1986), psychology has largely neglected any analysis of female sexuality, except as a dysfunction to be placed under the positivistic microscope.[5] In either case, in this heterosexually orientated discourse, woman's sexuality is positioned as passive, as problematic, but always seen in relation to men.

The central thesis of this chapter is that the psychological discourse on the subject of female sexual dysfunction occupies a central position in the regulation of women,[6] both because the limited, fragmented, and one-dimensional view of sexuality offered within psychology may be internalised by women, who subsequently experience their own sexuality as negative, and because the psychological discourse reinforces the positioning of woman's sexuality as liability within wider cultural discourse. Psychological theory and therapy are proffered by their protagonists as objective, rational, and scientifically validated, whilst in reality they operate within a specific ideological framework, which is both biased and short-sighted – denying the existence of alternative or competing discourses of sexuality (such as the cultural, social, or historical) – and thus is ultimately flawed.

Yet the conundrum feminists are faced with is that many women *do* experience difficulty and discontent associated with their sexuality, and turn to psychologists for help. Problems do exist – and, whilst they are certainly framed by the current discourse, for the individual women they are real. So psychology *may* have a place in providing some explanation and intervention for difficulties – if it can move away from a position in which female sexuality is either ignored or seen as a potential root for pathology.

HISTORY OF PSYCHOLOGY AND SEXUAL PROBLEMS

Theological doctrine

In order to understand the current psychological discourse associated with women's sexual problems, it is essential to have some understanding of the historical context which has led to our present practices and prejudices. From a Foucauldian standpoint, the roots of our current conceptions of sexual problems are seen as necessarily grounded in the past, as understandings of what is positioned as normal and abnormal sexuality, and therefore what constitutes a 'problem', are not historically or culturally invariant. The framing of female sexuality as problematic or as invisible is not confined to twentieth-century psychology.

Prior to the 'age of enlightenment' in the eighteenth century, sexuality was understood within the boundaries of theology, as a moral construct, where the teachings of the church served to define what was and what was not 'normal' sexual behaviour (Weeks, 1990). The most commonly accepted view was that sexuality was a biological, instinctive drive that was essentially male, directed at the passive, if seductive, female. Man was driven, woman received. Man's unholy desires, as the theologians clearly deemed them, were invariably attributed to the fatal attraction of the female, his impulses driving him to sow his seed, often forcing him to act against the doctrines of the Christian church. Control was deemed imperative, and was achieved through castigation of female sexuality. For, as psychiatric historians have argued, the collapse of feudalism potentially heralded a move away from theological control of mind and body and thus:

> it became increasingly imperative to the Church to start an anti-erotic movement, which meant that women, the stimulants of men's licentiousness, were made suspect . . . they [were seen as] carriers of the devil.
>
> (Alexander and Selesnick, 1966: 67)

Thus, whilst men were positioned as the active driving force, the 'naturally' sexual beings, women were seen to be playing a key role in arousing male desire. Woman's sexuality was therefore both fatal and flawed – paradoxically framed either as absent, within the archetype of the asexual pure Madonna, or as all-encompassing and dangerously omnipotent, an image represented most clearly by the witch or the whore (Ussher, 1991). The other side of this essentialist coin is that *normal* sexuality was seen as an 'instinct for reproduction' (Weeks, 1990: 143), firmly contained within marriage, the individual ultimately motivated by the desire to bear children. Both views clearly locate sexuality in the heterosexual act of intercourse. In its other forms it was invisible or, if acknowledged, perverse and therefore condemned.

Nineteenth-century science

The eighteenth and nineteenth centuries saw the establishment of the (male) expert who assumed the legitimacy which allowed him to pronounce upon the rights and wrongs of sexuality: what Foucault (1979) has termed the psychiatrisation of sex. Psychiatry was used to define the boundaries of normality and abnormality, effectively prescribing sexuality for both men and women. When previously those who were intent on preserving the institutions of the family and patriarchal power might have used theological discourse to curb and control women's supposedly abhorrent sexuality, in the nineteenth century they turned to science. So, in the same way as woman's unhappiness or despair was couched within psychiatric nosology (Showalter, 1987; Ussher, 1991), so was her sexuality. And, whilst many of the new 'disorders', such as masturbation, nymphomania, frigidity, homosexuality (termed 'inversion'), and a host of other 'minor perversions', were categories of illness which could be applied to men or women, female sexuality was undoubtedly more carefully scrutinised and controlled. For, after the eighteenth century:

> the female body was analysed – qualified and disqualified – as being thoroughly saturated with sexuality; whereby it was integrated into the sphere of medical practices, by reason of a pathology intrinsic to it.
> (Foucault, 1967)

Sexuality was reduced to what Foucault has termed 'aberrations, perversions, exceptional oddities, pathological abatements, and morbid aggravations' (1979: 53), most clearly exemplified in Krafft-Ebing's 1890 encyclopaedia which detailed the 'various psycho-pathological manifestations of sexual life' through the use of individual case histories. Sexuality outside the strictly prescribed bounds of normality was perceived to be the root cause of pathology, of madness, for, as Henry Maudsley (1873: 83) commented, 'we have to note, indeed, to note and bear in mind how often sexual feelings arise and display themselves in all sorts of insanity': an insanity which women were deemed to be more prone to experience (Ussher, 1991).

Within the scientific discourse the individual was clearly the focus of attention, social or historical context ignored. Sexual problems or deviancies (often seen as synonymous) were either deemed to have arisen from innate biological factors or were believed to be manifestations of some degenerative process (Bancroft, 1974). Yet there was also a school of thought which saw dysfunction as having been acquired through learning or childhood experiences: a foretaste of the split between the expert positions of today.

These different aetiological theories clearly had different implications for treatment, which at the essentialist extreme could be crude and disfiguring. For example, many women were subjected to Mitchell's rest cure, which involved enforced bed-rest in a darkened room with no stimulation and forced feeding of gruel, for disorders of hysteria and masturbation, both thought to be connected to an over-active sexuality (Tissot, 1769). Equally, ovariectomy was regularly offered for a host of female complaints, including nymphomania (Szasz, 1981). Its pioneer, Robert Battey, claimed:

> I have hoped through the intervention of the great nervous revolution which ordinarily accompanies the climacteric, to uproot and remove serious sexual disorders and reestablish general health.[7]

A treatment which literally removed the offending organ at the root of women's sexual dysfunction, clitoridectomy, was pioneered by the medic Issac Baker Brown for the 'sexual perversion of masturbation', but was thought to be efficacious in treating a host of other female complaints. Clitoridectomy exemplifies the contradiction wherein female sexuality is seen as the root of a host of pathologies, yet at the same time is denied or disregarded. For this barbaric surgery (with no proven efficacy), whilst offered as a panacea for a host of 'female complaints', was at the same time not expected to have any great effect on a woman's mood or self-esteem, as it was believed that it was 'irrelevant to a woman's feeling whether she had sex organs or not' (Barker-Benfield, 1976: 125). It implies that the very existence of the female sexual organs could only have a detrimental effect on the woman's psyche.

Yet the era of the 'little knife' as an antidote to dysfunctional or deviant sexuality was short lived, for, at the beginning of the twentieth century, psychological techniques were introduced.[8] As early as 1895 Schrenck-Notzing advocated psychological methods to 'create series of habits by means of direct persuasion, acts, imitation and admiration' (Bancroft, 1974: 23), using this technique primarily to 'treat' homosexuality. Yet it was in the early twentieth century that the research of the sexologists and the new therapeutic techniques of the psychologists really came into their own. Women's sexuality was finally bracketed, controlled, and – if problematic – able to be cured.

Twentieth-century sexology

In the early twentieth century the rapidly burgeoning discipline of sexology, which formed the foundation of our current psychological theories and practices, was dominated by the work of Havelock Ellis and Sigmund Freud. Both were initially vilified for their supposedly 'incorrect' or 'hazardous' theories (Weeks, 1990: 142), but were subsequently influential in analysing and proposing treatment of so-called 'normal' sexual difficulties. On the subject of women they were less than objective – despite their adoption of the mantle of neutral scientist.[9]

Ellis advocated and celebrated as 'natural' the traditional gender roles laid down for men and women, categorically stating that 'woman breeds and tends; man provides'.[10] In this view, women were designed with reproduction in mind, with female sexual pleasure (Ellis did at least acknowledge the existence of female orgasm) serving evolutionary ends in ensuring copulation. That female orgasm could exist outside a sexual relationship with a man was inconceivable: women were believed to become aroused only following 'the stimulation of the male at the right moment.[11]

It is not surprising then that the lesbian presented a particular challenge to Ellis's theory, for, as Jeffrey Weeks explains:

> Whilst he [Ellis] recognised the legitimacy of female homosexuality (his wife was a lesbian) he obviously found it difficult to conceptualise in terms of his sexual theories . . . it was as if he could only conceptualise lesbianism as a masculinization of the woman, whereas today many tend to see female homosexuality as the ultimate in female autonomy from men.
>
> (Weeks, 1990: 147)

As an inherent 'abnormality', female inversion (lesbianism) was reduced to hormonal imbalances or irregularities: a distortion of the *normal* 'courtship' ritual of the male wooing the female – an unwelcome challenge to the firmly held notion of the secondary nature of female sexuality. Yet, whilst he was convinced of the naturalness of the heterosexual (and it was assumed male-dominated) union, Ellis was not reactionary in his support of expression of active female sexuality, within marriage, unlike his Victorian predecessors. Believing that individuals were potentially 'polysexual', he advocated marriage predominantly as a keystone of social policy, which in Ellis's view should be egalitarian, moving away from the traditional model within which women's rights were ignored: certainly a radical view in its time.

Whilst Ellis, with his emphasis on a continuum between normality and abnormality, his potentially positive view of sexuality, and his acknowledgement of the existence of female pleasure, provided a benchmark for researchers and clinicians of the twentieth century, Freud was equally if not more influential. Freud finally moved the analysis of sexuality from the biological to the psychological arena. For, whilst the belief in a biological sexual drive was still present in his theorising, sexuality was conceived of as a socially located instinct, with central aspects repressed as a result of cultural norms and mores.

Freud's postulations on the subject of female sexuality have presented succeeding generations of scholars with ammunition for either a complete disavowal of psychoanalytic theories on the grounds of misogyny (e.g. Figes, 1970) or its adoption as the mainstay of a feminist re-analysis of women's sexuality and psyche (e.g. Mitchell and Rose, 1982: Irigaray, 1988). In arguing for a basic bisexuality which is only socially channelled into heterosexuality, Freud drew attention to the large element of repression in all sexuality. Through the experience of childhood, girl children came to experience their sexuality as a lack, their non-possession of a penis as a loss. Always seen in relation to men, following the Oedipal stage of development, women's sexuality was essentially castrated, the physical reality of the 'inferior' organs sentencing women to a lifetime of neurosis and unresolved conflict – which could be resolved only through psychoanalysis or through symbolic acquisition of the phallus following childbirth.

Recent feminist analyses (e.g. Mitchell, 1974) have rejected the view that Freud was misogynistic, arguing that in positioning woman's sexuality as castrated or as a lack, he was merely *reflecting* the dominant cultural discourse, rather than prescribing it. However, Freud's influence in laying the foundations of the late twentieth-century psychological discourse on female sexuality cannot be underestimated. With Ellis, he established once and for all the legitimacy of the scientific analysis of sexuality[12] – and reinforced the association between pathology and sexuality (Breuer and Freud 1895: 246). Both reaffirmed the right of the (male) expert to pronounce upon the subject of female sexuality, the right to frame it within a psychological prism.

PSYCHOLOGY AND THE PROBLEM OF FEMALE SEXUALITY

Women's sexuality under the microscope

In the late twentieth century the dominant discourse of psychology and psychiatry, if it considers women's sexuality at all, classifies it clearly, concisely, and clinically. 'Normal' female sexuality is certainly marginalised or ignored, for, as one commentator noted, 'the issue of female sexuality has been a puzzlement to male social scientists and they have usually elected to ignore it' (Plummer, 1984: 227).

The same could be said of clinicians. For, whilst the categorisation of male sexual problems is seen as relatively straightforward, with attention generally being focused on performance-related problems, such as premature or retarded ejaculation, or erectile dysfunction, as Cole (1988a: 35) comments:

> sexual disorders in women, with the possible exception of vaginismus ... are by their very nature less easily categorized because of the more complex nature of women's sexual responses.

So clinicians often ignore the sexual problems of women.

A further difficulty which psychologists face is that of quantifying the extent of sexual problems in women. The activity of arriving at accurate epidemiological statistics is fraught with difficulty, for sexuality remains an aspect of experience positioned very much in the private domain, and thus is rarely discussed by clinicians (Ussher, 1990) or by individuals who might experience difficulty (Friedman *et al.*, 1986). The two avenues of study for those collecting statistics are studies of clinic attenders or general surveys of the population, and, whilst questions have been raised in relation to the representative nature of the samples of women used and the validity and reliability of the results presented (Bancroft, 1983), prevalence rates are certainly high.

Quantifying sexual dysfunction

The female sexual problems which have been categorised are generally described thus:

a) anorgasmia
b) inhibited sexual desire/general sexual dysfunction
c) vaginismus and dyspareunia.

The host of disorders and minor perversions floridly described in the nineteenth-century literature have been reduced to these supposedly more objectively defined categories – apparently afflicting large numbers of women. For example, examining clinic attenders, Masters and Johnson (1966) reported that out of a sample of 342 women 91 per cent experienced orgasmic dysfunction and 9 per cent suffered from vaginismus or dyspareunia. Similarly, Bancroft and Coles (1976) in analysis of 102 women who attended a sex-therapy clinic over a three-year period claimed that 62 per cent of women experienced general sexual problems, 18 per cent were anorgasmic, and 12 per cent suffered from vaginismus or dyspareunia. Mears (1978) reported that out of 1330 clinic attenders 51 per cent experienced general sexual dysfunction, 22 per cent were anorgasmic, and 15 per cent suffered from vaginismus or dyspareunia.

When more general populations of women are questioned, such as through a sexual survey,[13] similarly high rates of problems are suggested. On the subject of anorgasmia in women the estimates range from Hite (1976) who claimed 29 per cent of 3000 women respondents never or almost never achieved orgasm, to Garde and Lunde (1980) who claimed only 4 per cent of their sample of 225 women were anorgasmic. Others report 19 per cent (Chester and Walker, 1980), 15 per cent (Frank *et al.*, 1978), 7 per cent (Hunt, 1974), 5 per cent (Pietropinto and Simenauer, 1977), and 4 per cent (Saunders, 1985) to be anorgasmic. Vaginismus is reported to affect between 1 and 4 per cent of women (Pasini, 1977; Catalan *et al.*, 1981), but exact figures are unknown.

Yet, despite the apparent certainty provided by the statistics, categorisation and diagnosis of sexual problems are far from incontrovertible. Firstly, the notion of dysfunction has been contested. One recent author has argued that 'identifying the absence of orgasm in a woman as "dysfunctional" is not only intellectually unacceptable but it can also be therapeutically counterproductive' (Cole, 1988a: 41) – thus challenging many of the theories and treatments currently directed at large numbers of women. Secondly, the type of difficulty necessary for diagnosis is not clear cut. For example, within current psychological discourse a problem is invariably defined as that which is related to pleasure or performance in sexual intercourse. Thus anorgasmia is diagnosed if a woman cannot achieve orgasm through intercourse, but not if she cannot achieve orgasm through masturbation, clearly defining orgasm during vaginal penetration as the normal experience for women. A woman's ability (or unwillingness) to give herself autonomous pleasure is not deemed an issue for the sex experts, unless she is being taught to masturbate as part of a programme of therapy. However, different surveys suggest that strikingly large numbers of women rarely or never achieve 'unassisted' orgasm during intercourse – up to 80 per cent in one study (Saunders, 1985),[14] suggesting that 'anorgasmia' may be experienced by a majority of women, thus challenging the notion of its being pathological. Yet, if Kinsey *et al.*'s (1948) estimate that three-quarters of men ejaculate (and therefore terminate intercourse) after only two minutes of penetration is in any way representative, perhaps it is not too surprising that women are anorgasmic without what is euphemistically termed 'assistance' (clitoral stimulation).

The dysfunction termed 'inhibited sexual desire', the general lack of interest in sex which is supposedly more common in women than in men (Hawton, 1985; Cole and Dryden, 1988), is equally problematic. The manifestations of this 'disorder' include lack of sexual appetite, boredom, anxiety, and frequently active avoidance of sex. An often related problem is the condition termed 'impaired sexual arousal' – in which women 'fail to become aroused when sexually stimulated by their partners' (Cole and Dryden, 1988: 6) even though *desire* may be present. This unambiguously refers to a pathology within the woman, rather than looking to her partner, or to the relationship, for reasons for her disinterest. Following in the path of the experts of the past, the woman is blamed for the problem of sex.

Whether women consider these so-called dysfunctions to be a problem is also ambiguous. In one American study which reported that 63 per cent of women experienced impaired arousal or anorgasmia (Frank *et al.*, 1978) it was found that 80 per cent of the couples rated their sexual relationship as satisfying. Whether this reflects low expectations of sexual satisfaction, or the adoption of an androcentric view which denies the importance of female arousal, is unclear. What it does suggest is that, whilst these particular 'problems' may be common, most women[15] will grin (or grimace) and bear them in silence.

The invisibility of difficulty

All of the aforementioned problems relating to female sexual dysfunction have vexed researchers and clinicians – as it is claimed that 'blocks in the sexual responses of a woman are *naturally* less conspicuous' than in a man (Cole and Dryden, 1988: 6, my emphasis). As the positivistic approach dominant within psychology invariably relies on accurate measurement and observable phenomena, female sexual responses create a conundrum – if they can't be seen and quantified (as male arousal and dysfunction more easily can) can they be studied?

It is perhaps for this reason that the more measurable problems of vaginismus and dyspareunia have received greater attention from many psychologists. Vaginismus is the term used to describe automatic constriction of the muscles of the vagina upon attempt at penetration by the penis – resulting in the impossibility of intercourse, or, if the man perseveres, extreme pain for the women. Dyspareunia is the diagnosis given to pain experienced by the woman during intercourse – and may include vaginal pain or more general symptoms such as nausea. Whilst positioned as physical problems, both have a clear psychological component. For, as Jehu (1984: 135) describes:

> This is one incidence of a sexual phobia in which certain specific features of sexual activities elicit intense irrational anxiety. The reaction often involves physiological components such as profuse sweating, nausea, vomiting, diarrhoea or palpitations. . . . Even purely affectionate acts, such as a hug or a kiss, may evoke anticipatory

anxiety unless the circumstances are such that a possible progression to sex is ruled out.

So, although vaginismus is statistically less common than the generalised 'disorders of desire', it provides a more amenable focus for research and intervention for many psychologists, as it is more easily identified and measured. It may also be deemed more problematic, as it interferes very directly with a man's ability to penetrate the woman – whereas absence of desire or anorgasmia does not.

Sexual phobias have possibly been a focus of interest for similar reasons – they act to interfere with sexual intercourse, and therefore are a problem for men. Described as 'more common' in women than in men, sexual phobias have been recently exemplified in a text book on sex therapy as:

> an aversion to touching her partner's penis or a fear of having her vulva stimulated by his hand. More common is an aversion in women to semen and of course oral sex, when the woman takes the penis into her mouth, is often totally unacceptable.
>
> (Cole and Dryden, 1988: 9)

This is an interesting example of the pathologisation of women's aversion towards, or unwillingness to engage in, particular sexual acts. In a different era (or in particular religious or cultural groups) the very act of oral sex may be deemed deviant: a problem in itself (in certain American states it is actually illegal). In the liberal world of the late twentieth-century sex experts, women's refusal to engage is the problem: elevated to the status of phobia and thus reified as dysfunction within the psychological discourse. And, as the epidemiological data on female sexual dysfunction make clear, vast numbers of women can be defined as dysfunctional – framed within a psychological framework as abnormal.

Denying 'perversion'

The converse function of this psychological regulation is to make certain aspects of female experience invisible, through exclusion from the agenda of research or therapy. For example, it is interesting that, despite the move to remove homosexuality from the annals of psychiatric nosology in the early 1970s, 'homosexual and related problems' and 'deviance' are included in a recent review (Cole, 1988a) as sexual problems of men, but are not mentioned in relation to women. This may be a relic of the Victorian era wherein lesbianism was maintained as an invisible issue, its existence denied for fear that women stray from the path of hetero-sexuality should they discover the notion of lesbianism (Weeks, 1990). Or it may be that the researchers are reflecting the fact that fewer women have traditionally been 'treated' for their homosexuality, either because their sexuality was more easily ignored by those who might encourage referral – parents and peers – or because there is less tradition in psychology associated with diagnosing and treating lesbianism.

Equally, the literature on 'sexual deviancy', focusing particularly on fetishism, sadomasochism, and related behaviours (cf. Gosselin and Wilson, 1984) invariably omits any mention of women. A textbook on 'the psychology of sexual diversity' (Howells, 1984) mentions women only in passing, referring to the gender-neutral 'subjects and patients' throughout the text, when in reality men are the focus of attention. If perversion is acknowledged (see Richards, 1990), it is often deemed more deviant in women than in men, or used as an indicator of psychiatric diagnosis (Ussher, 1991), for to be female and to be knowingly sexually perverse is an inherent contradiction. The general denial of such perversion in women may be because, as Gosselin and Wilson argue, 'females are much less prone to such distortions' (1984: 106). Or perhaps because women are deemed immune from deviancy, too innocent (or lacking in imagination?) for perversity.[16] Yet is it not more likely that in the main researchers and clinicians are merely concentrating their energies and resources on the sexuality and sexual problems of men, a process familiar within many areas of psychology where male behaviour is the sole focus of attention, at the unquestioned expense of any acknowledgement of the female (see Squire, 1989).

All of this is not merely an academic debate, for women clearly internalise these definitions of 'normal' sexual functioning and as a result refer themselves for help, thus reinforcing the notion of pathology and of the need for expert intervention (see Paula Nicolson's chapter in this volume). For, as Friedman et al. (1986: 69), in an analysis of sex therapy, point out:

> none of the couples stated that they wanted treatment because they believed sexual activity would be pleasurable if they could overcome their fears. Narcissistic motivation predominated, especially the desire to appear 'normal'.

The root of sexual difficulties

Psychologists have not confined themselves to the categorisation and classification of female sexual problems, for, either as researchers or clinicians, they have been active in proffering explanations for the aetiological root of sexual difficulties, invariably advocating particular courses of treatment on the basis of their analysis. Many of the theories are unidimensional, looking to biological factors, such as neurotransmitters (i.e. 5HT) (Riley et al., 1986) or testosterone (Dow and Gallagher, 1989), or to social factors, such as sexual abuse (Jehu, 1989) or marital difficulties (Zimmer, 1987). Table 1.1 provides a summary of some of the recent research to provide an indication of the range of different opinions.

Table 1.1 Aetiological theories of female sexual problems

Aetiological reason	Author	Date	
Sexual abuse:	Charmoli and Athelstan	1988	
	Feinauer	1989	
	Jehu	1989	
	Black	1988	
	Kilpatrick	1986	
	Becker *et al.*	1986	
	Rensick	1983	
	Gazan	1986	
	Gilbert and Cunningham	1986	
Psychological:	Weijmar-Schultz *et al.*	1986	(motivation)
	Stuart *et al.*	1986	(personality)
	Avery-Clark	1986	(career)
	Giovacchini	1986	(rage)
	Nutter and Condron	1983	(no fantasy)
	Masters and Johnson	1966	(religious orthodoxy)
Cognitions:	Phinney *et al.*	1990	
	Goldfarb *et al.*	1988	
	Alizade	1988	
Contraceptive anxiety:	Bruch and Hynes	1987	
Sociobiology:	Bixler	1983	
Marital problems:	Zimmer	1987	
	Stuart *et al.*	1987	
	Whitehead and Mathews	1986	
Menopause:	Cutler *et al.*	1987	
	Reyniak	1987	(osteoporosis)
	Myers and Morokoff	1986	
	Channon and Ballinger	1986	
	Sherwin *et al.*	1985	
Alcohol:	Klassen and Wilsnack	1986	
	Pinhas	1987	
	Covington and Kohen	1984	
	Peterson *et al.*	1984	
	Price and Price	1983	
Men:	Pietropinto	1986	
	Bancroft	1984	

Table 1.1 Continued

Aetiological reason	Author	Date	
Physical:	Stuntz	1986	
Hormones:	Schreiner-Engel *et al.*	1989	
	Benton and Wastell	1986	
	Whitehead and Mathews	1986	
Epilepsy:	Ndegwa *et al.*	1986	
Hyper-prolactinaemia:	Sobrinho *et al.*	1987	
Pelvic pain:	Black	1988	
Cancer:	Bos	1986	
	Weijmar-Schultz *et al.*	1986	
	Thomas	1987	
	Andersen and Jochimsen	1987	
Spinal cord lesion:	Bregman	1978	
Heart attack:	Crenshaw	1986	
	Papadopoulos	1985	
Diabetes:	Prather	1988	
	Schreiner-Engel *et al.*	1987	
	Newman and Bertelson	1986	
	Slob *et al.*	1990	
	Schreiner-Engel	1983	
Vulvectomy:	Stellman *et al.*	1984	
Urethritus/cystitis:	McCormick and Vinson	1988	
	Kaplan and Steege	1983	
	Melman	1983	
	Leiter	1983	
Hysterectomy:	Ananth	1983	
Post-partum:	Debrovner and Shubin	1985	
	Elliott and Watson	1985	(pregnancy)
	Alder and Bancroft	1983	
Menstruation:	Morris *et al.*	1987	
	Bancroft *et al.*	1983	
Arthritis:	Ferguson and Figley	1979	
Psychoanalytic:	Richards	1990	
Social:	Tiefer	1988	
	Piskorz-de-Zimerman	1983	

The different aetiological theories clearly have serious implications in terms of the way in which female sexuality is conceived, and consequently the way in which 'problems' are treated. For example, if we take the case of a woman presenting to a clinician with 'general sexual dysfunction', manifested by lack of desire, if she is deemed to be suffering from endocrine disorders, her treatment may be chemotherapy. If she is deemed to be suffering from the consequences of sexual abuse, her treatment may be psychotherapy, and acceptance that her 'problem' is understandable and normal.

This may seem unproblematic, merely a reflection of the different roots which lead to difficulty in individual women. In some cases, there *may* be a clear aetiological root for a woman's sexual difficulties, yet it is a rare case where one event or illness is the sole root of difficulty, and the assumption of a simple causal relationship between sexuality and physical or psychological factors is misleading (see pp: 25–6). Equally, each of these aetiological theories appears to conceive of the notion of sexual problems as an unproblematic construct, devoid of cultural or historical context, which is clearly inadequate.

In an attempt to move away from the one-dimensional view, a number of psychologists have advocated a more integrated or multidimensional approach, generally taking the view espoused by Bancroft (1983) that sexuality must be conceived of within a psychosomatic circle, where physiology and cognitions interact, which implies that treatment should operate on a number of different levels. This approach may seem the most eclectic in its attempt to move away from an artificially constrained view of female sexuality – yet it is clear that many of those who offer particular interventions for women are operating within narrow parameters, still offering unidimensional therapies, as Table 1.2 illustrates.

It may appear from the confident proclamations of many of these therapists that psychologists have rightly taken over as the gate-keepers of sexual functioning: diagnosing and categorising difficulty, offering explanations of aetiology and therapeutic intervention in order to effect a cure. Yet all is not as it seems. These seemingly uncontroversial analyses adopted by different psychologists invariably conceal an ideological stance which both colours their theory and determines their practice, and which may be detrimental to the needs of the individual woman. For, whilst psychology has traditionally adhered to the discourse of the rational and neutral scientist, there are clearly very different principles in operation within the various paradigms. Whether they can be reconciled, at present, in order to provide any understanding of female sexuality, or the difficulties of the individual woman in distress is debatable. It may be argued that much of the theorising is both misogynistic and misleading, a case which is never more clear than in the sociobiological theories of sexuality, which I will now examine in order to provide illustration of the argument.

Table 1.2 Therapies for sexual problems

Authors	Type of therapy; sample of women studied
Dow and Gallagher, 1989	Testosterone vs. counselling (latter more effective). 30 couples, sexual unresponsiveness in female partner.
Golubtsova and Polishchuk, 1988	Multi-modal: drugs/therapy/acupuncture/diet. 90 women with progressive schizophrenia.
Milan *et al.*, 1988	Group therapy. 38 women, orgasmic dyfunction.
Metz and Seifert, 1988	GPs as sex educators and assessors; women wanted more proactive GP input. 56 women, general population.
Gazan, 1986	Package: relaxation training, cognitive restructuring, treatment of the sexual dysfunctions. 5 sexually abused women and their partners, who sought therapy.
Zimmer, 1987	Cognitive-behavioural therapy: marital therapy vs. relaxation/information (marital more effective). 28 couples, wives secondary sexual dysfunction.
Whitehead *et al.*, 1987	Conjoint M&J therapy vs. women-focused method (both effective). 44 couples, lack of sexual response in women.
Jonsson and Byers, 1986	Graduated modelling in sexually anxious woman. One 22-year-old woman.
Whitehead and Mathews, 1986	M&J counselling plus placebo or testosterone (effective). 48 couples, lack of female sexual response.
Becker *et al.*, 1984	Time limited, behaviourally orientated treatment package. 68 sexually abused women.
Adkins and Jehu, 1985	Behavioural treatment. 6 couples, woman anorgasmic.
Nairne and Hemsley, 1983	Directed masturbatory training. Review.
Rust and Golombok, 1990	Stress reduction and global approach for women. Review.
Riley *et al.*, 1986	Better understanding of hormonal/chemical control of sexual desire in women needed. Review.

Biology as destiny

Our sexual behaviour is controlled by phylogenetically ancient parts of our brain and therefore is best understood at the level of instinct, within the concepts of ethology and sociobiology. In fact, the 'reproductive imperative' is the ultimate principle underlying all human behaviour, since animals survive in proportion to their breeding success.

(Wilson, 1988)

This is not the diatribe of a nineteenth-century patriarch, or a religious zealot, as one might imagine. Whilst it bears a striking resemblance to many of the nineteenth-century pronouncements on women and sexuality, it is the comment of a respected psychologist as recently as 1988. The reductionist belief in biology as destiny is clearly still prevalent in the late twentieth century. And, whilst its proponents may present the biological perspective as the most rational, that which adopts the perspective most closely resembling that of the natural sciences, in reality this paradigm may be the most damaging in reifying negative reductionist discourses associated with female sexuality.

The biological view conceives of sexuality as rooted in the body, as a biologically determined set of instincts and behaviours, which can be clearly differentiated between the sexes. Sex differences in behaviour are seen as 'natural' (Ussher, 1992) and tied to the different reproductive role of males and females, irrevocable and incontrovertible. For example, one theory which has been put forward to explain the apparent sex difference in sexual behaviour is 'parental investment theory', which, according to the psychologist Glenn Wilson, means that the goal of the male is 'to impregnate many females simultaneously, hence his interest in multiple mates of breeding age' (1988: 50). The female, on the other hand, needs to protect her offspring, 'and hence the coyness of the female and their need to build relationships' (1988: 50). The cynic might comment that this very neatly justifies male promiscuity, which in this view is normal, whilst female promiscuity would most certainly be 'abnormal'. It also legitimates a patriarchal social structure, which is seen as being based on 'natural' principles.

Equally, within this view, the choice of what is attractive in a sexual partner is seen as biologically determined. So, whilst men are programmed to seek 'physically attractive women', by which they mean indications of 'fertile ground in which to plant their seed' (Wilson, 1988: 51), women are 'seeking evidence that a man is superior breeding material which means physical strength and skills relevant to defence and provision and willingness to share the burden of child rearing' (Wilson, 1988: 51). Given the evidence that women still take the burden of child rearing even in so-called egalitarian couples (Social Trends, 1992), women are obviously going wrong somewhere.

Out of the current psychological perspectives on female sexuality, the sociobiological view is perhaps the most clearly prejudicial to the interests of women. It merely acts to give pseudo-scientific credence to particular constructions of female beauty, in this case the image of the voluptuous female who, Wilson declares, 'is more desirable with proportionately large breasts and hips . . . and the narrow waist'. The same psycho-biological explanations are used to justify 'the tendency for males to be sexually recharged by novel females' (p. 65). This deserves quotation at length, as an example of the bias in such theorising:

> The tendency for males to be sexually recharged by females has been observed in most mammals (Bermant and Davidson, 1974) and is another manifestation of their reproductively optimal 'promiscuity strategy'. This presents a problem, for men especially, over the course of a long marriage and is responsible for a great deal of adultery. Progressive 'contempt due to familiarity' (at least, as regards sexual excitement) is an almost inevitable outcome of sexually exclusive marriage. It is not unusual for sex therapists to see men who are unable to achieve erection with their wives but perfectly capable of stud like prowess with their new secretary. Once again, what is observed is not a disease but a normal biological phenomenon, and realistic solutions must be sought.
>
> (Wilson, 1988: 65)

It is startling to find this description of sexual behaviour in a mainstream textbook on sex therapy published in 1988. It is clearly misogynistic, conceiving of the man as a driven animal, planting his seed in the receptive female – her power defined by her subordinate status, typified by Wilson's use of the example of the 'attractive secretary'. The woman herself is represented as passive and invisible – interested only in protecting her offspring. How the woman who engages in this illicit liaison is viewed by the essentialist author is unknown; perhaps she is seduced by the 'physical strength and skills' he earlier describes as being most attractive in men.

The advice that 'realistic solutions must be sought' for man's lack of desire in marriage is tantalising. Perhaps it merely feeds into the argument for the provision of novel sexual material for the male, most clearly seen in the use of sexual surrogacy (cf. Cole, 1988b). Or validates and simultaneously excuses promiscuity – in men.

Within the biological model, the other, perhaps more acceptable view is that sexual problems are related to some physical illness or to endocrine function, as is illustrated above (see Table 1.1). Yet, whilst seemingly uncontroversial, are not the latter merely the modern successors to the theories which pronounced upon the hystericisation of women's bodies – the location of difficulty in the womb or the reproductive hormones? Equally, cancer, diabetes, or the menopause may seem simple causes of sexual difficulties, a consistent correlation between identified clinical populations and rates of sexual problems allowing for a strong case to be made for generalisable theories. Yet it is not so simple. As I argued above, it is not enough to posit a physical (or psychological) cause for a sexual difficulty and then treat it out of context of any other facet of a woman's experience. For example, cancer itself does not *cause* sexual difficulties, but the concomitant physical, psychological and social factors associated with disease may result in symptomatology (see Christine Baker's chapter in this volume).

The same critique could be levelled at different models, which might seem diametrically opposite, such as that positing that sexual abuse is the main precursor of sexual difficulty. Sexual abuse may clearly lead to later sexual difficulties in women, as attested by analyses of both clinical and more general population samples (see Table 1.1). But it is not enough to posit that sexual abuse in childhood *causes* anxiety around sexuality in adult women – this consequence is affected by a myriad of factors including the silence associated with sexuality, the differential power relations between men and women, the positioning of the individual woman within a heterosexual culture, and the many other psychological consequences of sexual abuse. Women who have been abused have been shown to be at risk of depression, anxiety, self-injurious behaviour or attempts to commit suicide.[17] They often experience a distorted sense of reality as the victimisation creates a negative sense of the world, where little seems meaningful[18] and where the woman herself feels weak, needy, frightened, and out of control. The woman's whole image of the world, and of herself, can become imbued with negative overtones (see Browne and Finkelhor, 1986, for a review). It is this complex interaction which affects her sexual identity and her sexual response.

The sociobiological view may seem extreme – most psychologists would steer clear of such reductionist explanations for behaviour, and sex therapists would be unlikely to adhere simply to such theories. Yet many of the underlying beliefs are reflected in the general psychological discourse, wherein female sexuality is dissected into disjointed fragments, where men are powerful and active, women powerless and passive, all viewed from above by the scientist-practitioner.

The rational researcher-clinician

In common with other realms of behaviour where experts have pronounced upon the female condition (e.g. madness (Ussher, 1991) or performance (Ussher, 1992)), the psychological analysis of female sexuality is fragmented, decontextualised, and offers less than a complete understanding of women's experiences. For, whilst outside psychology scholars were deconstructing the discourse associated with sexuality (Foucault, 1979) or providing critical analyses of the relationship between the social construction of sexuality and the oppression of women

(Jeffreys, 1990) or homosexuals (Weeks, 1990), psychologists appear to have reduced sexuality to its component parts: to 'incidence and frequency', to the cataloguing of dysfunctional symptoms, or to a variable able to be manipulated and measured in exact experimentation. Much of this research is used as supporting evidence for psychological theories and therapies associated with female sexuality, yet, as it is often esoteric or abstract, viewing female sexuality out of any social context, it must be considered with caution.

This is never more clear than in the laboratory-based experimental research wherein 'vaginal pulse amplitude' and the like are observed in the neutral detached manner beloved of the positivists – as is illustrated by some recent examples in Table 1.3.

As is clear from these experiments, female sexuality is literally reduced to the status of abstract experimental variable – the woman herself invisible behind the attention given to carefully selected aspects of her sexuality which are dissected and discussed. The vibration of her vaginal walls is of interest, her own experience of her sexuality ignored. Whether these intrusive experiments are meaningful or justifiable may be questionable, but the fact that this genre of research forms the bulk of psychological research on female sexuality is evidence of the denial of subjectivity at the expense of exact experimentation in mainstream psychology.

This approach is not confined to the experimental psychologists, for throughout the academic and clinical literature on the subject of sexual problems in women there is a curious distance and use of language which is devoid of any notion of the woman's own experience. It is always clinical, cool, and objective. Take this recent description of dyspareunia and vaginismus:

> [D]yspareunia in the female (pain in the vagina during intercourse) and vaginismus can be viewed as similar problems with varying degrees of intensity. They range from a dyspareunia of mild discomfort, through serious and perhaps intolerable pain, to vaginismus where the reflex contracture of the peri-vaginal muscles effectively prevents penetration by the penis. In more serious cases, any attempt to touch or approach the vagina leads to powerful reflex adduction of the thighs, thus precluding even the possibility of attempted penetration.
>
> (Cooper, 1988: 137)

That this is a description of a woman who cannot (or does not want to) have sexual intercourse could easily be overlooked in the discussion of peri-vaginal muscles and reflexes of the thighs. That penetration could be attempted, as the author implies, in such circumstances seems startling. Yet it is obviously not uncommon, given the comment. This seems to me

Table 1.3 Experimentation on female sexuality

Authors	Subject group	Methodology
Benton and Wastell, 1986	100 'healthy, heterosexual' women students	Ss reading neutral or sexually arousing passage wearing masks impregnated with androstenol or a placebo.
Myers and Morokoff, 1986	20 premenopausal Ss 14 postmenopausal Ss	Ss viewing neutral or erotic film; self report arousal and vaginal pulse amplitude and lubrication recorded. Estrodiol/testosterone/estrone, and luteinising hormone collected.
Meuwissen and Over, 1990	8 students.	Subjective and physiological sexual arousal in response to erotic film or sexual fantasies.
Perper and Weis, 1987	117 college students	Female proceptivity in sexual encounters measured through questionnaire of liberalism/conservatism, or essay describing 'how you would seduce a man'.
Loos *et al.*, 1987	87 women (aged 19–59 yrs)	Attributions for orgasm measured by questionnaire.
Beggs *et al.*, 1987	19 'sexually functional women' (aged 18–30 yrs)	Vaginal photoplethysmography in response to sexually arousing or anxiety-provoking narratives.
Bond and Mosher, 1986	104 undergraduate women	Affective and subjective sexual responses in relation to guided rape imagery.
Morokoff, 1986	92 'unmarried female undergraduates'	Volunteers in sex research: greater noncoital sexual experience, greater masturbatory experience, less sexual inhibition, and more experience with unusual sex.
Harrell and Stolp, 1985	65 women (aged 18–28 yrs)	Tapes of erotic guided imagery; committed or casual situation. Subjective measures of sexual arousal.
Rogers *et al.*, 1985	Two groups of women ages 26.7 yrs and 23.3 yrs	Vaginal pulse amplitude measured during waking erotic conditions and sleep.
Morokoff, 1985	62 female Ss (aged 18–53 yrs) 'high/low sex guilt'	Subjective sexual arousal and vaginal photoplethysmograph, response to erotic videos and sexual fantasy.
Alzate and Londono, 1984	'coitally experienced females' (32 non-paid, mean age 30.3 yrs, 16 paid, mean age 28.1 yrs)	Measured vaginal erotic sensitivity by means of systematic digital stimulation of both vaginal walls.
Hoon *et al.*, 1984	16 women (22–43 yrs old)	Construction and calibration procedures for vaginal photoplethysmography instrumentation for measuring female sexual arousal.

to be reminiscent of the misogynistic belief that a woman cannot be raped if she puts up a fight, if she closes her legs and refuses, because of the 'almost inexpugnable position she occupies on account of the topography in the female body' (Mendleson, 1956: 25).

This pseudo-scientific theorising merely conceals a phallocentric view which is also reflected in more recent clinical literature, such as in this recent discussion of sexual activity:

> [N]*aturally*, more responsibility falls upon the male than upon the female in relationship formation . . . moreover, to add to his problems the male needs to get an erection at least a minute or two before ejaculation in order to, as he sees it, 'have sex' and 'please his partner'.
>
> (Cole, 1988b: 277, my emphasis)

This advocate of sexual surrogacy,[19] Martin Cole, is quite blatant in his view of the *naturally* active male, the centre-stage penis, and the passive female who is 'pleased'. He may use inverted commas but his point is clear. The penis is the most important player in sex. This phallocentricism is undoubtedly detrimental to women, but is clearly also problematic for men, who cannot always 'perform', as Christine Baker illustrates in her chapter in this volume.

However, the dominant psychological discourse, with its emphasis on the penis, has certainly not remained unchallenged, as is clear particularly from the recent feminist critiques of sex therapy and sexology.

DECONSTRUCTING SEXUAL PSYCHOLOGY

> 'Scientific' sexology is a veritable Trojan horse: appearing to be modernity's gift to mankind in its struggle for freedom and dignity, it is, in fact, just another strategy for its pacification and enslavement.
>
> (Szasz, 1981: xiii)

Whilst psychological theories associated with psychopathology have been the object of scrutiny and criticism from a number of different camps (see Sedgewick, 1987; Ussher, 1991), the psychological discourse on the subject of sexuality has been a particular object of vilification.

One of the main arguments has been that the notion of sexual dysfunction is a social construction, for it has been claimed that the 'taxonomic and labelling zeal which attempted to classify "scientifically" the characteristics and increasingly the various forms of sexual variety . . . helped construct them as objects of study and as sexual categories' (Weeks, 1990: 20–1).

This process, endemic in the nineteenth century, acted very powerfully as a means of social control, as sex became 'a means of access both to the life of the body and the life of the species' (Foucault, 1979: 146). And, whilst these criticisms can be levied at the notion of sexual psychology in general, it has been argued that women were of particular interest to those who deemed it their duty to solve and cure the problem of sexuality, for through the 'hystericisation of sex' (Foucault, 1979) female sexuality was defined as inherently dysfunctional, liable to lead to female madness if suppressed, or if expressed (Ussher, 1991): a dangerous double-bind for women.

More recently, feminist critics have taken up this analysis, seeing that psychological theory on female sexuality functions to maintain women's sexual subordination. As Sheila Jeffreys has argued:

> The setting up of the marriage guidance council, the work of sexologists and the development of sex therapy are all instances of how men's power over women was to be supported through the regulation of marital sex.
>
> (Jeffreys, 1990: 5)

Theories of sexuality and definitions of sexual dysfunction within psychology have been seen as being based on misogynistic theorising, functioning to pathologise women who do not seek or achieve pleasure within the phallocentrically biased heterosexual relationship.

Sex therapy has been positioned as objectifying for women, 'tinkering with the husband/wife relationship so as to bolster the man's power and subordinate the woman' (Jeffreys, 1990: 11). It is argued that many women's understandable physical reaction to heterosexual sex, repugnance, is pathologised through being labelled as vaginismus, a syndrome elevated to the status of phobia, as a 'dread of the penis' (Jeffreys, 1990: 33). and that it is only when the woman cannot perform (i.e. receive the penis) during intercourse that her sexual difficulties are taken seriously. Underlying theories and therapies is 'the assumption of the primacy of erections over other sexual concerns' (Stock, 1988: 26). And, whilst the 'inability of the male to have a cylindrical tube of flesh between the legs become sufficiently rigid to insert in a vagina' (Stock, 1988: 31) is a major sexual dysfunction, problems with emotional intimacy, communication about sex, or female dissatisfaction with intercourse as the focus of sexual activity are invariably ignored. So whilst psychologists who theorise about female sexuality are maligned for narrowly defining what is legitimately a 'problem' for women (i.e. intercourse not intimacy), the therapists are condemned for being merely 'dedicated to the maintenance of marriage and heterosexuality' (Jackson, 1984).

One further important contributor to this debate, invariably ignored by psychologists, is the contribution of the interdisciplinary debate on the subject of sexuality, at its height during the 1970s and 1980s (cf. the journals *mf* and *Feminist Review*). Conceiving of sexuality as a construct far more complex than that framed by psychologists as problem or experimental variable, theoretical analysis from a number of different sources (psychoanalysis, film theory, literary criticism) moved understanding of female sexuality into the central arena of critical theory. That this debate has not in the main infiltrated into the psychological literature is a sad loss for psychology.

Moving forward: fictions, facts, realities

The notion of female sexuality as problem clearly cannot continue in the unquestioning, narrowly focused manner currently endemic within psychology. Psychology acts to define the boundaries of normal sexuality for women, to provide a legitimate discourse for those difficulties deemed of importance, those related to heterosexual intercourse, whilst marginalising or ignoring a myriad issues and questions which do not at present fit comfortably into the psychological debate. It is indefensible that psychological theory is presented as consisting of an objective, scientific analysis of female sexuality and its insidious function, that of regulation and control, denied. Equally, the notion that female sexuality, either as problem or as experimental variable, can be construed without reference to historical or cultural[20] considerations within psychology can no longer be defended. The cursory consideration of such factors in research papers or textbooks on sexuality (e.g. Bancroft, 1983) cannot be condoned in the light of the vast literature on the subject developed in other disciplines. If psychologists are to operate in the sphere of female sexuality, they cannot continue to do so within the narrow disciplinary dimensions as presently construed – the interdisciplinary framework is essential. The fictions of sexuality – the myths and mystifying discourses – can only be uncovered within this arena.

Yet, whilst psychologists must acknowledge the perspectives of the critics, it is also important to recognise that many women do experience sexual difficulties. The deconstruction of the dominant psychological discourse is important in allowing an appraisal of the narrow focus of current concerns and the nonsense of focusing on the penis, on heterosexual intercourse, in theories and treatments. Yet implicit within much of the critical theorising is the notion that the experts merely create difficulties by a process of definition. This position cannot be defended, for, limited as the research statistics are in terms of methodology and focus of concern, they do present striking evidence of dissatisfaction and discontent associated with sexuality for many women. These women cannot be ignored because of the fact that the continued existence of their difficulties cannot be easily reconciled with critical perspectives. It is not enough to suggest that women have been coerced into believing that their sexuality is secondary, is deviant, is inherently dysfunctional, and that their aversion for the penis is normal and healthy. Many women experience the reality of distress associated with their sexuality, and will continue to turn to psychologists for help. It is therefore not enough merely to dismiss psychologists, their theories and their therapies, as many of the critics appear to have done (e.g. Jeffreys, 1990).

Current theories outlining the causes of sexual problems may appear to be one-dimensional and limited, but taken together they suggest a number of different roots which may lead to dissatisfaction or difficulty for the individual woman. Physical illness, psychological distress, relationship problems, and negative social discourse may all be contributory factors. But none can be considered on its own. Psychologists *can* contribute to the debate on female sexuality – through demonstrating that these myriad roots can cause real distress and that psychological therapies may have an ameliorative influence. Yet only if the current psychological agenda is widened can it offer anything more than simplistic and one-dimensional analyses and answers. Equally, women's sexuality must not be considered within a disease model, wherein dissatisfaction is pathologised and reified as dysfunction through the too frequent diagnosis of the sexual syndrome. Whilst women's sexuality is positioned as negative, as liability, as that which marks woman as other, it cannot be conceived of in the objective pseudo-scientific way beloved of psychologists.

Female sexuality, in its many manifestations and forms, does not have to be a negative aspect of identity, serving to mark woman as eternal other, as lack, as dysfunctional. One of the most positive movements in recent years has been the reclamation of female sexuality as a positive empowering force for women, allowing women to understand and express their own sexuality, as individuals, with women or with men (e.g. Irigaray, 1988; Cixous, 1986). Psychology has thus far ignored this debate, choosing to concentrate on the traditional notion of difficulty and dysfunction. Perhaps the first step for a new psychology of female sexuality would be to acknowledge the positive potential of female sexuality, to examine sexuality outside the realms of pathology, and to integrate the feminist theorising into an interdisciplinary framework which works for women, not merely seeing sexuality as a variable to be manipulated by the sex experts. Psychology does have the potential to offer much to the debate on sexuality, but it is time for psychologists to remove the narrow disciplinary restrictions which have provided such blinkered theories for so long.

NOTES

1 In this context 'woman' refers to the signifier woman, rather than to the individual woman. Yet the individual woman is positioned as sexual/asexual because of this signification.

2 In this context discourse, in the Foucauldian sense, is used to refer to academic and theoretical arguments, attitudes, beliefs, and practices within the disci-

pline of psychology. There may be competing discourses, but I am referring to the dominant ones.

3 See Ussher, 1991.

4 It is not uncommon for experimenters to justify their sole use of male subjects by countering that factors such as menstruation would only contaminate experimental conditions and results.

5 The only exception seems to be the inclusion of sexuality as a variable in an experimental study, to be measured and manipulated as any other.

6 As Foucault argued, both power and knowledge are maintained and realised through discourse, the regulated system of statements and beliefs which determine all social structure, actions, and thoughts. And three of the four specific discourses which Foucault identified as central to the apparatus of power and knowledge are still central to the psychology of sexual problems: the hystericisation of women's bodies, the socialisation of procreative behaviour, and the psychiatrisation of perverse pleasures. The fourth is the pedagogisation of children's bodies.

7 Longo, 1979: 244-67.

8 See Bancroft (1974), Chapter 4, for a discussion of the history of the modification of so-called deviant sexual behavour.

9 See Weeks (1990), Chapter 8, for an analysis of this early twentieth-century history of sexology.

10 Ellis, 1894: 440.

11 Ellis, 1936: 24.

12 Despite the criticisms of latter-day scientists that psychoanalytic theory is suspect because it can not be subjected to scientific (positivistic) analysis (see Kline, 1977), Freud was adamant that his approach was scientific.

13 See Cole (1988a), Chapter 2, Table 2.1 for a summary of the various studies.

14 This was a magazine survey of 4,000 women (randomly selected sample of 15,000 replies), where 80 per cent of unmarried women and 60 per cent of married women claim never to have achieved unassisted orgasm during intercourse.

15 Men also fail to complain: in Kinsey's (1948) survey of the men who ejaculated within two minutes of intercourse, only 6 per cent felt that they experienced a problem.

16 A recent text on female perversions (Kaplan, 1991) clearly goes some way towards redressing this balance.

17 Koss, 1990.

18 Taylor, 1983.

19 The practice wherein sexual dysfunction can be treated with a partner provided by the therapist.

20 Female sexuality is a central construct in the regulation of woman across cultures.

REFERENCES

Adkins, E. and Jehu, D. (1985) 'Analysis of a treatment program for primary orgastic dysfunction', *Behaviour Research and Therapy* 23(2): 119–26.

Alder, E. and Bancroft, J. (1983) 'Sexual behaviour of lactating women: a preliminary communication', *Journal of Reproductive and Infant Psychology* 1(2): 47–52.

Alexander, F.G. and Selesnick, S.T. (1966) *The History of Psychiatry*, London: Allen & Unwin.

Alizade, A.M. (1988) 'Ensayo psicoanalitico sobre el orgasmo femenino' (A psychoanalytic essay on the subject of female orgasm), *Revista de Psicoanalisis* 45(2): 337–52.

Alzate, H. and Londono, M.L. (1984) 'Vaginal erotic sensitivity', *Journal of Sex and Marital Therapy* 10(1): 49–56.

Ananth, J. (1983) 'Hysterectomy and sexual counselling', *Psychiatric Journal of the University of Ottawa* 8(4): 213–17.

Andersen, B.L. and Jochimsen, P.R. (1987) 'Research design and strategy for studying psychological adjustment to cancer, reply to Thomas', *Journal of Consulting and Clinical Psychology* 55(1): 122–4.

Avery-Clark, C. (1986) 'Sexual dysfunction and disorder patterns of husbands of working and nonworking women', *Journal of Sex and Marital Therapy* 12(4): 282–96.

Bancroft, J. (1974) *Deviant Sexual Behaviour: Modification and Assessment*, Oxford: Clarendon Press.

Bancroft, J. (1983) *Human Sexuality and its problems* London: Churchill Livingstone.

Bancroft, J. (1984) 'Interaction of psychosocial and biological factors in marital sexuality: differences between men and women', *British Journal of Guidance and Counselling* 12(1): 62–71.

Bancroft, J. and Coles, L. (1976) 'Three years' experience in a sexual problems clinic', *British Medical Journal* i: 1575–7.

Bancroft, J., Sanders, D., Davidson, D., and Warner, P. (1983) 'Mood, sexuality, hormones, and the menstrual cycle: III. Sexuality and the role of androgens', *Psychosomatic Medicine* 45(6): 509–16.

Barker-Benfield, G.J. (1976) *The Horrors of the Half Known Life: Male Attitudes Towards Women and Sexuality in Nineteenth Century America*, New York: Harper & Row.

Becker, J.V., Skinner, L.J., Abel, G.G., and Cichon, J. (1984) 'Time limited therapy with sexually dysfunctional sexually assaulted women', *Journal of Social Work and Human Sexuality* 3(1): 97–115.

Becker, J.V., Skinner, L.J., Abel, G.G., and Cichon, J. (1986) 'Level of postassault sexual functioning in rape and incest victims', *Archives of Sexual Behavior* 15(1): 37–49.

Beggs, V.E., Calhoun, K.S., and Wolchik, S.A. (1987) 'Sexual anxiety and female sexual arousal: a comparison of arousal during sexual anxiety stimuli and sexual pleasure stimuli', *Archives of Sexual Behavior* 16(4): 311–19.

Benton, D. and Wastell, V. (1986) 'Effects of androstenol on human sexual arousal', *Biological Psychology* 22(2): 141–7.

Bermant, G. and Davidson, J.M. (1974) *Biological Basis of Sexual Behaviour*, New York: Harper & Row.

Bixler, R.H. (1983) '"X" and the single girl: of parental investment, reproductive strategies, and the overly cautious female', *Psychological Reports* 53(1): 279–82.

Black, J.S. (1988) 'Sexual dysfunction and dyspareunia in the otherwise normal pelvis', *Sexual and Marital Therapy* 3(2): 213–21.

Bond, S.B. and Mosher, D.L. (1986) 'Guided imagery of rape: fantasy, reality, and the willing victim myth', *Journal of Sex Research* 22(2): 162–83.

Bos, G. (1986) 'Sexuality of gynecological cancer patients: quantity and quality', *Journal of Psychosomatic Obstetrics and Gynaecology* 5(3): 217–24.

Bregman, S. (1978) 'Sexual adjustment of spinal cord injured women', *Sexuality and Disability* 1: 85–92.

Breuer, J. and Freud, S. (1895) *Studies on Hysteria*, New York: Bias Books, 1957.

Browne, A. and Finklehor, D. (1986) 'Impact of child sexual abuse: a review of the literature', *Psychological Bulletin* 99(1): 66–77.

Bruch, M.A. and Hynes, M.J. (1987) 'Heterosocial anxiety and contraceptive behavior', *Journal of Research in Personality* 21(3): 343–60.

Catalan, J., Bradley, M., Gallwey, J., and Hawton, K. (1981) 'Sexual dysfunction and psychiatric morbidity in patients attending a clinic for sexually transmitted diseases', *British Journal of Psychiatry* 138: 292–6.

Channon, L.D. and Ballinger, S.E. (1986) 'Some aspects of sexuality and vaginal symptoms during menopause and their relations to anxiety and depression', *British Journal of Medical Psychology* 59(2): 173–80.

Charmoli, M.C. and Athelstan, G.T. (1988) 'Incest as related to sexual problems in women', *Journal of Psychology and Human Sexuality* 1(1): 53–66.

Chester, R. and Walker, C. (1980) 'Sexual experience and attitudes of British women', in W.H.G. Armytage, R. Chester, and J. Peel (eds) *Changing Patterns of Sexual Behaviour*, London: Academic Press.

Cixous, H. (1986) 'Sorties', in E. Marks and I. Courtivron (eds) *New French Feminisms*, Sussex: Harvester Press, pp. 90–9.

Cole, M. (1988a) 'Normal and dysfunctional sexual behaviour: frequencies and incidences', in M. Cole and W. Dryden (eds) (1988) *Sex Therapy in Britain*, Milton Keynes: Open University Press.

Cole, M. (1988b) 'Sex therapy for individuals', in M. Cole and W. Dryden (eds) (1988) *Sex Therapy in Britain*, Milton Keynes: Open University Press.

Cole, M. and Dryden, W. (1988) 'Sexual dysfunction: an introduction', in M. Cole and W. Dryden (eds) (1988) *Sex Therapy in Britain*, Milton Keynes: Open University Press.

Cooper, G.F. (1988) 'The psychological methods of sex therapy', in M. Cole and W. Dryden (eds) (1988) *Sex Therapy in Britain*, Milton Keynes: Open University Press.

Covington, S.S. and Kohen, J. (1984) 'Women, alcohol, and sexuality', *Advances in Alcohol and Substance Abuse* 4(1): 41–56.

Crenshaw, T.L. (1986) 'A woman's persistent fear of sex two years after a heart attack', *Medical Aspects of Human Sexuality* 20(12): 50–1.

Cutler, W.B., Garcia, C.R., and McCoy, N. (1987) 'Perimenopausal sexuality', *Archives of Sexual Behavior* 16(3): 225–34.

Debrovner, C.H. and Shubin, R. (1985) 'Pregnancy and postpartum: II. postpartum sexual concerns', *Medical Aspects of Human Sexuality* 19(5): 84–90.

Dow, M.G. and Gallagher, J. (1989) 'A controlled study of combined hormonal and psychological treatment for sexual unresponsiveness in women', *British Journal of Clinical Psychology* 28(3): 201–12.

Elliott, S.A. and Watson, J.P. (1985) 'Sex during pregnancy and the first postnatal year', *Journal of Psychosomatic Research* 29(5): 541–8.

Ellis, H. (1894) *Man and Woman*, London: Contemporary Science Series.

Ellis, H. (1936) *Studies in the Psychology of Sex*, Vol. 1, part 2, New York: Random House.

Feinauer, L.L. (1989) 'Sexual dysfunction in women sexually abused as children', *Contemporary Family Therapy: An International Journal* 11(4): 299–309.

Ferguson, K. and Figley, B. (1979) 'Sexuality and rheumatic disease: a study', *Sexuality and Disability* 2: 130–8.

Figes, E. (1970) *Patriarchal Attitudes*, London: Faber.

Foucault, M. (1967) *Madness and Civilization: A History of Insanity in the Age of Reason*, London: Tavistock.

Foucault, M. (1979) *The History of Sexuality*, Vol. 1, London: Allen Lane.

Frank, E., Anderson, C., and Rubinstein, D. (1978) 'Frequency of sexual dysfunction in "normal" couples', *New England Journal of Medicine* 299: 111–15.

Freud, S. (1886-99) *The Standard Edition of the Complete Psychological Works of*

Sigmund Freud Vol. 1. *Pre Psycho-analytic Publications and Unpublished Drafts*, London: Hogarth and the Institute of Psycho-Analysis.

Friedman, D., Clare, A.W., Rees, L.H., and Grossman, A. (1986) 'Should impotent males who have no clinical evidence of hypogonadism have routine endocrine screening?', *The Lancet* i: 1041 (letter).

Garde, K. and Lunde, I. (1980) 'Female sexual behaviour: a study in a random sample of 40 year old women', *Maturitas* 2: 225–40.

Gazan, M. (1986) 'An evaluation of a treatment package designed for women with a history of sexual victimization in childhood and sexual dysfunctions in adult-hood', Special Issue: women and mental health, *Canadian Journal of Community Mental Health* 5(2): 85–102.

Gilbert, B. and Cunningham, J. (1986) 'Women's postrape sexual functioning: review and implications for counseling', *Journal of Counselling and Development* 65(2): 71–3.

Giovacchini, P.L. (1986) 'Promiscuity in adolescents and young adults', *Medical Aspects of Human Sexuality* 20(5): 24–31.

Goldfarb, L., Gerrard, M., Gibbons, F., and Plante, T. (1988) 'Attitudes toward sex, arousal, and the retention of contraceptive information', *Journal of Personality and Social Psychology* 55(4): 634–41.

Golubtsova, L.I. and Polishchuk, Y.I. (1988) 'Multiple modality therapy of sexual disorders in women with slowly progressive schizophrenia', *Zhurnal Nevropatologii i Psikhiatrii* 88(2): 110–14.

Gosselin, C.C. and Wilson, G.D. (1984) *Sexual Variations: Fetishism, Transvestism and Sadomasochism*, London: Faber.

Harrell, T.H. and Stolp, R.D. (1985) 'Effects of erotic guided imagery on female sexual arousal and emotional response', *Journal of Sex Research* 21(3): 292–304.

Hawton, K. (1985) *Sex Therapy: A Practical Guide*, Oxford: Oxford University Press.

Hite, S. (1976) *The Hite Report*, New York: Macmillan.

Hoon, P.W., Murphy, W.D., Laughter, J.S., and Abel, G.G. (1984) 'Infrared vaginal photoplethysmography: construction, calibration, and sources of artifact', *Behavioral Assessment* 6(2): 141–52.

Howells, K. (1984) *The Psychology of Sexual Diversity*, Oxford: Blackwell.

Hunt, M. (1974) *Sexual Behaviour in the 1970's*, Chicago: Playboy Press.

Irigaray, L. (1986) 'The sex which is not one', in E. Marks and I. de Courtivron (eds) *New French Feminisms: An Anthology*, Sussex: Harvester Press, pp. 99–106.

Irigaray, L. (1988) 'Interview', in E.H. Baruch and L. Serrano (eds) *Women Analyse Women: In France, England and the United States* London: Harvester Wheatsheaf, pp. 149–66.

Jackson, M. (1984) 'Sex research and the construction of sexuality: a tool for male supremacy?', *Women's Studies International Forum* 7: 43–51.

Jeffreys, S. (1990) *Anticlimax: A Feminist Perspective on the Sexual Revolution*, London: The Women's Press.

Jehu, D. (1984) 'Impairment of sexual behaviour in non-human primates', in K. Howells (ed) *The Psychology of Sexual Diversity*, Oxford: Blackwell.

Jehu, D. (1989) 'Sexual dysfunctions among women clients who were sexually abused in childhood', *Behavioural Psychotherapy* 17(1): 53–70.

Jonsson, B.D. and Byers, E.S. (1986) 'Treatment of sexual anxiety with graduate modeling', *Journal of Sex Education and Therapy* 12(1): 60–4.

Kaplan, D.L. (1991) 'Female perversions', *Journal of Counseling and Development* 65(2): 71–3.

Kaplan, D.L. and Steege, J.F. (1983) 'The urethral syndrome: sexual components', *Sexuality and Disability* 6(2): 78–82.

Kilpatrick, A.C. (1986) 'Some correlates of women's childhood sexual experiences: a retrospective study', *Journal of Sex Research* 22(2): 221–42.

Kinsey, A.C., Pomeroy, W.B., Martin, C.E., and Gebhard, P.H. (1948) *Sexual Behaviour in the Human Male*, Philadelphia and London: Saunders.

Klassen, A.D. and Wilsnack, S.C. (1986) 'Sexual experience and drinking among women in a US national survey', *Archives of Sexual Behavior* 15(5): 363–92.

Klein, M. (1952) 'Some theoretical conclusions regarding the emotional life of the infant', in M. Klein and J. Riviere (eds) *Developments in Psycho-Analysis*, London: Hogarth.

Kline, P. (1977) *Fact and Fantasy in Freudian Theory*, London: Methuen.

Koss, M. (1990) 'The women's mental health research agenda: violence against women', *American Psychologist* 45(3): 374–80.

Lacan, J. (1977) *Ecrits: A Selection*, London: Tavistock.

Leiter, E. (1983) 'Urethritis: clinical manifestations and inter-relationship with intercourse and therapy', *Sexuality and Disability* 6(2): 72–7.

Longo, L.D. (1979) 'The rise and fall of Battey's operation: a fashion in surgery', *Bulletin of the History of Medicine*, 53: 244–67.

Loos, V.E., Bridges, C.F., and Critelli, J.W. (1987) 'Weiner's attribution theory and female orgasmic consistency', *Journal of Sex Research* 23(3): 348–61.

McCormick, N.B. and Vinson, R.K. (1988) 'Sexual difficulties experienced by women with interstitial cystitis', Special issue: women and sex therapy, *Women and Therapy* 7(2–3): 109–19.

Masters, W.H. and Johnson, V.E. (1966) *Human Sexual Response*, Boston, MA: Little, Brown & Co.

Maudsley, H. (1873) *Body and Mind*, London: Macmillan.

Mears, E. (1978) 'Sexual problem clinics: an assessment of the work of 26 doctors trained by the Institute of Psychosexual Medicine', *Public Health* 92: 218–33.

Melman, A. (1983) 'The interaction of urinary tract infection and sexual intercourse in women', *Sexuality and Disability* 6(2): 93–8.

Mendleson, B. (1956) 'The victimology', *Etudes Internationale de Psycho-Sociologie* July: 25–6.

Metz, M.E. and Seifert, M.H. (1988) 'Women's expectations of physicians in sexual health concerns', Special issue: human sexuality and the family, *Family Practice Research Journal* 7(3): 141–52.

Meuwissen, I. and Over, R. (1990) 'Habituation and dishabituation of female sexual arousal', *Behaviour Research and Therapy* 28(3): 217–26.

Milan, R.J., Kilmann, P.R., and Boland, J.P. (1988) 'Treatment outcome of secondary orgasmic dysfunction: a two- to six-year follow-up', *Archives of Sexual Behavior* 17(6): 463–80.

Mitchell, J. (1974) *Psychoanalysis and Feminism*, London: Allen Lane.

Mitchell, J. and Rose, J. (1982) *Feminine Sexuality: Jacques Lacan and the Ecole Freudienne*, London: Macmillan.

Morokoff, P.J. (1985) 'Effects of sex guilt, repression, sexual "arousability", and sexual experience on female sexual arousal during erotica and fantasy', *Journal of Personality and Social Psychology* 49(1): 177–87.

Morokoff, P.J. (1986) 'Volunteer bias in the psychophysiological study of female sexuality', *Journal of Sex Research* 22(1): 35–51.

Morris, N.M., Udry, J.R., Khan-Dawood, F., and Dawood, M.Y. (1987) 'Marital sex frequency and midcycle female testosterone', *Archives of Sexual Behavior* 16(1): 27–37.

Myers, L.S. and Morokoff, P.J. (1986) 'Physiological and subjective sexual arousal in pre- and postmenopausal women and postmenopausal women taking replacement therapy', *Psychophysiology* 23(3): 283–92.

Nairne, K.D. and Hemsley, D.R. (1983) 'The use of directed masturbation training in the treatment of primary anorgasmia', *British Journal of Clinical Psychology* 22(4): 283–94.

Ndegwa, D., Rust, J., Golombok, S., and Fenwick, P. (1986) 'Sexual problems in epileptic women', *Sexual and Marital Therapy* 1(2): 175–77.

Newman, A.S. and Bertelson, A.D. (1986) 'Sexual dysfunction in diabetic women', *Journal of Behavioral Medicine* 9(3): 261–70.

Nutter, D.E. and Condron, M.K. (1983) 'Sexual fantasy and activity patterns of females with inhibited sexual desire versus normal controls', *Journal of Sex and Marital Therapy* 9(4): 276–82.

Papadopoulos, C. (1985) 'Sexuality of women after myocardial infarction', *Medical Aspects of Human Sexuality*, 19(3): 215–23.

Pasini, W. (1977) 'Unconsummated and partially consummated marriage as sources of procreative failure', in J. Money and H. Musaph (eds) *Handbook of Sexology*, Amsterdam: Elsevier/North Holland.

Perper, T. and Weis, D.L. (1987) 'Proceptive and rejective strategies of U.S. and Canadian college women', *Journal of Sex Research* 23(4): 455–80.

Peterson, J.S., Hartsock, N., and Lawson, G. (1984) 'Sexual dissatisfaction of female alcoholics', *Psychological Reports,* 55(3): 744–6.

Phinney, V.G., Jensen, L.C., Olsen, J.A., and Cundick, B. (1990) 'The relationship between early development and psychosexual behaviors in adolescent females', *Adolescence* 25(98): 321–32.

Pietropinto, A. (1986) 'Male contributions to female sexual dysfunction', *Medical Aspects of Human Sexuality* 20(12): 84–91.

Pietropinto, A. and Simenauer, J. (1977) *Beyond the Male Myth: A Nationwide Survey*, New York: Times Books.

Pinhas, V. (1987) 'Sexual dysfunction in women alcoholics', *Medical Aspects of Human Sexuality* 21(6): 97–101.

Piskorz-de-Zimerman, S. (1983) 'La mujer segun el psicoanalisis', (The female as viewed by psychoanalysis), *Revista de Psicoanalisis* 40(5–6): 1155–72.

Plummer, K. (1984) 'Sexual diversity: a sociological perspective', in K. Howells (ed.) *The Psychology of Sexual Diversity*, Oxford: Blackwell.

Prather, R.C. (1988) 'Sexual dysfunction in the diabetes female: a review', *Archives of Sexual Behavior* 17(3): 277–84.

Price, J.A. and Price, J.H. (1983) 'Alcohol and sexual functioning: a review', *Advances in Alcohol and Substance Abuse* 2(4): 43–56.

Resick, P.A. (1983) 'The rape reaction: research findings and implications for intervention', *Behavior Therapist* 6(7): 129–32.

Reyniak, J.V. (1987) 'Sexual and other concerns of the woman with osteoporosis', *Medical Aspects of Human Sexuality* 21(1): 16I–J.

Richards, A. (1990) 'Female fetishes and female perversions', *Psychoanalytic Review* 77(1): 11–23.

Riley, A.J. and Riley, E.J. (1986) 'The effect of single dose diazepam on female sexual response induced by masturbation', *Sexual and Marital Therapy* 1(1): 49–53.

Riley, A.J., Riley, E.J., and Brown, P.T. (1986) 'Biological aspects of sexual desire in women', *Sexual and Marital Therapy* 1(1): 35–42.

Rogers, G.S., Van-de-Castle, R.L., Evans, W.S., and Critelli, J.W. (1985) 'Vaginal pulse amplitude response patterns during erotic conditions and sleep', *Archives of Sexual Behavior* 14(4): 327–42.

Rose, J. (1986) *Sexuality in the Field of Vision*, London: Verso.

Rust, J. and Golombok, S. (1990) 'Stress and marital discord: some sex differences', *Stress Medicine* 6(1): 25–7.

Saunders, D. (1985) *The Woman's Book of Love and Sex*, London: Sphere.
Schreiner-Engel, P. (1983) 'Diabetes mellitus and female sexuality', *Sexuality and Disability* 6(2): 83–92.
Schreiner-Engel, P., Schiavi, R.C., Vietorisz, D., and Smith, H. (1987) 'The differential impact of diabetes type on female sexuality', *Journal of Psychosomatic Research* 31(1): 23–33.
Schreiner-Engel, P., Schiavi, R.C., White, D., and Ghizzani, A. (1989) 'Low sexual desire in women: the role of reproductive hormones', *Hormones and Behavior* 23(2): 221–34.
Sedgewick, P. (1987) *Psychopolitics*, London: Pluto Press.
Sherwin, B.B., Gelfand, M.M. and Brender, W. (1985) 'Androgen enhances sexual motivation in females: a prospective, crossover study of sex steroid administration in the surgical menopause', *Psychosomatic Medicine* 47(4): 339–51.
Showalter, E. (1987) *The Female Malady*, London: Virago.
Slob, A.K., Koster, J., Radder, J.K., and and Van der Werff ten Bosch, J.J. (1990) 'Sexuality and psychophysiological functioning in women with diabetes mellitus', *Journal of Sex and Marital Therapy* 16(2): 59–69.
Sobrinho, L.G., Sa-Melo, P., Nunes, M.C., Barroco, L.E., et al. (1987) 'Sexual dysfunction in hyperprolactinaemic women: effect of bromocriptine', *Journal of Psychosomatic Obstetrics and Gynaecology* 6(1): 43–8.
Social Trends (1992), London: HMSO.
Squire, C. (1989) *Significant Differences: Feminism in Psychology*, London: Routledge.
Stellman, R.E. et al. (1984) 'Psychological effects of vulvectomy', *Psychosomatics* 25(10): 779–83.
Stock, W. (1988) 'Propping up phallocracy: a feminist critique of sex therapy and research', *Women and Therapy* 2–3: 23–41.
Stuart, F.M., Hammond, D.C., and Pett, M.A. (1986) 'Psychological characteristics of women with inhibited sexual desire', *Journal of Sex and Marital Therapy* 12(2): 108–15.
Stuart, F.M., Hammond, D.C., and Pett, M.A. (1987) 'Inhibited sexual desire in women', *Archives of Sexual Behavior* 16(2): 91–106.
Stuntz, R.C. (1986) 'Physical obstructions to coitus in women', *Medical Aspects of Human Sexuality* 20(2): 117–34.
Szasz, T. (1981) *Sex: Facts, Frauds and Follies*, Oxford: Blackwell.
Taylor, S.E. (1983) 'Adjustment to threatening events: a theory of cognitive adaptation', *American Psychologist* 38: 1161–73.
Thomas, J. (1987) 'Problems in a study of the sexual response of women with cancer: comment on Andersen and Jochimsen', *Journal of Consulting and Clinical Psychology*, 55(1): 120–1.
Tiefer, L. (1988) 'A feminist critique of the sexual dysfunction nomenclature', Special issue: women and sex therapy, *Women and Therapy* 7(2–3): 5–21.
Tissot, S. (1769) *Advice to the People with General Respect to their Health*, Bristol: Pine.
Ussher, J.M. (1990) 'The future of sex and marital therapy in the face of widespread criticism: caught between the devil and the deep blue sea', *Counselling Psychology Quarterly* 3(4): 317–24.
Ussher, J.M. (1991) *Women's Madness: Misogyny or Mental Illness*. Hemel Hempstead: Harvester Wheatsheaf.
Ussher, J.M. (1992) 'Sex differences in performance: fact, fiction or fantasy?', in D. Jones and A. Smith (eds) *Studies in Human Performance*, Chichester: Wiley.
Weeks, J. (1990) *Sex, Politics and Society: The Regulation of Sexuality since 1800*, London: Longman.
Weijmar-Schultz, W.C., Wijma, K., Van-de-Wiel, H.B., and Bouma, J. (1986)

'Sexual rehabilitation of radical vulvectomy patients: a pilot study', *Journal of Psychosomatic Obstetrics and Gynaecology* 5(2): 119–26.

Whitehead, A. and Mathews, A. (1986) 'Factors related to successful outcome in the treatment of sexually unresponsive women', *Psychological Medicine* 16(2:) 373–8.

Whitehead, A., Mathews, A., and Ramage, M. (1987) 'The treatment of sexually unresponsive women: a comparative evaluation', *Behaviour Research and Therapy* 25(3): 195–205.

Wilson, G.D. (1988) 'The sociobiological basis of sexual dysfunction', in M. Cole and W. Dryden (eds) *Sex Therapy in Britain*, Milton Keynes: Open University Press.

Wilson, R.J., Beecham, C.T., and Carrington, E.R. (1975) *Obstetrics and Gynecology*, St Louis: Mosby.

Zimmer, D. (1987) 'Does marital therapy enhance the effectiveness of treatment for sexual dysfunction?', *Journal of Sex and Marital Therapy* 13(3): 193–209.

Chapter 2

The seeds of masculine sexuality

Stephen Frosh

DECONSTRUCTING MASCULINITY

Finding a starting point is itself a gendered act, for there is a sense in which all points are masculine, at least once they are symbolised. For ever, it seems, but definitely since Kant (Seidler, 1989) and since the Reformation, the world has been viewed through masculine eyes; masculinity has defined the world. Often, therefore, discussions of masculinity and femininity in terms of behavioural and role differences miss the point, the starting point: they assume the existence of sexual difference and take too little account of its construction. Man is man and woman woman, they suggest, and then set out to describe what they do, not to speculate on how they come to be. Thus the chasm between the sexes is taken as given, the task of investigation is to categorise and control in that way with which we are all familiar, to pin down the flow of differences and make them all reduce to one. Male is male and female female; there is something which is 'masculine' and something which is not. Moreover, something else that is important is missed. We look from the outside, distancing ourselves from the sexuality of those we study: male sexuality looks like this, this is what men do – and ugly sometimes it seems, when sexual abuse is the focus. But what does it mean, what is at its centre, what does it feel like to have this possession, this masculine sexual being?

Masculine sexuality and masculinity: these belong together, the former cannot be talked about as distinct from the latter, as a set of behaviours having no bearing on emotion. There is an interior point of view to be uncovered here, a way of exploring masculine sexuality from the perspective of the development of masculine subjectivity: the doing only makes sense in the context of the being.

This is jumping ahead, however. In this chapter I try to set up a few signposts pointing towards the interior view of masculine sexual subjectivity using, as the most developed and challenging set of ideas of this kind currently available, some contemporary psychoanalytic theories. Some of this work will be used to offer an explanatory account of the links between masculine sexuality and sexual abuse, particularly abuse of children. An important place to start if ever there was one: the next section of this chapter looks at the impact of increased awareness of sexual abusiveness for theories of masculinity. Following this, there is an account of one set of psychoanalytic perspectives on masculine development, a set informed particularly by feminist consciousness. Finally, I return to the issue of sexual abuse and try to apply to it some of the insights gleaned from this work, arguing that a full understanding of abusiveness can only be built on the basis of a general theory of masculinity.

ON DOMINANT ABUSE

One source of the contemporary dissatisfaction with traditional masculinity is the specific awareness that the domination so long associated with masculinity is linked with violence and abusiveness. Women have, of course, always known this and have been shouting it for some time; children may well have known it too, but they have more often been silent or, rather, silenced, double-bound into corners ('Don't tell, but why didn't you tell?'), each thinking they were the only one to know. There are, of course, women who abuse children, but they are a small minority of abusers, despite women, through their caretaking roles, generally having more opportunity to abuse (Haugaard and Reppucci, 1988). It is with masculinity that the links are systematically made.

The nature of the domination/abusiveness/sexuality network is a major theme throughout this chapter, but the impact of its recognition needs to be acknowledged here. For women, it has legitimised anger and separateness – at times a radical repudiation of all things male, a closing of female ranks around mutual support and hostility towards the other. Maybe this has a mirroring flavour, perhaps also a narcissistic one: denying difference is not in itself a means of overcoming difference; rejecting masculinity is too close a parallel to the male rejection of femininity to offer anyone full comfort. In addition, as the following quotation from Seidler (1991) suggests, the rejectionist stance neglects the differentiations currently entering into masculinity, which themselves undermine masculine claims to universal dominance. That is, by lumping us all in one dumpable basket, radical feminism reiterates the 'one and whole' mythology of masculinity – univocal command, homogeneous demand, smooth and violent force.

> It has been an enduring feature of radical feminist work to place issues of male violence at the centre of an understanding of social relations, although often this has been done in a way that forecloses the possibilities of men to change. In this context it is crucial not to treat

masculinity as a unified and homogeneous category, fixed within particular relations of power, but to explore the emergence and experiences of different masculinities.

(Seidler, 1991: 142)

Them-and-us: this is a mentality which is apparent not just in fascism, but also more generally in masculine ideology, with its fantasy of a truly rational state of masculine authority. Undifferentiating rejectionism misses the opportunity to carve out a space for the worm of doubt to enter into this fantasy, the worm carrying the suggestion that, 'We are not all, every one of us, the same'. Consequently, rejectionism shares in the ideology of wholeness: there is nothing you can do with masculinity except oppose it, it is so monolithic, it will always strive to dominate; some men may seem like allies, but in the end they will stick to their own. Well, maybe they/we will; but their small own, not all other men, not necessarily the big Other.

But the radical feminist critique is not easily dismissible. Functionally, it offers solidarity for women and resistance to men. Being resisted, we men may try to force some more, but we also know that opposition exists, that our domination is not pre-ordained, a simple state of nature; it is something that is forced, that is part of a struggle against a recalcitrant other, who will not take it lying down. Moreover, the content of the critique has been deeply shocking for men. 'You do not want or need us?', 'You can have babies without us?', 'You really want us to move out?'. Being resisted, we may try to force some more, but awareness of the hatred we have engendered, of how desperately we use force because we have no other strategies for overcoming that hatred, makes more cracks in the masculine armour. 'Do we deserve all this?', 'Is this really how they feel?', 'In every step I take, do I really tread on someone else?'.

Of course the self-hating man is just as irritating as the macho. Again denying difference: 'I have seen the light and become like you, I am no longer manly, I have all these feminine attributes – intimacy, care, nurture, loving kindness.' Who needs him? There may as well not be any difference if no difference is allowed to be. Narcissism is regression, escape: denial of difference ends back in the womb, where maybe we would all like to be, but that is Thanatos, not Eros, that is withdrawal not engagement with life. But the critical examination of masculinity in the light of the feminist critique, the analysis of what it is that feeds our abusiveness, why the force has to be so much with us – that is a different project, one that can move us on, different but towards togetherness. About time too.

MASCULINITY DISSOLVED

Theories aspiring to articulation of the interior point of view are not necessarily immune from androcentric assumptions. Lacan, for example, identifies the woman as 'Other', deep in the psyche and deeply rejected from the Symbolic web of culture, but Lacan is no innovator here. Freud, too, has a misogynistic way about him: 'The little girl is a little man,' he writes (1933: 152); sexual libido is active, therefore masculine, it operates on, it does things to, it pushes and shoves and thrusts and achieves. The feminine is other; mysterious, yes – like nature, a state which is engulfing and threatening, but also a site of great riches, to be explored and conquered. We need to understand it, to struggle with it, precisely because it is so alien: the masculine is the starting point.

Take this passage, from Moore's articulation of the Lacanian stance on gender inequality.

> If the phallus is the key signifier of difference . . . then masculinity becomes set up as the norm and femininity can only exist as absence, as what masculinity is not. Of course no-one actually possesses the phallus but men are able to make identifications with this symbol in a way that women are not.
>
> (Moore, 1988: 172)

'If', Moore writes, 'If': an understatement, an unnecessary qualification. The phallus is taken to be the key signifier of difference, wantonly, perhaps wrongly, but it sticks its head in everywhere. It's what he has and she wants, they say; the absence that marks her as other, just because there is a vacancy where it is taken to matter. Well, if we are thinking about masculine sexuality, we must start somewhere, at some point; it might as well be phallic.

But starting with the phallus turns out to lead us nowhere.

> The phallus is the privileged signifier of that mark where the share of the logos is wedded to the advent of desire. One might say that this signifier is chosen as what stands out as most easily seized upon in the real of sexual copulation, and as also the most symbolic in the literal (typographical) sense of the term, since it is the equivalent in that relation of the (logical) copula. One might also say that by virtue of its turgidity, it is the image of the vital flow as it is transmitted in generation.
>
> All these propositions merely veil over the fact that the phallus can only play its role as veiled.
>
> (Lacan, 1958: 82)

It is neither one thing nor another: the phallus, which we take as the mark of masculine authority, only 'plays its role as veiled' – it is hidden, not amenable to pinning down, not a reliable starting point after all. Women may indulge in masquerade (Lacan, 1958: 84), thus not having any real essence, but if men claim dominance through the phallus they are in for a sore surprise. The penis, which men do have, is not the phallus, for the phallus is a symbol rather than a substance; all those bemusing male impotences are linked to this. So inscrutable, so unavailable to possession – the real organ cannot match the imaginary one, and the more you try to make it do so, the more incorrigible is the failure likely to be.

Male dominance is a fantasy; that is a genuine starting point. Fantasies, of course, have effects, but they are fantasies none the less – or perhaps myths would be a better term. In this myth, the stability and rationality of the world is incorporated into the masculine state of oneness: the up-swelling, integrated, whole being to be found in the psychiatric and humanistic imagination, all things undappled, unfreckled, and pure. 'Masculinity is an essentially negative identity learnt through defining itself against emotionality and connectedness,' writes Seidler (1989: 7). As Grunberger (1989) tells us, anything that pursues purity and despises anality, despises the real dirt and confusion of the world, is regressively narcissistic, possibly fascistically so. It operates by refusing conflict, denying heterogeneity, making what is different out of bounds, the object of aggressive assault. This kind of regressiveness enforces rigid, turgid values; it fights for itself, it is at the centre of racism (Frosh, 1989) and misogyny (Theweleit, 1977). It is, also, desperate: a staving off of the world in which we live, because its heterogeneity and complexity cannot be borne.

For the world does not any more, if ever it did, work like that: the masculine order, the rational stance, cannot sustain its own. 'To be modern,' writes Berman (1982: 15), 'is to find ourselves in an environment that promises us adventure, power, joy, growth, transformation of our-selves and the world – and, at the same time, that threatens to destroy everything we have, everything we know, everything we are.' The world spirals away, our reality cannot be grasped, by power neither of mind nor of will; narcissism and psychosis become the orders of the day (see Frosh, 1991). There is too much fluctuation, too much contradiction; those who once were dubbed minorities can now speak; including, amazingly, those designated by some as most outside language (because language is, say Lacanians, fixed into the patriarchal systems of culture): women. And what they have to say, amongst other things, is: 'Come on, stop pretending; you have no answer, you are a whole only in your head.'

There are many possible responses to this challenge to the mythology of a rigorous, rational masculinity. Seidler's (1991) claim concerning the heterogeneity of masculinity, quoted earlier, is such a response, worth taking seriously as it arises from the penetrating analysis of male sexual abusiveness offered by feminist writers. This claim hits at a core feature of masculine ideology: the assumption of universality, of sameness, of the reality of phallic authority. '[It] is crucial,' writes Seidler, ' . . . to explore the emergence and experiences of different masculinities' (1991: 142): 'different masculinities', meaning, for instance, black and white, homosexual, bisexual and heterosexual, Jewish and Gentile – powerless and powerful. Already, this is a deconstruction: the apparently monolithic nature of masculinity begins to fragment as soon as one investigates it; multiplicity enters in, differences abound; just like women, men are not all the same. In the whirlpool of the modern environment, everything comes into play; there is no starting point, no fixed point at all, but only a fragmentation of what once might have been taken as whole. The 'point' here, phrased formally and academically, is that the received tradition identifying masculinity with rationality is giving way in the face of feminist and other cultural critiques, to problematise the entity 'masculinity' just as it problematises the experience of each individual man. Critical analysis of masculine sexuality, no longer taken as 'natural' or subject unquestioningly to the discourse of the biological drive (Hollway, 1989), is part of this larger fragmenting or 'deconstructive' process.

HIS-STORY

This might come as a surprise. The words of a woman:

> Whatever the meanings attached to 'the act' of sexual intercourse, for many men it confirms a sense of ineptness and failure: the failure to satisfy women . . . for many men it is precisely through sex that they experience their greatest uncertainties, dependence and deference in relation to women. . . . And certainly for many men it is precisely through experiencing themselves as powerless and submissive that they experience the greatest sexual pleasure.
>
> (Segal, 1990: 212)

So much for unequivocal domination. Anyway, 'Domination begins with the attempt to deny dependency' (Benjamin, 1988: 52), so it is not a positive in its own right – like masculinity itself, it is defined negatively, against that which it is not. Perhaps the two issues are linked like this: to dominate, dependence must be kept at bay; but in sex, there is a recognition by the other which is needed as part of the domination, and the woman can always deny this to the man. There is, indeed, a dual dependency in sex: to have pleasure oneself, to pleasure the other – to be the object of the other's desire. Not being desired, not being 'successful' in generating the woman's jouissance, as all those smart and elegant French theorists put it, is a failure of masculine domination. 'The failure to satisfy women': what could be a more forceful indictment of masculine power?

Moreover, if Segal is right (and she sounds sure, with her 'certainly for many men it is precisely') that men often desire passivity in the sexual encounter, that they want to be done to more than be doers, then something else is being undermined in the sphere of domination. The woman freely acting on the man? This does not sound like masculine independence and autonomy, the superiority of the rational mind. The phallus as fraud, again: it appears to dominate, to be the primary signifier, but it is dependent on the good will of the other – of that which, according to Lacan at least, does not really exist.

There are two related elements to explore here in rather more detail: firstly, that of men's difficulties with dependence; secondly, the sense of degradation which, for men, seems often to accompany sex. What was suggested above is that sex places men in a dependent position that undermines the ideology of masculine autonomy and domination. This is due partly to the familiar paradox that 'the master needs the slave', or else he is no longer master – needs recognition from the dominated one if his mastery is to mean anything. It is also, however, that men's sexual enjoyment is often organised around passivity, making the other 'master': 'Men's fantasies, desires and experiences of sex in actual relationships with women are not, it seems, so very different from women's in terms of images of submission – presumably recalling pre-pubescent fantasies in both sexes' (Segal, 1990: 214). So, let us follow a descriptive path here, and then a causal one.

First, the description. Sex is a threat to masculine autonomy, because it generates and is built around relationships characterised by dependence. This is true even in the most sadistic of contacts: the search for the recognition of the other is that much more desperate, the need to prove oneself separate and in control is so much more out of control. In a reciprocally sadomasochistic relationship the confusions of mastery and dependence are even more obvious (see Benjamin, 1988). And in 'ordinary', non-abusive sex, dependence on the other for pleasure and for a pleasured response is acute, intense, paramount. So why is this such a problem for men?

> Since the Reformation, masculinity has been identified with notions of 'self-control'. . . . It is in forsaking our own needs that we prove we have the self-control that makes our masculinity secure . . . our sexuality connects to our sense of masculinity and remains at some deep structure in the culture identified with the animal or the 'beastly'. Our sense of our lives can be so fragmented that sexual feelings can easily be identified as 'weakness', as giving in to temptation.
>
> (Seidler, 1989: 45–7)

So far removed from the body, masculine ideology idealises the life of the rational mind. Action: moving forward, progress, thrusting with force into the future, untrammelled by emotion, liberated from the confusions of womanly feeling, balanced, critical, self-assertive, free. In masculinist thought, the body is what holds us back, keeps us in the muddle of nature; the body is what is par excellence feminine, to be seen and owned, but not to be intrinsic to us. The gains for men lie in the apparent freedom this repudiation of the body gives us from the constraints and ties of nature – as superman, we can master everything. Through control of emotion, through passionless enterprise, we can always make the best, the most rational, the most 'objective' decisions. (And, of course, we can give ourselves up to the demands of production and profit, but that is another story.) The cost? 'We lose any sense of grounding ourselves in our own embodied experience as we identify our sense of masculinity with being objective and impartial' (Seidler, 1989: 129). Separate from the body, the body is repressed: we act as if we do not know it, as if it has no part in our experience. Self-control, mastery of nature and of our nature, is a defining marker of the masculine state. Consequently, when the repressed returns, when the body makes its mark through sex, it is experienced as failure, as a dangerous giving in to the bestial elements in our make-up.

This means that sex is both dangerously 'basic' and also somehow external – not part of what defines the man as 'man', as that advanced creature of rational mastery. Sex is always there, an obsession, but it is not part of us; being repudiated and repressed, it paradoxically threatens to take control. Here, as it happens, is a massive shaft of metaphorical connections, linking the body, sex, nature, women, and the fear of femininity.

> Underneath the image of nature in modern science as passive and entirely knowable is a suppressed signifier of nature as the ultimate force, capable of wreaking havoc over mind and culture. It contains intimations of something which always resists being fully known (like woman) and fully controlled (like woman) – else why the emphasis on pursuit and control?
>
> (Hollway, 1989: 115)

To the extent that sex is absorption in the body, is giving up of self-control and inhibition of desire, is jouissance, it represents the return of the repressed – of nature and all its feminine flows. The body-armour of the man falls away, is itself penetrated by the fantasised and repudiated femininity of boundary-less, unbound energy – with all its threats of devastation and havoc. 'All that's solid melts into air': the body's return is one that sweeps away the control on which masculine mastery is based.

Even in this description there is some causality: the signifier[1] 'sex' sets up signifieds that undermine the culture of masculinity as it has evolved over the centuries, producing in men terror, shame, a sense of failure, and – inevitably – anger and a drive to retribution. If we cannot tame the body, we can at least hit back at the body's representative, the woman. (So that is how she ends up outside language: not allowed a voice, she can be pure nature, to be acted on and exploited, justifiably kept within – or out of – bounds.) This is all culturally given: masculinity equals rationality, femininity equals nature/body; sex is the overcoming of the former by the latter, hence is unbearable and disowned. But how, in the life of each individual man, does this algebra become experience? How indeed, if not through relationships, beginning with the first relationship of all.

DESIRE AND THE MOTHER

For man, writes Olivier:

> what is at issue in sexual love is the re-enactment of his earliest love relation, that with his mother . . . hence the seriousness of impotence for the man: it both prevents him from taking possession of the second woman and signifies that he is not yet separated from the first, the forbidden mother.
>
> (Olivier, 1980: 99)

The first relationship, what is it? Often, it is thought of as something outside culture, something unmediated by the third term of the Oedipal progression (me–mummy–daddy; self–other–law), something purely of the body, absorbing, 'symbiotic', not yet constructed by language, that great constructor of identity. Developmentally speaking, this is an impossible relationship, consisting of complete oneness with the other yet holding in it the potential for, even the first moment of, separation. This is the Lacanian Real which can never be encountered, the moment before Kristeva's (1983) 'abject' marks some boundary between subject and object. Empirically, perhaps, we are speaking in Kleinian terms here, of the investment of desire in a bodily space, of an experiential world full to overflowing of anxiety and love, bounded desperately by the struggles of the psyche to survive. Jacobus (1990: 160) comments: 'One response to the current return to Klein: it feels like eating one's words.'

Eating one's words, yes, that which structures I and you, subject and object, disappears into a space of oneness in which there are no differentiations. This is 'thinking through the body', the feminine mode again (Gallop, 1988). Grunberger talks of it as the 'monad', the post-natal continuation of pre-natal oneness, in which the baby experiences her or himself as still perfectly linked with the mother. But the monad has a dual task: it both preserves pre-natal bliss and prepares the infant for something new.

The monad is a nonmaterial womb which functions as though it were material; on the one hand, it encloses the child in its narcissistic universe; on the other, it prepares it for the partial dissolution of that universe – or, in other words, for the dissolution of its own essence.

(Grunberger, 1989: 3)

Grunberger identifies the monad as a preserver of infantile sanity in the face of the assaults of the post-natal environment; but it is also a continuing pull backwards during development, a source of regressive narcissism as a fantasised solution to all problems presented by reality. Put bluntly, misogynistically, the opposition is between Narcissus and Oedipus, with the former identified as a maternal principle of oneness, an unattainable fantasy, and the latter as an encounter with paternal reality – the reality of the world as it is. Engaging with the conflicts of Oedipus is engaging with difference, with how the world is actually structured, and with the necessity for toleration of constraint and uncertainty; resisting Oedipus, staying with the fantasy of the maternal monad, is narcissistic regression, wanting everything pure, whole, and uncontaminated.

Let us leave aside all the epistemological problems with this set of claims and note its genderedness. First, an intriguing side issue: a gendered dispute over the nature of anality. For Grunberger, as mentioned earlier, anality opposes narcissism, which tends towards a fantasy of purity and which is consequently opposed to corporeality and toleration of the messy nature of reality. 'The triumph of narcissism over anality means not only an apparent liberation from Oedipus and from conflict, but also a liberation from reality – or, in a phrase, from the human condition' (1989: 155). So anality is a positive move, towards reality. But see this, from the woman Olivier: 'The man's anal game comes down to this: how to stop the other from existing; how to remove all trace of her desire; how to kill her in fantasy' (1980: 64). There is more than a disagreement here, there is a radical difference of interpretation of what constitutes 'reality', and of the extent to which the masculine order – the Oedipus, if it must be – can be tolerated. For the man, the choices apparently forced by reality are necessary; for the woman, they are ways of exerting control.

Perhaps this is not so much a side issue after all, but a front and back one. The argument concerning masculine development goes like this. Freud was wrong in thinking that feminine development is the harder path (e.g. 1933), a mistake generated by his failure to look far enough back from the Oedipus complex. Certainly, if one takes the Oedipal view, one has to explain how the girl shifts her object of desire from the mother to the father. But this makes gender development contingent on the nature of the object, when it makes more sense to see it in terms of the subject, in particular of the identifications around which subjectivity is constructed. Looking at the pre-Oedipal period one is impressed not so much with the directions in which the infant expresses her or his desire, but with the incorporations, internalisations, identifications which she or he demonstrates – the psychological procedures, modelled on bodily ones, of building up the ego through taking in material from outside. Seen like this, it is masculinity which is the more precarious achievement. Incorporation of the mother is the natural position for all infants – the first relationship – making identification with femininity easy; indeed, object-relations theorists suggest that it is so easy that girls and women consistently show difficulties in becoming separate (e.g. Eichenbaum and Orbach, 1982). Releasing oneself from the mother and finding a father with whom to identify, on the other hand, is a task much more difficult to achieve, yet this is the boy's task, at least under social conditions in which gender development and self-development go hand in hand.

So let us think through what might happen here. There is, at first, a tremendously powerful bond, an absorption of the infant in the mother, an almost-oneness, infused with anxieties (if the Kleinians are right), bodily, relatively unmediated, but perhaps already marked with the horror of potential dissolution. Girls have many problems with this – of differentiation, of finding a place which is both bodily and yet autonomous, of entering the world of symbols, of becoming true subjects in their own right. But this chapter is not concerned with girls' experiences, except as fantasised by boys. For boys, attaining masculinity is a desperate striving towards something unknown and unknowable: a state of difference from the mother, yet grounded in her. The trend of early experience is to suck the boy in, to make him fused with the mother; but, as fused, he cannot master her, cannot take on the vague but intensely felt promise of phallic mastery, cannot conquer nature – his own or her's. Consequently, his activity is that of repudiation of the mother, a repudiation helped both by her own fantasy of him as other, as separate from her (hence a potential object of desire, because not the same, not already-owned) and also the Oedipal fantasy that the masculine order dominates the feminine, that the boy can grow into a phallus of his own.

But here's the rub, if we can. The phallus is not to be his; as discussed earlier, the phallus is itself fraudulent, there is no mastery that is complete. The boy knows this from his own experience already, but cannot bear it.

> The father's phallus stands for the wholeness and separateness that the child's real helplessness and dependency belie. . . . The devaluation of the need for the other becomes a touchstone of adult masculinity.
>
> (Benjamin, 1988: 171)

Repudiating the mother, the boy turns his back on the intense contact with the other that she represents. Because of the precariousness of his own sense of mastery, he must battle continually to assert himself against her, against the feminine principle of oneness, against 'regressive narcissism', against anything that smells of the maternal. Sexually, the boy learns to fear his desire, because it brings back the loss of mastery; converting it into conquest and performance, it becomes 'an individual achievement that reflects upon the position of a man within the pecking order of masculinity' (Seidler, 1989: 39), a way of establishing oneself rather than making contact with another. All intimacy is potentially dangerous, because the boundaries of the masculine self are so fragile that they can be all too easily overwhelmed. Paradoxically, this explains the apparent rigidity of so much masculinity: one cannot bend at all, for fear of disappearing into the mire. Oh those images of feminine luxuriousness, multiplicity, and multifariousness, how easily they switch into the demonic vision of the overtaking, overcoming, engulfing mother who will not let us breathe. Most poignantly, when faced with feminine desire, the male backs away – mastery is all.

ABUSE AGAIN

So, back we are with domination. Here is Benjamin's summary statement.

> Erotic domination represents an intensification of male anxiety and defence in relation to the mother. The repudiated maternal body persists as an object to be done to and violated, to be separated from, to have power over, to denigrate. . . . The vulnerability of masculinity that is forged in the crucible of femininity, the 'great task' of separation that is so seldom completed, lays the groundwork for the later objectification of women. The mother stands as the prototype of the undifferentiated object. She serves men as their other, their counterpart, the side of themselves they repress.
>
> (Benjamin, 1988: 77)

Why do men sexually abuse women and children? If there is any validity to the analysis presented above, sexual abuse is a function of men's own abhorrence of the feminine within – it is a kind of continuing assault on the body of the mother. In both forms of abuse, the nexus is one of hostility/rage/sexuality (see MacLeod and Sarraga, 1988), centring on that splitting off of sex from intimacy which is a crucial element in masculine sexual socialisation. Women are the primary recipients of the offshoots of this splitting: 'If women are not enough of a problem in their own right, they become so in their role as the bearers or symbolic representatives of various disavowed, warded off, unacceptable aspects of men' (Fogel, 1986, quoted in Segal, 1990: 75). The man's rage as he experiences sexual desire, associated with a breaking down of masculinity and a sucking back into the body of the powerful mother, is extruded on to the woman, who is, both individually and socially, the sanctioned recipient of violence. The growing strength of women and the declining power of traditional masculine modes of character organisation (declining through the dismantling of old authority structures, the disbanding of traditional and reliable work environments, and the general heterogeneity of contemporary capitalism – see Seidler, 1991), reinforce this rage, now more like an infantile despair at the loss of power than the fully formed expression of mastery.

But children, why should they be abused? There are some persuasive descriptive accounts of the pathways to abuse, for example, in Finkelhor (1984); also some which link powerfully with feminist analyses of gender relationships (e.g. MacLeod and Sarraga, 1988). The powerful cultural associations of children and sexuality should also not be denied, even though they usually are (see Glaser and Frosh, 1988). But here, let us keep to the implications of the earlier analysis of masculine development. Renouncing the mother and striving for the father, but also living in the exquisitely painful consciousness of the impossibility of attaining the phallus – of being truly rational and masterful – the male has only a fragile armour of masculinity, kept desperately in place by repression of emotion, desire, and intimate connection with others. Sex, then, becomes a tremendously important channel for the expression of emotion, which is denied any other channel; but it is also a terrifying threat. This is because it makes the man dependent on the other and also represents the overwhelming of control by desire. Masculine sexuality may then, if alienated enough, seek the least threatening, the most controllable of objects – which may not be the adult woman. As Olivier (1980) points out, having to deal with the desire of the other/mother is terrifying to the man, because it carries with it the threat of fusion, of being sucked back into her narcissistic womb and thus losing all the laboriously built boundaries of masculinity: 'There is no greater threat to the man than the express desire of the woman, which for him invariably takes on the form of an evil trap (evil because linked to the desire of the all-powerful mother)' (1980: 96). Searching for a more controllable object, one which can be silenced, forced, made in fantasy into anything at all, some men alight upon a child.

Of course not all men abuse children, and the differences between those who do and those who do not are crucial for theory and therapeutic practice. These differences may arise from a number of sources: the quality of early relationships as well as of those formed during adulthood; challenges to emotional distancing faced during development; differences in patterns of gender socialisation; and specific experiences of trauma or reparation (see Frosh, 1987). But most abusers of children are men, and this takes some explaining. The suggestion here is that the systematic links are given not only through the organisation of society along patriarchal lines, but also in the more micro-cosmic patterns of

relationship and desire that are characteristic of masculine sexual socialisation. The painful mixture of impulse and over-control, of separation
and intimacy, of fear and desire – this mixture so common in men is also
something that infiltrates men's relationships with children, sometimes
leading to abuse. As sex is the only form of intimacy allowable to many
men, all intimacy tends to turn into sex; as emotion is so linked with
mastery and power, so threatening to it, then power is used where emotion would be more appropriate; as nurture is so feared, it is renounced,
denied, brutalised. This is not true of all men, of course not. But this is
what all men struggle with, at least now, at least here, at least while our
experience is so pervasively, so damningly gendered.

SEX AND SEXUALITY

So sex is not all there is to sexuality; sexuality is a broader term, it carries with
it a heavy baggage of connections with identity, with socialisation, and with
culture. The manner in which we understand masculinity influences the
manner in which we understand masculine sexuality; sexuality is a psychological entity, not just a set of biological urges or behavioural techniques.
The formulation given here suggests that the separation of sex from
sexuality, a separation characteristic of much sex therapy, is itself part of the
ideology of masculinity: sex is decontextualised, isolated from the dangers of
emotion and boundary dissolution. It becomes something out there, to be
achieved or performed, a mark of mastery. Success and failure: these are the
terms of alienation in any discussion of what sex means.

The seeds of masculine sexuality are embedded deeply in relationships, both concretely and figuratively. In domination and fear, in
ambivalence towards intimacy, in a desire for an other who both is and is
not the mother, in awareness of the space that a father might fill. In a
cultural order built around fantasies of wholeness and rational perfection,
safe from dissolution but also bereft of emotion. In certain kinds of
specific family relationships. For therapists, all this suggests the need for
exploration of the significance of sex in the life of male clients; in the
context of abuse, it means a challenge to all manifestations of domination
and force. Most of all, it means opposition to that splitting, that fearful
turning away, seen so often when men's emotional life is the issue.
Rationality, mastery, control: exploration of masculine sexuality is as
much about these issues as it is about sexual 'performance'. Focusing only
on the latter is, indirectly or directly, a masculinist strategy; it says, 'this
far will I go, but I will not really challenge what is, not really try to make
the differences speak'.

NOTE

1 Signifier refers to the form of a sign – the sound of a spoken word or sight of a written one. Signified refers to the mental representation produced by this signifier.

REFERENCES

Benjamin, J. (1988) *The Bonds of Love*, London: Virago, 1990.
Berman, M. (1982) *All That is Solid Melts into Air*, London: Verso, 1983.
Eichenbaum, L. and Orbach, S. (1982) *Outside In . . . Inside Out*, Harmondsworth: Penguin.
Finkelhor, D. (1984) *Child Sexual Abuse*, New York: Free Press.
Freud, S. (1933) *New Introductory Lectures on Psychoanalysis*, Harmondsworth: Penguin, 1973.
Frosh, S. (1987) 'Issues for men working with sexually abused children', *British Journal of Psychotherapy* 3: 332–9.
Frosh, S. (1989) *Psychoanalysis and Psychology*, London: Macmillan.
Frosh, S. (1991) *Identity Crisis: Modernity, Psychoanalysis and the Self*, London: Macmillan.
Gallop, J. (1988) *Thinking Through the Body*, New York: Columbia University Press.
Glaser, D. and Frosh, S. (1988) *Child Sexual Abuse*, London: Macmillan.
Grunberger, B. (1989) *New Essays on Narcissism*, London: Free Association Books.
Haugaard, J. and Reppucci, N. (1988) *The Sexual Abuse of Children*, San Francisco: Jossey-Bass.
Hollway, W. (1989) *Subjectivity and Method in Psychology*, London: Sage.
Jacobus, M. (1990) '"Tea Daddy": poor Mrs Klein and the pencil shavings', *Women* 1: 160–79.
Kristeva, J. (1983) 'Freud and love', in T. Moi (ed.) *The Kristeva Reader*, Oxford: Blackwell, 1986.
Lacan, J. (1958) 'The meaning of the phallus', in J. Mitchell and J. Rose (eds) *Feminine Sexuality*, London: Macmillan, 1982.
MacLeod, M. and Sarraga, E. (1988) 'Challenging the orthodoxy: towards a feminist theory and practice', *Feminist Review* 28: 16–55.
Moore, S. (1988) 'Getting a bit of the other: the pimps of postmodernism', in R. Chapman and T. Rutherford (eds) *Male Order*, London: Lawrence & Wishart.
Olivier, C. (1980) *Jocasta's Children*, London: Routledge, 1989.
Segal, L. (1990) *Slow Motion: Changing Men*, London: Virago.
Seidler, V. (1989) *Rediscovering Masculinity*, London: Routledge.
Seidler, V. (1991) *Recreating Sexual Politics*, London: Routledge.
Theweleit, K. (1977) *Male Fantasies*, Cambridge: Polity, 1987.

Chapter 3

Public values and private beliefs
Why do women refer themselves for sex therapy?

Paula Nicolson

INTRODUCTION

> The high priests of sexual theory *have* contributed to the world we
> inhabit . . . they promoted the belief that sex was of crucial importance
> to individual health, identity and happiness . . . they set an agenda for
> sexual change which, to a remarkable degree, has been completed.
>
> (Weeks, 1985: 7)

The last thirty years have seen an increase in 'expert knowledge' on
human sexual response and development of techniques and enthusiasm
for sexual counselling and therapy. This knowledge, based on sexological
theory and research, has contributed to cultural expectations that each
individual has a right and a duty to achieve and give maximum
satisfaction in their sexual relationships. The uptake of sex therapy by
both women and men may be seen as a trend towards well-being and
self-care. It may be, however, that seeking help of this kind obscures a
more complex human problem – that is, that the discourse on human
sexuality constrains individuals, particularly women, in ways that
potentially stimulate distress.[1]

Lesbian social scientists have already identified and challenged sexology, which, while claiming to liberate both women and men, has been
effective in upholding an oppressive patriarchal mythology about female
sexuality – ensuring women's 'availability' as the objects of male desire
(e.g. Jackson, 1987; Jeffreys, 1990). This invaluable feminist analysis
clarified historical and political dimensions underlying the knowledge
base of the sex experts, thereby challenging the 'objectivity' of patriarchal
science (see also Jane Ussher's chapter). Thus we need to be aware that:

> The implications of . . . sexual liberation are profoundly anti-feminist,
> and the main reason for this lies in the failure to make problematic the
> concept of sexual pleasure. What counts as sexual pleasure, who de-
> fines it, who has the power to insure that certain definitions prevail?
>
> (Jackson, 1983: 2)

And:

> This 'sexual liberation' was the freedom for women to take pleasure in their own erotic subordination. Sexology . . . is the idea that sex is and should be a way of expressing and maintaining male dominance and female enthusiasm. The sexologists of the twentieth century have been the high priests who have organised the worship of male power.
>
> (Jeffreys, 1990: 1)

In this chapter I look specifically at heterosexual women's sexuality and assess the sexological discourses available to explain why women seek treatment for psycho-sexual 'disorders'. I argue that the emphasis on sexual intercourse as the medium through which sexual desire and pleasure are obtained needs to be understood ideologically rather than biologically, and, in order to do this, assumptions about what constitute 'normal' or 'natural' desires and pleasures for women need to be deconstructed.

Women's sexuality, their desires and responses have been defined and dictated by men. Women are expected to engage with heterosexuality enthusiastically, and take what is an essentially passive/responsive role in which, most important, they are ever 'available'. But why should women collude in this humiliating sexual ritual – and more so – why should they seek therapy if their distaste becomes unmanageable? Here, I explore the ways in which the dominant discourses on heterosexuality have penetrated women's self-concepts so that they evaluate themselves and hold beliefs according to accepted, but value-laden indices which potentially lead to self-pathologisation and consequent self-referral for therapy.

SCIENCE AND POWER

Initially, it is important to ask how such an apparently male-orientated perspective on heterosexuality has become universally influential. The main philosophical and historical influences upon sexology have been outlined in Chapter 1, and it is through these clerical/theological and medical/scientific discourses that women's sexuality is regulated. But how do these discourses enter the perceptions of ordinary women?

The intrinsic relationship between claims to knowledge of dominant groups and commonly accepted, taken for granted understandings and practices has been explored and well documented among Foucauldian philosophers, and this perspective is relevant here (see Foucault, 1973; Philp, 1985). The essence of this is that, following Foucault, knowledge derives from power, and that knowledge reproduces itself through the social mechanisms of norm-setting which in turn have a psychological dimension; that is, they penetrate self-cognitions. This occurs through the cyclical interrelations between science, the media, and those professionals (in this case sex and psychotherapists) who are agents of social control.

In the case of sex, it appears that men, via science, have gained control of what is considered 'normal' and 'healthy'. As a consequence they have gained control of social norms which regulate behaviour and influence women's as well as men's self-concepts. Thus, alternative sexual or social practices or rejection of the 'normal' in private may lead women to be assessed by others and themselves as pathological (see also Ussher, 1990, 1991, 1992a; Nicolson, 1992a).

As very little evidence has been produced to challenge male constructions of female sexual desire and behaviour, both women and men, scientists and others, evaluate women's sexuality according to beliefs which confine women's sexual expression within a *passive/submissive* framework, and women's sexual desire within one which is essentially *responsive* to male desire and behaviour (Nicolson, 1992b). In as far as we are all bound by the values and ideas of the societies in which we live, sexologists (sexual scientists) derive their validity from investigations of individuals who *respond in some relation to socially accepted norms*. Thus traditional paradigms are upheld through the power of knowledge 'cycles'.

The 'knowledge cycle'

> To define the regime of power–knowledge–pleasure that sustains the discourse on human sexuality in our part of the world . . . to account for the fact that it is spoken about, to discover who does the speaking, the positions and viewpoints from which they speak, the institutions which store and distribute the things that are said. What is at issue, briefly, is the over-all 'discursive fact', the way in which sex is 'put into discourse'.
>
> (Foucault, 1978: 11)

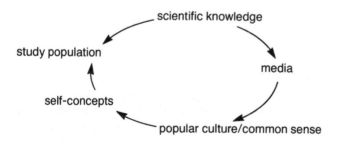

Figure 3.1 The knowledge cycle
Source: Nicolson, 1991a.

The way that knowledge claims about human sexuality are structured and the power of dominant social groupings employing vested interests to set norms and influence popular knowledge are also crucial for understanding the genesis of research paradigms and human socialisation. The priority Western society attributes to science is more problematic in the late twentieth century than ever before because of the relationship of science and the media which influences socialisation (e.g. White, 1977).

Sexology, as in any discipline which studies human behaviour, relies for its data on the practices of socialised and culture-bound individuals, so that to explore 'natural' or 'culture-free' behaviour (i.e. that behaviour unfettered by culture, social structures, and power relations) is by definition – impossible. As Jane Ussher points out, though, this is frequently not even acknowledged by scientists themselves (see also Ussher, 1992b).

The diagram of the 'knowledge cycle' clarifies the interconnectedness of science and self-concept, demonstrating the fallacy of measuring 'natural' behaviour, and illustrates the danger of not challenging the dominant discourses on human sexuality. As with Foucault above, it is the way sex is put into discourse that influences what we believe is 'natural' in ourselves and others. If this model is applied to the belief that orgasm during sexual intercourse is natural/normal for women, the problem may be represented as in Figure 3.2.

While this is a simplistic representation, it does go some way to explaining the interrelationship of science and individual women's self-concepts. However, the power relationship between research funding,

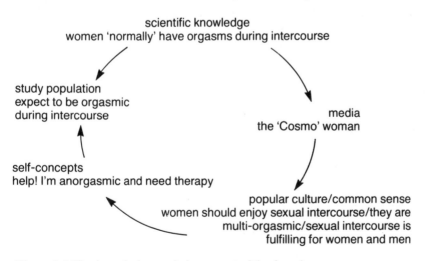

Figure 3.2 The knowledge cycle in respect of the female orgasm
Source: Nicolson, 1991a.

institutional approval, serious media attention, and the everyday popular influence of feminist critiques of science in relation to female psychology is frequently overridden by the superordinate status of male-dominated science (see Ussher, 1992b; Nicolson, 1992b). Thus feminist critiques have little impact on 'serious' research, where reductionist theories are perpetuated, and positivist ideas continue to reign supreme.

DECONSTRUCTING SEXUAL DESIRE

The method of *deconstruction*, developed from literary criticism, psychoanalysis, and linguistic theory, enables an exposure of the ideological premises underlying scientific discourse (see Ussher, Chapter 1, this volume; Hollway, 1989; Fox, 1991). Here I want to deconstruct twentieth-century sexological discourse to demonstrate its unflinching adherence to notions of male power and the desire to have women as passive objects of pleasure or derision; and then suggest how emergent ideas become embedded in everyday knowledge and from there women's self-concepts which may lead to self-pathologisation.

There are three clear dominant discourses operating around human sexual behaviour, and the ideology underlying texts on human sexuality which may be identified in theories which in themselves are not linked – such as sociobiology and psychoanalysis.

The first key discourse concerns the nature of heterosexuality which is structured as biologically driven (and therefore 'natural'), positioning women in a passive/responsive role and men as active. This discourse refers to both sexual intercourse and heterosexual courtship.

The second key discourse is the one surrounding the *orgasm* for both partners as the goal of sexual engagement. In this discourse the required physiological consequence of intense stimulation to the penis, clitoris, and (questionably) the vagina would 'normally' be an orgasm, and orgasm is taken to be both the *climax* (in the sense of being the most intense part of the experience) and the *goal* (in that it is the point to which all behaviours lead).

The third discourse surrounding *penetration* may be distinguished from, although clearly linked to, the other two. Not only has the male to be active and the female passive, but the male has to prove his masculinity and overcome the female's feigned resistance. The woman has to demonstrate her femininity by allowing herself to be conquered through the act of penetration.

The extracts discussed below are intended as illustrations of these discourses identified through deconstruction of the texts that these extracts represent (see Nicolson, 1990).

Active versus passive

The discourse which posits heterosexuality as natural has been identified and discussed by Jane Ussher (Chapter 1), and Jeffrey Weeks (1985) has provided an excellent account of the politics of sexology in relation to this. Here, I focus on the aspects of this discourse which relate to female/male roles surrounding the act of sexual intercourse (the apparent focus of heterosexual desire, see p.60): that is the *activity* of the male and the *passivity* of the female. These 'complementary' behaviours occur at various levels of heterosexual interaction: during heterosexual intercourse where the penis *actively* penetrates the passive vagina; in courtship where the male actively pursues the passive, waiting female; in reproduction where the ovum passively receives the active sperm; and, on a wider perspective, where women are valued for their feminine/passive qualities and men for their masculine/active ones (see Nicolson, 1992a).

Within the traditional sexological discourse, women are positioned as the nurturers and carers of men and children dependent on 'achieving' a male partner. Thus women need to make themselves attractive to men by fitting in with male desires: in other words, individual women need to defy any inclinations to independence, self-centredness, or ignoring the fine-tuning of their appearance in order to be seen as feminine (Brownmiller, 1984). Women are encouraged to make themselves passive so that male activity, social and sexual, may be facilitated.

Yet the notion of feminine passivity is paradoxical – it seems easy, potentially a haven for the feminine woman to await the male in pursuit. But, as Brownmiller asserts:

> Femininity always demands more. It must constantly reassure its audience by a willing demonstration of difference, even when one does not exist in nature. . . . To fail at the feminine difference is to appear not to care about men, or to risk the loss of their attention and approval. To be insufficiently feminine is viewed as a failure in core sexual identity, or as a failure to care sufficiently about oneself, for a woman found wanting will be appraised (and will appraise herself) as mannish or neutered or simply unattractive as men have defined these terms.
>
> (Brownmiller, 1984: 15)

So feminine sexual passivity is a passivity which men prescribe and desire, and male scientists 'observe' and then describe, but in reality involves an active struggle by women attempting to play this male-defined game. Men not only dictate women's 'natures', and thus how they behave, but 'objectively' describe this behaviour in a way which fits in with the patriarchal paradigm. Women either actively pursue passivity or self-pathologise.

This wider perspective on the construction of gender roles directly influences heterosexual sexual behaviour, and early twentieth-century sexology focused enthusiastically upon this dichotomy. For example, Ellis (1905), who claimed concern with the 'neglected area' of women's sexuality set out to overturn assumptions that women did not engage actively with sexuality, through defining women's 'sexual impulses' as having distinctive characteristics. Ellis suggests that women's apparent passivity is really a contrived role!

So:

> Except where the male fails to play his part properly, she is usually comparatively passive; in the proper playing of her part she has to appear to shun the male, flee from his approaches – even actually to repel them. Courtship resembles very closely indeed, a drama or game; and the aggressiveness of the male, the coyness of the female, are alike unconsciously assumed in order to bring about in the most effectual manner the ultimate union of the sexes. The seeming reluctance of the female is not intended to inhibit sexual activity either in the male or in herself, but to increase it in both. The passivity of the female, therefore, is not a real, but only an apparent passivity, and this holds true of our own species as much as of the lower animal.
>
> (Ellis, 1905: 229)

Men have to be aggressive, and women to be passive and withdrawn or else they fail. It is this contrast between women's *role* and women's apparent *nature* that is at the heart of the sexual paradox, and contributes to a discourse where women's sense of what they actually mean when they say 'no' to intercourse becomes negated.

Ellis draws attention to the *active* nature of women's desire (as opposed to behaviour) by suggesting that:

> The true nature of the passivity of the female is revealed by the ease with which it is thrown off, more especially when the male refuses to accept his cue. Or if we prefer to accept the analogy of a game, we may say that in the play of courtship, the first move belongs to the male, but that, if he fails to play, it is then the female turn to play.
>
> (Ellis, 1905: 232)

This male-centred interpretation of sexual behaviour underlies subsequent ideas made explicit by Freud – that women are mysterious, unpredictable, and potentially dangerous if they should step outside the bounds of passivity. Following Ellis's argument, women are somehow *responsible* for male potency, but only if they remain in a passive, unwakened state, while remaining *unavailable*. Freud's well-rehearsed version of female sexuality has rendered Ellis's view unproblematic because Freud evoked notions of normal/desirable versus pathological/undesirable states of women's being. The normal woman was essentially *passive* in terms of her personality, speech, and behaviour which were mirrored through her body in order for her to gain sexual pleasure in Freud's view. Women's genitals were biologically located and structured to be *penetrated* by a man so that it would be unnatural and against her passive nature and biological make-up for her to seek pleasure *actively* through male penetration.

> More constraint has been applied to the libido when it is pressed into the service of the feminine function . . . the accomplishment of the aim of biology has been entrusted to the aggressiveness of men and has been, to some extent, independent of women's consent.
>
> (Freud, 1933: 131–2)

It may sound to the modern ear that this is equivalent to a justification for male rape, and indeed some psychoanalytic literature does carry indications that women potentially welcome such violations in both fantasy and reality (Deutsch, 1944). It is easy and necessary to repudiate Freud's model, and many modern sex therapists would argue that early sexology has little impact upon their theorising. But it would be mistaken to imply that it lacks salience, as more recent researchers such as Gagnon and Simon have echoed Freud.

> At the present time the main determinant of adult rates of heterosexual activity in our society is the level of male commitment.
>
> (Gagnon and Simon, 1973: 198)

Patriarchal beliefs about women's sexuality are paradoxical: women are seen as both 'needing to be awakened' and rampant, lustful 'consumers' of men. Women's sexuality is not only potentially dangerous to men in this unpredictable way, but is also dangerous to their own reputation if they should err too much in the direction of sexual enjoyment or initiate a sexual relationship with a man outside the confines of marriage (Ussher, 1990). Underlying all, remains the contradiction that rape is psychologically (if not now legally) acceptable.

Within this active/passive discourse, women are portrayed, despite their subordinate role, as *essentially responsible for male potency.* By definition a woman is available to men, and, although passive, may be awakened according to male desires. What is not possible within this discourse is for a woman to be actively uninterested in sex with men, or active but not 'alluring', or always unavailable to be aroused. If a woman should actively not want sex with men or a particular man at a particular time or want sex with a man who does not want sex with her – she is pathological and requires treatment; and because of the powerful constraints of patriarchal knowledge claims, she believes in her own pathology.

The female orgasm

The second powerful discourse to emerge concerns the orgasm and, in particular, questions about the existence and site of the female orgasm. Ideas about repression of sexual instincts and sexual inhibition emerged through the European psychoanalytic movement, particularly the work of Wilhelm Reich in the 1930s. In *The Function of the Orgasm*, Reich stated:

> Psychic health depends upon orgasmic potency ie. upon the degree to which one can surrender to and experience the climax of exaltation in the natural sex act. It is founded upon the healthy character attitude of the individual's capacity for love. Psychic illnesses are the result of a disturbance of the natural ability to love. In the case of orgasmic impotence, from which the overwhelming majority of people suffer, damming-up of biological energy occurs and becomes the source of irrational actions.
>
> (Reich, 1942: 70)

Reich himself was concerned with social repression under fascism, coming from within the Freudian psychoanalytic tradition where there was a general concern with the psychopathological results of repressed instincts. Reich's creed represented the template for 1960s 'liberated' sexuality: that biological demand for orgasmic gratification needs to be fulfilled. It is the only way to peace and love![2]

The 'discovery' of female orgasmic capacity has had a problematic history: it was 'naturally' located in the vagina, as occurring when penetrated by a penis. Thus, there was a 'biological basis' for female passivity (i.e. reception of the penis) linked to 'mature' and 'normal' femininity. Freud has argued that females would transfer their sexuality from the clitoris to the vagina with adulthood (Freud, 1931). Masters and Johnson (1966) and feminist writers (e.g. Koedt, 1973) have challenged the universality of the vaginal orgasm, arguing that the clitoris is biologically charged for orgasmic capacity while the vagina is not. However, Birke suggests that:

> Nonetheless, the myth persists that women's sexuality is centred on the vagina, a myth that has provoked much anxiety among women believing themselves to be 'frigid'. If prevailing orthodoxy had been that women learnt their sexual responses, then presumably there might be acceptance of the idea that women could learn to reach orgasm during intercourse. Unfortunately for women, the prevailing orthodoxy has been that sexuality is an inborn trait, in which vaginal penetration somehow releases the biological potential. As a result women often feel guilt or a sense of failure if they do not achieve orgasm during vaginal penetration.
>
> (Birke, 1986: 17–18)

Thus, this biological essentialist discourse throughout the twentieth century progressively disempowered and pathologised women, who in turn felt themselves to be 'unnatural'.

Concern with 'natural' sexual expression emerged strongly in the decades preceding the 'sexually liberated 1960s', and the original studies by Kinsey and colleagues (1948, 1953) have been taken to demonstrate the end of Victorian sexual repression and part of the move towards allowing humans their natural rights to sexual expression.

The Kinsey research thus stressed 'sexual outlets' as a main variable which tended to mean 'orgasms'. Although they 'counted' orgasms through masturbation as outlets, the data were organised so that men were seen to experience more frequent 'successful' expressions of their sexuality than women. In their favour though, Kinsey's research team did indicate a serious place for clitoral rather than vaginal orgasms.

Kinsey and colleagues' research in the 1940s set out to collect explicit data from a cross-section of the North American population – first men and then women – about their sexual desires and behaviours. Although criticisms of this work are legion, the concern of other scientists has been with sampling and method rather than the underlying assumptions and their prescriptive nature, and particularly the facts that they failed to explore women's own perspectives on female sexuality, and emphasised the orgasm as the 'goal' or index of sexual achievement.

Their second volume, on the human female was largely considered as a comparison to the first, on the male, the implicit assumption being that women were complementary to men and male behaviour set the norms. The volume on women dedicated itself to comparisons, with no attempt to explore an independent female sexuality. The researchers concluded that women may be less overtly sexual than men (see Kinsey *et al.*, 1953: 687–8), in that they needed a specific context in which to express their sexuality.

Yet this research did give a proportion of its time to the female orgasm, drawing the telling conclusion that women's orgasmic capacity 'matures' with age, a situation which contrasts sharply with that of men. Although this conclusion has passed into everyday understanding and continues to occupy a significant place in popular ideas about older women's sexual relationships with younger men, this knowledge claim has shaky foundations, extrapolated from a series of unmarried and married women's experiences of sexual intercourse, where the married women tended to be drawn from an older population. The problem with this research (as with all) is the kind of questions which were asked and the subject population itself. In the case of orgasmic maturation, for example, they base their assertions on the following data:

Unmarried women (ie. not living in a sexual relationship with a man)
40.3% had never experienced sexual climax during intercourse,
54.6% experienced an orgasm on less than 50% of the occasions they
had sexual intercourse,

Married women
13% of married women reported never experiencing orgasm under
these conditions.
47.3% experienced orgasm on less than 50% of the occasions they had
sexual intercourse
33% said they always had orgasms.

(Gebhard and Johnson, 1979)

Although this demonstrates that more married women reported orgasms
coinciding with sexual intercourse than unmarried, the conclusion that a
higher rate of reported orgasms means maturity needs to be deconstructed as it makes explicit the belief that orgasms during intercourse are
'better' than other sexual experiences. The data itself are also problematic
in relation to the conclusions reached. Firstly, it is likely that most married
women had more opportunity to 'practise', within a relationship they
hopefully continued to find satisfying in itself. Secondly, it may be that,
as the married women had more invested in that relationship, they
reported what they considered to be the stereotypical notion of 'good'
sex, for their own self-image or for their partner's sake. Thirdly, the
analysis of this data failed to emphasise the fact that sexual intercourse did
not *normally* result in the woman's orgasm.

The question of orgasmic frequency during intercourse has become
central in the norm setting about women's sexuality and women's sexual
problems. Despite the relatively low frequency of reported orgasms
during intercourse for married women, 40 per cent said they were happy.
This might suggest that women have other criteria to apply in evaluating
a relationship – both in terms of what makes sex satisfying and in how far
sexual intercourse is central to marital happiness.

Interviews with men in this study showed that around 45 per cent of
married men claimed that their wives had orgasms 100 per cent of the
time when intercourse took place! Although this group did not comprise
the partners of the women in the study, it certainly indicates that either
both sets of statistics are problematic or they are distorted by women
lying, by wishful thinking, or by the fact that men wanted to indicate to
the interviewers that they were sexually accomplished. Whichever of
these is the case, it seems that men have a greater investment in the notion
of women's orgasms than do women. This is fundamental to the orgasm
discourse, and underpins all the 'scientific' debate on sexuality: i.e. men
can *make* women have orgasms and orgasms during sexual intercourse
not only represent a sexual union, but are good for both women and men.

But how far does the idea of women's orgasms coinciding with the penetration of the vagina by a man's penis serve women's interests? Is this a ploy to ensure women's availability by making them feel pathological if they cannot achieve this or a device to ensure heterosexuality?

While men appear to have orgasms on most occasions that they have sexual intercourse, there is little evidence that women have the same experience. Yet despite the contradictions, in practice, women's 'failure' to achieve orgasm during penetration has been consistently pathologised and the term 'frigid' applied to such women.

McVaugh (1979) claimed frigidity was a disease and, from Kinsey's figures, he generalised that around 13 million married women in the USA must be 'frigid'. If this is the case, instead of pathologising women, perhaps questions need to be asked about sexual intercourse itself. Why is it seen as 'real' sex? Whose interests are served by promoting this view? (See Jeffreys, 1990.)

Certainly, the myth of the female orgasm became pervasive following Masters and Johnson (1966) despite their declaration of a high proportion of anorgasmic subjects (see Chapter 1, this volume). In their study of human sexual response, efforts went towards showing similarities rather than differences between women and men. Their original work was criticised for its small and potentially unrepresentative sample, but possibly more important was the way their ideas passed into everyday understanding: for from their work the multi-orgasmic 'Cosmopolitan' woman emerged – ever available and ever demanding of sexual satisfaction.

Masters and Johnson's work, which demonstrated women's physical potential for multiple orgasm, involved the collection of physiological and psychological measures and observations. They concluded:

> There are so many variables of sexual response that no possibility exists for establishing norms of sexual performance for the study subject population
>
> (Masters and Johnson, 1966: 311)

Also:

> Female study subjects' orgasmic inadequacy has also been primarily coitally oriented . . . female orgasmic experience usually is developed more easily and is physiologically more intense (although subjectively not necessarily satisfying), when induced by auto-manipulation as opposed to coition.
>
> (Masters and Johnson, 1966: 314)

The contrast between what they say here and the everyday understanding of their work is marked. They suggest that sexuality is varied and that women are more likely to experience intense orgasms from masturbation. The radical potential of this conclusion has been supplanted and ignored in the wake of the more 'liberating' (to men) discovery of clitoral and multi-orgasms. Women do appear to have multi-orgasmic capacity, but, in contrast to men's orgasmic capacity, issues of incompatibility appear more persuasive than the possibility of most women and men achieving orgasms together during intercourse. Thus norm setting occurred, informing sex therapy and media images. Women's and men's popular magazines and sex manuals focus on how to turn women on, both in terms of women being able to articulate what they require and men finding the 'key'. Far from liberating women, new chains have been developed – women appear to have become slaves to the image of the multi-orgasmic woman. Their *physiological capacity* (a concept developed through research on overtly sexually interested women) has supplanted any possible exploration of the variety of sexual pleasures which might be sought. For heterosexual women the possibility of warm, close, not necessarily penetrative, physical relations with men are off the agenda. Orgasmic performance is what counts for the sexually normal woman.

The confusion is apparent in contemporary research on sex therapy (Haslam, 1988). 'Liberal' therapists have suggested that women's orgasms may be different from men's.

> It is sometimes difficult for the male to conceptualise, however, what a non-ejaculatory orgasm would be like, since in the male there is almost invariably an end-point which can be identified, even though the experience of orgasm on some occasions may be much more exciting than others. For a woman a relatively unexciting climax which is non-ejaculatory may be identified as a minor peak during sexual excitement; further, since the female is on some occasions capable of multiple orgasm, that is, the experience of one peak running into a further peak over a period of time . . . for women there may be problems in identifying the very nature of orgasm itself. Women may on some occasions experience an acute peak which satisfies, precluding the desire for further orgasm – more like that experienced by the male. Despite controversy over the existence of the G-Spot, orgasmic response is usually triggered by clitoral stimulation either direct or indirect, the inside of the vagina being relatively insensitive in this respect . . . a number of women can only develop sexual arousal under particular conditions, though these conditions may lack quite the same sort of clear-cut physical or visual stimulatory cues as tend to occur in males with similar problems.
>
> (Haslam, 1988: 96)

This extract provides an overview of the confusion surrounding female sexuality when examined through the patriarchal microscope. 'What really turns women on and what do they want?' is a question that concerns men and renders women themselves unable to answer. Women are not an homogeneous group, and there may be many answers, but until scientists ask these questions *of women* sexological knowledge will be no more accurate.

Penetration: power or pathology?

Contained within sexological discourses on heterosexuality is that which most severely pathologises women: the 'virgin wife' discourse in which penetration of the vagina by the penis represents the 'natural' awakening to womanhood. Friedman's (1971) review of clinical studies of virgin wives (during the 1950s) suggests that this 'condition' is unexpected, but not uncommon (Friedman estimated that there were around 700 new clinical cases per year in the UK). It is, he means, rarely discussed in everyday conversations.

> That a woman may need a doctor's help before she can have sexual intercourse after marriage, may be surprising. Newspapers occasionally report the annulment of unconsummated marriages, but these seem rare. The drive to have sexual intercourse has powerful, instinctual forces. When it is supported, in marriage, by strong cultural and social values as well, one might think that only the most severe organic pathology could block this drive. For most people it is true, but occasionally emotional conflict completely prevents sexual intercourse.
>
> (Friedman, 1971: 11)

It is clear that he finds resistance to penetration so amazing that it can only mean that the woman concerned is out of her own (as well as her partner's) control. Because the most common practice is for intercourse to occur within marriage, he assumes that it is instinctual, despite his acknowledgement of the social nature of marriage. While it may be that the woman does feel that her resistance is pathological, that she cannot control or keep charge of her body to enable penetration, Friedman and other clinical writers he quotes fail to examine the value and symbolism surrounding intercourse. Perhaps it is the woman's last remaining chance to keep some control over her *life*.

In order to understand what invariably is seen as the psychopathology of these women, Friedman quotes Michel-Wolfromm (1954):

> The patients . . . are generally of above average intelligence, often with a lively imagination, they had chimeric dispositions, or else were very ambitious . . . in general they could be grouped into two character types, those with strong masculine tendencies and those with infantile attitudes.
>
> (Friedman, 1971: 29)

Michel-Wolfromm says these women were of the masculine type, exhibiting an independence which seems to prevent them from passively giving themselves to their partner and that deliberately/consciously resisting penetration, or being unable to stop the involuntary spasms of the outer third of the vagina as with vaginismus, expresses *aggressiveness* and serves as a revenge for *day to day enslavement* (Friedman, 1971: 29). Others have distinguished vaginismus, a functional disorder which is seen in the highly strung and over-anxious woman who may be physically attractive but 'spoilt' from other forms of resistance to penetration. The effects are often similar (Jeffcoate, 1957, cited in Friedman, 1971: 18). This position remains visible today, more than thirty years after Jeffcoate's comments. Adler, a sex therapist, suggests:

> Less commonly seen today is the primary vaginismic patient, sleeping beauty: an emotionally immature woman awaiting a sexual awakening without taking responsibility for it. These 'good girls' have often been brought up to believe that sex is bad or dirty; she had to save herself for marriage! This type can appear 'little girl like', pristine, clean and tidy, and very controlled generally; or she may look quite sexy, enjoy sex play and experience orgasm with clitoral stimulation. Her partner is often 'a gentleman' in every sense: an unassertive, gentle, literally non-pushy man who may well have hidden anxieties about his own sexual abilities.
>
> (Adler, 1989: 420)

As Sheila Jeffreys has commented elsewhere in relation to the text on virgin wives:

> Power and domination by men in marriage would have been normal and not worthy of any comment, but anything apart from submission by wives was an upsetting of the patriarchal apple-cart which required not only comment but therapy.
>
> (Jeffreys, 1990: 33)

Within this discourse the bones of patriarchy seem to be laid bare. For a man, penetration of a woman's vagina demonstrates his right to be a real man. For a woman, resistance to penetration means she is not feminine, but while, for the man, this unproven masculinity is inevitably problematic, for a woman, resistance is potentially emancipatory. It is a woman's attempt to resist passivity that is being treated in sex therapy where a successful outcome means she agrees to submit to male power. The fact that, in law, marriage requires penetration of the vagina by the penis suggests the level of male fear of women's resistance: it is a legal rather than interpersonal matter. As discussed above, even in cases of male impotence, women are held psychologically 'responsible'.

The most severe punishments are directed towards women who

actively (consciously or unconsciously) resist penetration: such as inserting penis-shaped instruments of ever-increasing size into the vagina in the name of gynaecological therapy (i.e. graduated glass vaginal dilators). More important though for many women is that resisting sexual intercourse effectively removes her right and ability to become pregnant and have a child (there was a furore in the UK recently which outlined the fear and hostility directed towards a woman who had never had intercourse but wanted to become a mother through 'artificial' insemination; see Nicolson, 1991b). However, for some women, the 'punishments' in the form of treatment do not seem to outweigh the desire to avoid submission and, far from vaginismus being 'expunged', some gynaecologists and sex therapists have reported its increase (Adler, 1989).

The extent to which a woman is refused the right to resist, or fear, intercourse is further revealed by deconstruction of therapeutic accounts of how to 'cure' the condition. There are indications of gynaecologists revealing their hostility to women, and the *need to assert their own masculinity* in making women conform. Some reports of techniques have more in common with pornographic accounts of seduction than a desire to emancipate a distressed woman and enable her to explore her own sexuality. The following extract demonstrates this most clearly. The author (a man) is a Fellow of the Royal College of Obstetricians and Gynaecologists who works in London. He includes the following recommendation for treating the female partner (or 'girl', see below) in an 'unconsummated marriage':

> She is asked just to remove her lower underwear and to keep her skirt on, as she will feel much less exposed if examined with a skirt on. If this is impractical, then, as the patient lies on the bed, she could be covered with either a blanket or a sheet so that her vulva is hidden at least from herself, though not from me the examining doctor. My own practice is then to place the under side of my hand firmly on the bed, near, but not touching the vulva, and to explain to the patient that I will not proceed to introduce my fingers into her vulva, let alone her vagina, but that with these organs she herself should try to examine my outstretched finger. I keep my elbow, forearm and fist firmly on the bed, and initially extend only the index finger. I then persuade the girl to lower herself onto the finger by making wriggling movements down towards the hand. The finger, of course, is gloved and lubricated. If the lips of the vulva are closed or if the girl has difficulty in abducting her legs, I usually tell her to point one knee towards the wall, and then to separate her knees as far as she can. . . . It is surprising how quickly the vast majority of patients agree to 'examine' the doctor's fingers with their vulvas providing the doctor himself promises not to move his hand or finger.

(Phillip, 1988: 86)

This quote continues in the same vein with the woman eventually being persuaded to lower herself further on to the finger and the 'doctor' introducing more fingers. Phillip ends this section of his paper with the declaration that 'this technique has been found to work in the vast majority of patients' (1988: 86).

This clinical account seems to represent a case of male rivalry and male bonding. The 'doctor' here is challenging the masculinity and prowess of the husband, while at the same time substituting for him. The woman is objectified and the clinical aim is to conquer through making her infant-like by playing games, as well as through seduction. But the women agree to take part, and are cured! Who is gaining pleasure from this therapeutic experience? The gynaecologist, the woman, the woman's partner, and the reader all collude in a sexual drama, verging on the pornographic (cf. Jeffreys' (1990) account of Masters and Johnson's use of dilators).

From penetration of the vagina to penetration of the mind

Sexology makes clear the nature of the heterosexual discourse: women desire sex with men, they are passive which 'attracts' men, they are satisfied by responding to penetration and that satisfaction is represented by orgasm. Women who are lesbian or bisexual, socially and/or sexually 'active', unconcerned or careless as to whether they attract men, unable to experience orgasm during penetration, or who refuse to be penetrated at all are 'sick'. Such women need treatment. But, despite the problematic nature (for women) of fulfilling the requirements of these overlapping patriarchal discourses, women's resistance fails. Perhaps more significant is that *women actually collude with these patriarchal perspectives on femininity, masculinity, and sexuality.* Women seem to choose to believe in their own sexual failure rather than challenge the premises on which measures of normality are built. Images of the bitter virgin/spinster or the frustrated wife or the miserable 'ugly' woman who does not attract men are ever present (Ussher, 1989), while the beautiful, 'desirable' woman, both passive and responsive, abounds. Not only is she 'attractive' but she is sexually capable – the 'multi-orgasmic Cosmopolitan woman'. Women and men revile the unattractive woman, the woman who cannot be sexually satisfied because of her lack of responsiveness. However, this revulsion is also applied to a woman who cannot be satisfied because no *one* man has the stamina.

Not only is the sexually 'inadequate' woman pathologised, but so is the sexually' rampant' and lustful woman (Brownmiller, 1984; Ussher, 1991, Chapter 1, this volume). Most medical/therapeutic texts and papers do not focus on 'nymphomania' but there is a growing discourse – contributing to the process of regulation (see Chapter 1). Despite some women's accounts of enjoying sexual intercourse and the sense of conquest, psychologists and other experts are more than happy to pathologise these women. One example in a teenage magazine illustrates this (*More* February 1991). Young women interviewed said they did not necessarily want a relationship in order to have sex: 'I couldn't be faithful to one person because of all the temptations' (Vanessa, 21); 'How I feel the next day depends on the sex. If it was great, then I feel fantastic. If it's very bad, I think "when's the next bus?" I shrug it off. My main satisfaction comes from knowing that I got him into bed rather than the other way round' (Nancy, 21); 'Lesley (20) gets a kick out of sleeping around. When she meets a boy she fancies, if she wants to and he wants to, they usually end up having sex.'

But: 'Psychosexual counsellor Tricia Kreitman says there's a basic bio-logical difference in the make-up of males and females which enables boys to readily do it with just about anyone, anywhere and any time' (*More* February 1991: 16–17). The article goes on to say that boys have uncomplicated sexual urges which are normal, but girls do not and therefore 'promiscuous' girls are short-circuiting their emotions, by-passing closeness and the vulnerability that this brings. In other words, women who enjoy sex for its own sake are being coerced by other women (through the patriarchal media) to be what men want them to be – available but faithful, and certainly not active. Such magazines aimed at adolescents are clearly in the business of directly shaping behaviour. The experiences and desires of the women in this article are deemed 'un-natural' and the women themselves dismissed as promiscuous. They are active and unfeminine. Their punishment occurs not only through their 'disposal' under patriarchy where sexual women are dismissed as 'whores' (Ussher, 1991). But their real feelings are contested: 'She can't distinguish between sex where just bodies are touching and sex where the mind is involved' says the resident sex expert (*More* February 1991: 16).

From adolescence and early sex education we are taught directly that women are not sexually proactive; they are responsive and emotional. However, when women experience sexual pleasure as emotional rather than physical (i.e. orgasm) they are also pathologised as they are expected (by men) to have orgasms. This conundrum, described in more detail in Jane Ussher's chapter, penetrates women's consciousness. *Women know they cannot rely on their own feelings about what is right for them.* Unless they fit the feminine image with the sexological and social/sociobiological discourses they are sexually inadequate. Their only recourse is to with-draw, feel guilty and unhappy, or seek to rectify *their* problem through sex counselling and therapy. The knowledge claims of male science pene-trate all our self-concepts: women's and men's. We are all subject to and positioned within the dominant discourses and, until their decon-struction is taken seriously in a popular way, the psychological trap will continue to spring.

CONCLUSIONS

Women, in order to make sense of their own sexuality, draw upon three major scientific discourses surrounding sexual behaviour and desire: active/passive heterosexuality; orgasm as goal for sexual encounters; and the dominance of penetration. These discourses are demonstrably patriarchal in origin and, as I argued above, some therapists and researchers have employed these in ways which subordinate individual women and female sexuality in general. Central to this chapter is the problematic relationship between these patriarchal discourses and women's self-concepts, with an attempt to explain how and why women appear to collude in their own pathologisation. That women are pathologised whether or not they enjoy sexual intercourse emerges clearly from media messages which pass into everyday understanding and the popular consciousness of women and men.

The dominant and enduring discourses on sexual morality (outlined in Jane Ussher's chapter) serve to maintain these messages, which subsequently become reiterated through data collected from respondents in mainstream, patriarchal, and thus high-status sex studies. Lesbian feminists have made a major contribution to explaining ways that twentieth-century sexual science and 'liberation' have positioned women as subordinate within heterosexual relationships. However, the radical lesbian debate has failed to engage with the problems faced by women opting for heterosexuality, and this chapter is intended to extend the debate and explore heterosexuality through the issues that lesbian feminists have raised.

Deconstruction of the patriarchal discourses on female and male sexuality enable theorists, researchers, therapists, and their clients to go beyond the constraints that sexology has imposed. Heterosexuality must be explored from a perspective that allows both women and men to experience variety and freedom in their desires and behaviours, and to face up to issues of dominance and inequality. Only if the ideologies underlying sexology are exposed and challenged can sexual emancipation occur within heterosexual relationships.

NOTES

1 See Jane Ussher's chapter in this volume.
2 See page 71 in Brake, 1982.

REFERENCES

Adler, E. (1989) 'Vaginismus – its presentation and treatment', *British Journal of Sexual Medicine* November: 420–4.

Birke, L. (1986) *Women, Feminism and Biology: The Feminist Challenge*, Brighton: Harvester.
Brake, M. (ed.) (1982) *Human Sexual Relations: A Reader*, Harmondsworth: Pelican.
Brownmiller, S. (1984) *Femininity*, London: Simon & Schuster.
Deutsch, H. (1944) *The Psychology of Women*, New York: Grune & Stratton.
Ellis, H. (1905) *Studies in the Psychology of Sex*, Vol. 1, New York: Random House.
Foucault, M. (1973) *The Archaeology of Knowledge*, London: Tavistock.
Foucault, M. (1978/90) *The History of Sexuality*, Vol. 1, Harmondsworth: Penguin.
Fox, N.J. (1991) 'Postmodernism, rationality and the evaluation of health care', *Sociological Review*, 39: 707–44.
Freud, S. (1931) 'Female Sexuality', in *Three Essays on the Theory of Sexuality*, trans. J. Strachey, New York: Norton, 1977.
Freud, S. (1933) *New Introductory Lectures in Psychoanalysis*, trans. J. Strachey, New York: Norton, 1965.
Friedman, L.J. (1971) *Virgin Wives: A Study of Unconsummated Marriages*, London: Tavistock.
Gagnon, J.M. and Simon, W. (1973) *Human Sexual Conduct: The Sources of Human Sexuality*, Chicago: Aldine, excerpted in M. Brake (ed.) (1982) *Human Sexual Relations: A Reader*, Harmondsworth: Pelican.
Gebhard, P.M. and Johnson, A.B. (1979) *The Kinsey Data: Marginal Tabulation of the 1938–1963 Interviews Conducted by the Institute for Sex Research*, Philadelphia: Saunders.
Haslam, M.T. (1988) 'The assessment of sexual dysfunction, Part II: Male and female perspectives', *British Journal of Sexual Medicine* March: 94–9.
Hollway, W. (1989) *Subjectivity and Method in Psychology*, London: Sage.
Jackson, M. (1983) 'Sexual liberation or social control?', *Women's Studies International Forum* 6(1): 1–18.
Jackson, M. (1987) 'Facts of life or the eroticisation of women's oppression? Sexology and the construction of heterosexuality', in P. Caplan (ed.) *The Cultural Construction of Sexuality*, London: Tavistock.
Jeffcoate, T.N.A. (1957) *Principles of Gynaecology*, London: Butterworth.
Jeffreys, S. (1990) *Anti-Climax*, London: The Women's Press.
Kinsey, A.C., Pomeroy, W., and Martin, C. (1948) *Sexual Behaviour in the Human Male*, Philadelphia: Saunders.
Kinsey, A.C., Pomeroy, W., and Martin, C. (1953) *Sexual Behaviour in the Human Female*, Philadelphia: Saunders.
Koedt, A. (1973) 'The myth of the vaginal orgasm', in A. Koedt, E. Levine, and A. Rapone (eds) *Radical Feminism*, New York: Quadrangle.
McVaugh, G.S. (1979) *Frigidity*, Oxford: Pergamon.
Masters, W.H. and Johnson, V.E. (1966) *Human Sexual Response*, London: Churchill.
Michel-Wolfromm, H. (1954) 'Causes et traitment du vaginisme', in L.J. Friedman (1971) *Virgin Wives: A Study of Unconsummated Marriages*, London: Tavistock.
Nicolson, P. (1990) 'The psychology and biology of women's sexual desire: sexual intercourse, sexual problems and women's self-cognitions', paper presented at the BPS London Conference, City University.
Nicolson, P. (1991a) 'The social construction of female sexuality: understanding sex therapy', paper presented at the BPS Psychology of Women Conference, University of Edinburgh.
Nicolson, P. (1991b) 'Virgins and wise women', *Newsletter of the Psychology of Women Section* of the British Psychological Society, Spring, 7: 5–8.
Nicolson, P. (1992a) 'Towards a psychology of women's health and health care',

in P. Nicolson and J.M. Ussher (eds) *The Psychology of Women's Health and Health Care*, Basingstoke: Macmillan.

Nicolson, P. (1992b) 'Feminism and academic psychology: towards a psychology of women?', in K. Campbell (ed.) *Critical Feminism*, Milton Keynes: Open University Press.

Philp, M. (1985) 'Madness, truth and critique: Foucault and anti-psychiatry', *PsyCritique* 1: 155–70.

Phillip, E. (1988) 'Non-consumation of marriage', *British Journal of Sexual Medicine* March: 84–7.

Reich, W. (1942) *The Function of the Orgasm* excerpted in M. Brake (ed.) *Human Sexual Relations: A Reader*, Harmondsworth: Pelican.

Ussher, J.M. (1989) *The Psychology of the Female Body*, London: Routledge.

Ussher, J.M. (1990) 'Negative images of female sexuality and reproduction: reflecting misogyny or misinformation?', *Newsletter of the Psychology of Women Section* of the British Psychological Society: 17–29.

Ussher, J.M. (1991) *Women's Madness: Misogyny or Mental Illness?*, Brighton: Harvester.

Ussher, J.M. (1992a) 'Reproductive rhetoric and the blaming of the body', in P. Nicolson and J.M. Ussher (eds) *The Psychology of Women's Health and Health Care*, Basingstoke: Macmillan.

Ussher, J.M. (1992b) 'Gender issues in clinical research', in J.M. Ussher and P. Nicolson (eds) *Gender Issues in Clinical Psychology*, London: Routledge.

Weeks, J. (1985) *Sexuality and Its Discontents*, London: Routledge & Kegan Paul.

White, G. (1977) *Socialisation*, London: Longman.

Part II

Practice: widening horizons

The critiques of traditional sexology and sex therapy, and of the current psychological models of sexuality, do not mean that psychology has nothing to say about sexuality or about sexual problems. We cannot merely deconstruct the psychological theories and rid ourselves of sexual difficulties. For many individuals sexuality is problematic, and help may be sought. Yet psychology has traditionally confined itself to a limited sphere of sexuality: to heterosexual, able-bodied individuals, whose difficulties slot into the current notion of problems amenable to psychological intervention. However, this is changing. Clinical psychologists are widening their horizons and addressing sexuality in individuals previously marginalised or ignored. They are also moving away from the traditional reductionist view of sexuality as a biological pre-given entity, and developing new paradigms and practices, as the chapters in this section demonstrate.

This section contains a number of contributions from clinical psychologists who are critically evaluating current theories and practices at the same time as addressing the needs of individuals to receive help for problems associated with sexuality. Padmal de Silva examines the sexual problems of women with eating disorders, demonstrating the need to look at sexuality in individuals referred to psychologists for therapy for problems other than those related to sexuality. Christine Baker examines male sexual dysfunction, and moves away from the behavioural approaches to assessment and treatment previously dominant in sex therapy, demonstrating the efficacy of cognitive-behavioural models in this field. The subsequent chapters examine groups of individuals previously ignored, including people with learning difficulties, considered by Jan Burns, and those with a physical disability, considered by Chris Williams. These two contributions clearly demonstrate the need for empowering psychological interventions for individuals whose sexuality has often been denied.

Sexuality has been discussed only as deviancy or dysfunction in certain groups, including sex offenders, discussed by Derek Perkins, injecting drug users, considered by Geraldine Mulleady, and gay men affected by AIDS, considered by Heather George. These three groups of individuals are often positioned as being problematic or difficult, their sexuality outside the 'normal' remit of psychologists. Yet, as these three chapters illustrate, this is an inaccurate assumption, as psychologists have much to say.

Chapter 4

Sexual problems in women with eating disorders

Padmal de Silva

INTRODUCTION

The relationship between sexual problems and eating disorders is clinically well known (e.g. Bancroft, 1989; Kolodny, Masters, and Johnson, 1979; Russell, 1983a). Even the descriptions of anorexia written half a century ago (e.g. Waller, Kaufman, and Deutsch, 1940) referred to the loss of sexual desire and sexual functioning in the women afflicted by this disorder. More recently, both in the clinical and research fields, the close links and overlap between the two sets of problems have come to be fully recognized (e.g. Beumont, Abraham, and Simson, 1981; Crisp, 1980, 1984; Dally and Gomez, 1979). This chapter will start with descriptions of the major eating disorders and of female sexual problems. It will then discuss links between the two areas, and go on to consider their implications. Finally, it will then explore the issue of therapy for sexual problems in patients with eating disorders. A number of illustrative cases will be cited.

EATING DISORDERS

Historical aspects

The main eating disorders found among females are anorexia nervosa and its relatively recently recognized variant – bulimia nervosa. Obesity may also be added to this list, although only some cases of obesity can truly be regarded as an eating disorder (Russell, 1983b). Anorexia nervosa and bulimia nervosa are well recognized and their prevalence in modern Western societies has been extensively studied (e.g. Cooper and Fairburn, 1983; Fairburn, 1984; Fairburn and Belgin, 1990; Kendell *et al.*, 1973; King, 1989; Szmukler *et al.*, 1986; Theander, 1970), and varying rates have been estimated. Anorexia nervosa has shown an increase in incidence in the last few decades (e.g. Russell, 1985: Szmukler, 1985; Theander, 1970), and the appearance of this disorder in a few non-Western cultures has also been documented (e.g. Buchan and Gregory, 1984; Thomas and Szmukler, 1985). The victims are primarily young women. The pressure to be thin and slim in contemporary Western society is considered to be a major factor contributing to the increase in anorexic cases in recent decades. Gordon (1990) has argued that, in addition to a preoccupation with appearance and body image that is associated with the rise of mass fashion and consumerism, two other factors in Western industrialized culture may have contributed to the increase in eating disorders. These are: a culturally pervasive preoccupation with weight control; and a changing female role, where women find themselves struggling to find a balance between new ideals of achievement and traditional female role expectations. Di Nicola (1990a, 1990b), on the basis of an extensive survey of the literature on the historical and cultural aspects of anorexia nervosa, concludes that it is essentially a culture-reactive syndrome.

The descriptions of anorexia nervosa in the clinical literature go back several centuries (cf. Bliss and Branch, 1960). The earliest medical report of a case of anorexia nervosa is widely considered to be that given by Richard Morton in 1694 (Morton, 1694; see also Silverman, 1983). His patient, 'Mr. Duke's daughter' as he identified her, suffered from a 'Nervous Consumption'. Morton wrote of her great state of emaciation, and remarked that she was 'like a skeleton only clad with skin'.

In the 1870s, Sir William Gull and Charles Lasegue, independently of each other, gave descriptions of the illness. Gull, who was at the Guy's Hospital in London, first used the term 'anorexia nervosa' (Gull, 1874). Lasegue, a neurologist in Paris, used the term 'anorexie hysterique' (hysterical anorexia) (Lasegue, 1873, 1874). These authors noted a clear pattern of self-starvation which characterized these patients. Gull commented on the hyperactivity and excessive energy of these girls, and was aware of the occurrence of amenorrhoea. Lasegue observed the anorexic girl's peculiar attitudes to food and eating, and her family dynamics. While both used the word 'anorexia' (lack of appetite), neither emphasized a marked preoccupation with body weight and a fear of fatness, which today are seen as central to this illness. As Russell (1985) has pointed out, this may well have been because the psychopathology of the illness has changed over the decades, rather than due to any lack of perceptiveness on the part of these pioneering clinicians.

The medical literature of the subsequent decades is patchy and uneven; many considered anorexia nervosa to be a physical illness. Psychological interpretations and explanations began to come to the forefront about fifty years ago (e.g. Ryle, 1936; Sheldon, 1939), and the influence of psychoanalytic thinking made this a fertile ground for psychological theorizing (e.g. Rahman, Richardson, and Ripley, 1939; Waller, Kaufman, and Deutsch, 1940).

It is only in the last thirty years, however, that major developments began to emerge in the literature which have shaped the current under-standing and views of anorexia nervosa. Hilde Bruch (1962), in a key paper, referred to a disturbance of body image in anorexic patients, which has since been recognized as a major feature of the illness. Other major contributions came from, among others, Arthur Crisp and Gerald Russell, in addition to further work by Bruch (e.g. Bruch, 1973; Crisp, 1965; Crisp and Kalucy, 1974; Russell, 1970).

Bulimia nervosa, which is related to anorexia nervosa, came to be clinically recognised only relatively recently. The term was introduced by Russell in 1979, who also gave the first definitive description of the disorder. He called it 'an ominous variant of anorexia nervosa' (Russell, 1979). The term 'bulimia' means binge eating, and in bulimia nervosa this is a central feature, followed by attempts to counteract the effects of the eating by vomiting, laxative abuse, and so on. Cases of bulimia nervosa have increased dramatically in the last decade (Szmukler, 1989).

Both these conditions are now the major focus of attention of many psychologists, psychiatrists, and other health professionals. There is also an enormous public and media interest in them, and the literature, both technical and popular, is vast and still growing. Conferences on anorexia nervosa and/or bulimia attract large audiences (cf. Szmukler, 1989). An international conference held in Cardiff in 1984 was attended by over 250 participants, and there were over 150 scientific papers in the programme (Szmukler et al., 1986). There is also, understandably, widespread feminist interest in these disorders (e.g. Orbach, 1979).

Definitions and diagnoses

Perhaps the best way to understand the distinctive features of these disorders is to take a close look at the diagnostic criteria that are com-monly used.

The criteria for the diagnosis of anorexia nervosa suggested by Russell (1970) have been quite influential. These are as follows:

1. the deliberate induction of weight loss through self-starvation, some-times accelerated by other means such as vomiting, excessive physical exercise, and the abuse of laxatives;
2. evidence of an endocrine disorder – i.e. amenorrhoea; and
3. characteristic psychopathology which involves a marked fear of fat and distorted judgement of body size.

The criteria proposed in the American Psychiatric Association's *Diagnostic and Statistical Manual, 3rd Edition, Revised (DSM-III-R)* are as follows:

1. refusal to maintain body weight over a minimal normal weight for age

and height – e.g. weight loss of 15 per cent below expected level; or failure to make expected weight gain during period of growth, leading to a weight 15 per cent below expected;
2. intense fear of gaining weight or of becoming fat, despite being under-weight;
3. disturbance in the way body weight, size or shape is experienced, e.g. 'feeling fat' even when quite thin, or believing an area of body to be 'too fat' even when clearly underweight; and,
4. absence of at least three consecutive menstrual cycles when otherwise expected to occur.

As can be seen, despite some differences the two sets of criteria agree on the basic features: deliberate maintenance of a low weight; distorted view of weight, fat, body size and shape; and loss or lack of menstrual periods. Clinicians find that the diagnosis of anorexia nervosa is usually quite easy to make.

For bulimia nervosa, Russell (1979) suggested the following diagnostic criteria:

1. preoccupation with food, irresistible cravings for food, and recurrent episodes of overeating;
2. devices aimed at counteracting the following effects of food – e.g. self-induced vomiting, laxative abuse;
3. psychopathology similar to that of anorexia nervosa – i.e. a morbid fear of becoming fat; and,
4. a previous overt or cryptic episode of anorexia nervosa.

Once again, the *DSM-III-R* offers broadly similar criteria:

1. recurrent episodes of binge eating – i.e. rapid consumption of a large amount of food in a discrete period of time;
2. a feeling of lack of control over eating during such binges;
3. regular resort to self-induced vomiting, use of laxatives or diur-etics, strict dieting or fasting, or vigorous exercise to prevent weight gain;
4. a minimum of two binge episodes per week for at least three months; and
5. persistent overconcern with body shape and weight.

Apart from the details, the main difference between the two sets of criteria is the stipulation by Russell (1979) that the patient must have a history of anorexia nervosa, either overt or cryptic. There is disagreement in the literature on this point, and some authors have stated that the require-ment of the history is not met by some patients who nevertheless display all the other features (cf. Halmi, 1985). Robinson (1986) has taken the view that a clear distinction of anorexia nervosa and bulimia nervosa into separate categories may be misleading and that there is multiplicity of bulimic disorders. It is also important to note that bulimia, or binge eating, can and does occur in a relatively large number of females who do not have the full clinical features of bulimia nervosa, let alone a history of anorexia nervosa (e.g. Halmi, Falk, and Schwartz, 1981). Bulimia is also found in a proportion of obese persons (Russell, 1983b; Stunkard, 1959).

Aetiological factors

A few comments are in order at this point about the aetiology of these disorders.

The literature suggests very clearly that the origins of anorexia nervosa are best viewed as multi-factorial. Social, cultural, familial, psychological, and biological factors all seem to have a role to play (Russell, 1983a; Szmukler, 1989). We have already noted the pressures for women in contemporary Western culture to maintain a slim figure (e.g. Di Nicola, 1990b; Gordon, 1990). We have also noted that anorexia nervosa is extremely rare in societies that are not industrialized and are relatively free from Western influence. The social and cultural pressures to be slim operate both openly and more subtly. The widespread pressure to diet felt by young women and adolescent girls is well known and well documented: for example, studies of adolescent schoolgirls have shown a very high rate of dieting among them (e.g. Nylander, 1971; Patton, 1988; Szmukler, 1985; Wardle, 1980). Women's identity and developing sexuality are clearly affected by the changing body and the body image, and the way the female body is perceived in society (Ussher, 1990). Family factors have been shown to be important in the aetiology and maintenance of the disorder. Several authors have highlighted various interactional patterns, such as over-protection and enmeshment, found in these families (e.g. Selvini-Palazzoli, 1974; Yager, 1982; Yager and Strober, 1985). In addition, familial preoccupations with weight and fatness have been identified (Kalucy, Crisp, and Harding, 1977). The vicarious effects of mother's dieting is often found in clinical histories. Psychological factors, some of which are closely related to family factors, include the need for control, striving for independence, a sense of helplessness, and so on. More obvious and more general among many of these patients are the disturbances of body image, reflected in the misinterpretation of size and weight (cf. Bruch, 1973; Slade, 1985). A phobia of weight, food phobia, widespread food aversion, and obsessional features have also been highlighted by several authors (e.g. Crisp, 1980; Solyom, Freeman, and Miles, 1982). Some of these psychological factors, however, are considered more as part of the clinical picture rather than as having an obvious aetiological role. As for biological factors, clearly there is an endocrine disturbance which develops when the body reaches a low level of weight, which then contributes to the perpetuation of the illness (cf. Russell, 1970). The search for a primary biological explanation of anorexia nervosa has led to numerous studies and an array of theories. The hypothalamus and related systems have been considered by many as the main focus needing further investigation (for a review, see Szmukler, 1989).

It is important to recognize the complex interactions between the psychological factors of anorexia nervosa, the clear endocrine disturbance, and the malnutrition. In Russell's view (1970, 1983a), it is likely that the psychological or mental disorder causes the reduced food intake and weight loss, which in turn interfere with the hypothalamic–pituitary–gonadal axis and cause amenorrhoea, while malnutrition worsens the psychological disorder. It is also likely that non-nutritional factors contribute in some way to the hypothalamic disorder, although their nature is far from clear. The clearest evidence for this is that in many cases the amenorrhoea occurs before significant weight loss (Russell, 1983a).

As for bulimia nervosa, the considerations discussed with regard to anorexia nervosa clearly apply to those who satisfy the diagnostic criteria of Russell (1979). In addition, there is evidence of certain other factors which may have a role in the genesis of this disorder. There is clear evidence that the attempt by the person to maintain a very low weight tends to promote bulimic episodes, and thus a persistent cycle of bingeing and restriction may get established (e.g. Wardle, 1980). Laxative abuse and vomiting develop as secondary means of keeping the weight low, by helping to rid the body of the quantities of food consumed in a binge. There is also some evidence that there may be personality differences that distinguish bulimics from anorexics (e.g. Abraham and Beumont, 1982; cf. Andersen, 1985). Bulimics tend to show a failure of impulse control and disturbed mood more than anorexics (e.g. Casper *et al.*, 1980; Fairburn and Cooper, 1985). They also tend to be higher on extraversion scores and addictiveness, as measured by the Eysenck Personality Questionnaire (de Silva and Eysenck, 1987). There is a significant incidence of alcohol and drug abuse among bulimics, and they tend to be sexually more active (e.g. Beumont, Abraham, and Simson, 1981; Dally and Gomez, 1979; Pyle, Mitchell, and Eckert, 1981). There is also a higher incidence of stealing among bulimics (e.g. Norton, Crisp, and Bhat, 1985). Finally, bulimics tend to have a higher pre-morbid weight and/or a family history of obesity (e.g. Beumont, George, and Smart, 1976).

Obesity is not in itself an eating disorder, but can be associated with one. Garrow (1988) gives an excellent discussion of obesity. In practice, an excess body weight of 20 per cent over what is expected for height and body frame is considered obese (Russell, 1983b). Stunkard (1989) has offered a classification of obesity into mild (20–40 per cent excess weight), moderate (41–100 per cent), and severe (100 per cent). There is a strong genetic component in obesity but other factors also operate. There is no unanimity about the role of psychological factors in obesity. It is known, however, that neurotic symptoms are often associated with obesity, but this is not in every case. Each obese patient must be assessed individually to ascertain whether or not psychopathological features are present. While psychological factors cause or contribute to obesity in some cases, there are also numerous cases where the obesity itself is a cause of psychological disturbance for the person. Impaired social relationships and low self-esteem are among such psychological factors. It is also known that strict dieting in order to lose weight may be accompanied by mood disturbance (cf. Stunkard, 1989).

SEXUAL PROBLEMS

Sexual problems found in females are manifold and have been classified in numerous ways. Our interest here is in sexual dysfunction, and not in sexual deviations or paraphilias, which in any case are relatively rare in women. As the issues relating to the nature and types of sexual dysfunction are addressed more fully elsewhere in this book, only a brief discussion is offered here (for further discussion, see Ussher, Chapter 1, this volume).

The *DSM-III-R* categorizes sexual dysfunction into *Sexual Desire Disorders, Sexual Arousal Disorders, Orgasm Disorders*, and *Sexual Pain Disorders*. Under *Sexual Desire Disorders* two conditions are given: hypoactive sexual desire disorder (deficient or absent sexual fantasies and desire for sexual activity) and sexual aversion disorder (extreme aversion to, and avoidance of, genital sexual contact with a partner). Under *Sexual Arousal Disorders* for females, the following are given: partial or complete failure to attain or maintain lubrication–swelling response of sexual excitement; and lack of subjective sense of sexual excitement during sexual activity. Under *Orgasm Disorders*, inhibited female orgasm is described. This refers to delay or absence of orgasm following a normal and adequate sexual excitement phase during sexual activity. Finally, under *Sexual Pain Disorders*, dyspareunia and vaginismus are listed. The former refers to genital pain before, during, or after sexual intercourse, while the latter is described as involuntary spasm of the muscles of the outer third of the vagina which interferes with intercourse.

A simpler classification is offered by de Silva (1987a): loss of libido, lack of physiological arousal, anorgasmia, vaginismus, and sexual aversion. Cole and Dryden (1988) classify female sexual problems into: impaired sexual desire, impaired sexual arousal, orgasmic dysfunction, vaginismus, dyspareunia, and sexual phobias. A similar classification is given by Hawton (1985, 1988).

All of these problems may be either total or situational, referring to whether the impairment occurs in all or only in some situations.

Similarly, they may be primary or secondary, referring to whether the problem has been present throughout the person's life or whether it is a change from a previous non-impaired state.

Impaired sexual interest, or low libido, is the commonest sexual dysfunction in females (e.g. Garde and Lunde, 1980). Not surprisingly, this is the condition for which most seek help at clinics (Hawton, 1985, 1988). Impaired arousal is not a frequent presentation in women whose interest is undiminished, except when hormonal problems occur, for example in the post-menopausal period. Anorgasmia is commonly complained of, and several studies show a high rate of women seeking help for this. Hawton (1985) reported that 19 per cent of all women in a series of clinical cases present with this dysfunction. Vaginismus is the commonest cause of unconsummated marriage presenting for help (Duddle, 1977). The proportion of cases in sexual dysfunction clinics with this problem is almost as high as for those with anorgasmia. Dyspareunia may be due either to lack of arousal or to mild vaginismus; it can also be the result of physical causes. On its own, it is relatively uncommon in sex clinics. In Hawton's (1985) series, 4 per cent of women had dyspareunia as the main dysfunction. As for sexual aversions and phobias, which are closely related, no reliable figures are available. They often occur in the context of other sexual dysfunctions, or in some cases lead to these other problems. On their own, their clinical presentation is rare.

SEXUAL PROBLEMS IN EATING DISORDERS

Links between eating disorders and sexuality

The loss of sexual interest and deficient sexual functioning in anorexia nervosa has long been clinically recognized. Several early authors (e.g. Rahman, Richardson, and Ripley, 1939) made the observation that anorexic patients lacked normal sexual interest and in some cases even positively disliked it. Given the occurrence of amenorrhoea and other bodily changes, the reduction in sexuality is not surprising. Garfinkel and Garner wrote: 'Anorexic women may first contact physicians because of amenorrhoea or infertility and some present to sexual dysfunction clinics for vaginismus and frigidity' (1982: 15–16). The general effects of starvation or severe low nutrition on sexual desire and functioning have been established in many studies. Perhaps the most striking is the much-quoted Minnesota experiment. Thirty-six male volunteers on semi-starvation diets for six months showed many changes, prominent among which was a marked loss of sexual interest. Subjects reported marked reduction in dating, masturbation, fantasies, and sexual desire. One volunteer reported: 'I have no more sexual feeling than a sick oyster' (Keys et al., 1950).

Amenorrhoea, loss of vaginal secretions, and dyspareunia are commonly reported in anorexics (e.g. Andersen, 1985; Kolodny, Masters, and Johnson, 1979). The loss of interest in sex is, however, not always secondary to this. Many authors have made the observation that many anorexic females dislike pubertal changes, and are 'disgusted' by menstrual periods – and in some cases even by their bodies.

Psychodynamic and other theoretical views

It is worth noting at this point that psychodynamic theories of anorexia nervosa consider this disorder as a defence against unacceptable sexual impulses. Rahman, Richardson, and Ripley (1939), for example, stated that the condition served as a protection against the assumption of normal sexual relationships. Eating is considered as symbolic of impregnation and fatness as symbolic of pregnancy. The widely cited paper by Waller, Kaufman, and Deutsch (1940) gives an elaborate interpretation of the illness along these psychodynamic lines. Fantasies of oral impregnation are considered central. Related to this is the fantasy of a child in the abdomen. Their theoretical account refers both to starvation and bulimic behaviour.

> We see, then, a syndrome the main symptoms of which represent an elaboration and acting out in the somatic sphere of a specific type of fantasy. The wish to be impregnated through the mouth which results, at times, in compulsive eating, and at other times, in guilt and consequent rejection of food, the constipation symbolizing the child in the abdomen and the amenorrhoea as direct psychological repercussion of pregnancy fantasies. This amenorrhoea may also be part of the direct denial of genital sexuality.
>
> (Waller, Kaufman, and Deutsch, 1940: 15)

The notion of sexual symbolism, food and eating, and how it might contribute to anorexia is also found in Bliss and Branch (1980).

A somewhat different theoretical view linking sexuality and anorexia nervosa is given by Crisp (1984). He highlights the links between female pubertal development and the development of body fat. It is well established that the development of the menstrual cycle is connected to the development of a certain critical level of body fat. Further, the development of secondary sexual characteristics in the form of curves also depends on the development of a certain degree of fatness. Given these factors, the concern of a young female to control bodily shape and size and appetite may be seen as linked to the self-control of sexual desires. Anorexia thus reflects a regression to a prepubertal state, where sexual feelings are effectively kept away. In many ways, anorexia nervosa thus represents a fear of growing up and the femininity that comes with growing up.

Many feminist therapists and writers have also argued that there is a clear link between sexuality and eating in women (e.g. Orbach, 1978). Liss-Levinson says, quite bluntly: 'There is a profound relationship for women between sex and food. When it comes right down to it, women are not supposed to like food or sex very much' (1988: 121). Social and role pressures make this link, it is argued, often manifest itself in the form of problems in both areas.

These theoretical accounts, while speculative, essentially emphasise the link between anorexia and the suppression or rejection of sexual desires. The argument is that the lack or diminution of sexual desire is not the simple result of bodily changes that are caused by poor nutrition. In fact, as many authorities have pointed out (e.g. Russell, 1983a), the loss of menstrual periods in many cases happens well before severe weight loss; similarly, menstrual functioning is not always restored quickly upon weight gain to a satisfactory level. Equally important, many recovered anorexics, even after the full re-establishment of menstrual periods, do not easily regain a normal sexual desire or sexual functioning. Thus the sexual difficulties of anorexia cannot be seen as a simple consequence of bodily changes occurring due to poor nutrition, although these do often have a role to play.

Empirical studies of the links between eating disorders and sexual problems

Several empirical studies are available that throw useful light on the sexuality and sexual problems of women with eating disorders.

In a study carried out in Australia, thirty-one consecutive female anorexic patients treated in a specialist psychiatric unit were studied (Beumont, Abraham, and Simson, 1981). All of them satisfied the diagnostic criteria of Russell (1970). The mean age was just under 22 years. Data were collected through interview, using a standardized questionnaire. Some of the relevant findings are as follows.

Twenty of the patients had poor knowledge of sexual matters. Six patients deliberately avoided reading sexual material. Nine patients expressed a clearly negative attitude towards menstruation, while eight had a positive attitude; the rest were unsure. Eleven patients expressed a negative attitude towards premarital intercourse.

As for personal sexual experiences, twenty had experienced intercourse. Nine had indulged only in kissing and light petting. Of those who had had intercourse, most described the first experience in negative terms ('painful', 'disgusting', etc.). Eight said they much regretted ever having had coitus. Only seven reported ever having experienced orgasm during intercourse. Thirteen patients viewed sexual problems as major precipitants of their illness. The problems commonly cited in this context included anxiety, feelings of guilt, parental disapproval of partner, and insistence by partner on having sex.

The effects of the illness on their sexuality were also enquired about. The vast majority (twenty-five) reported that their sex drive had definitely decreased; they also reported that their change in libido had preceded feelings of general malaise and tiredness due to weight loss. All but two of the patients who had masturbated reported that this activity had ceased or decreased. As for heterosexual activity, of the seventeen patients who had not experienced sex prior to onset of the illness, six had their first intercourse after the illness started. Four showed little change, while seven clearly withdrew from all sexual contact after onset of illness. Of the fourteen who had experienced coitus before the illness, seven continued to have sexual contact, once ceased completely, while the remaining six showed a considerable decrease.

When the patients were divided into two groups on the basis of those who vomited or purged regularly to aid weight loss as against those who only restricted food intake, the former group (those with bulimia) emerged as including a significantly higher proportion of those who had experienced sexual intercourse, indulged in oral genital sex, and had more than one sexual partner.

Beumont, Abraham, and Simson state:

> [O]ur findings suggest that, as a group, anorexia nervosa patients show a wide spectrum of sexual experience, knowledge and attitude. No one type of psychosexual history is common to all. Hence it would seem unlikely that sexual factors have a specific role in the aetiology of the condition, although in some individual patients there may be a direct relationship between the onset of eating difficulties and concurrent sexual problems.
>
> (Beumont, Abraham, and Simson, 1981: 138)

They also comment on the higher level of sexual activity in the bulimic sub-group.

A further interview study of twenty-eight of these females is reported by Abraham and Beumont (1982). On the basis of their psychosexual histories, the investigators were able to categorise them into four groups. The patients in the first group clearly displayed what the authors called 'denial of sexuality'. They had negative attitudes to all aspects of sex and had little or no actual sexual experience. The second group were characterised by slow psychosexual development and were 'unsure of sexuality'. They had a history of limited sexual activity. The third group, the authors describe as characterised by 'passive sexuality'; they were reported as 'sexually active but unresponsive'. They showed swings in weight, reflecting bulimic behaviour. Finally, those in the fourth group were characterised by the 'mirroring of sexual activity in the eating behaviour'. Bulimia and vomiting were prominent in them. They had sex early, and were sexually quite active, but had negative feelings about sex. They tended to get into casual sexual relationships. Abraham and Beumont (1982) observe that the patients falling into the first and second groups (56 per cent) were the ones who showed many of the features of sexual behaviour commonly referred to in the literature as typical of anorexia.

These two studies generally confirm the low and deficient sexual activity in the histories of anorexic patients, but also point towards the lack of homogeneity in eating-disordered women with regard to this variable. It appears that pure anorexics tend to show the classical practice of low sexuality, while those with bulimia nervosa or bulimic features tend to have a richer, if still disordered, sexual history. This is in keeping with the clinical observations of Dally and Gomez (1979).

Further empirical data on the level of sexual activity in clinical anorexic patients come from the studies of Jiri Raboch in Czechoslovakia. A large-scale study was carried out of several groups of female patients in whom sexual development and sex life were studied with the aid of an interview schedule and several questionnaires (Raboch, 1986). The sample, who were all in-patients, included twenty women suffering from anorexia nervosa, with a mean age of 23.9 years. The anorexics were clearly higher than the other clinical groups on the variable of 'no steady partner'. Sixty per cent of anorexics had no partner, well above the figure for the other groups. The nearest was the schizophrenic group, with a percentage of 33. A control, non-psychiatric, group had none who had no steady partner. On the variable of a 'balanced relationship with a partner', the anorexics again emerged the lowest (35 per cent). The controls had a corresponding figure of 92.1 per cent. A further variable was whether the woman was coitally orgasmic. The figure for the anorexics was the lowest (45 per cent; normal controls, 78.2 per cent). They also scored lowest on the Sexual Arousability Index and on the Sexual Function of Women Inventory. There were no differences in sexual knowledge and attitudes as measured by the Sexual Knowledge and Attitudes Test. Raboch, and Faltus (1984, cited by Raboch, 1986) had previously reported that a large population of anorexics had insufficiencies in their sex life even before the onset of illness.

A recent paper by Raboch and Faltus (1991) reports data on thirty adult anorexic women and fifty controls. The main finding was that psycho-sexual adaptation was impaired in the anorexic group, when compared to the controls. Sexual disturbances were found in 80 per cent of the patient sample.

Impressive evidence for sexual problems in bulimic women comes from the German longitudinal study of Fichter and his colleagues in Munich (Fichter, 1991). In this large-scale study which included over 200 patients, about one half complained of a clear reduction of their sexual drive and associated difficulties.

Explanations of the link

The obvious question arises as to why a reduction in libido and other sexual difficulties arise in anorexia nervosa. Part of the answer is, of course, equally obvious. The endocrinal changes marked by loss of menstruation would be expected to lead to some difficulties, including lack of lubrication and thus pain in intercourse. Severe emaciation is also likely to lead to loss of interest by partner. But this is not the entire story. First, as noted in an earlier section, menstrual change sometimes occurs prior to severe weight loss so it cannot be explained entirely by the effects of poor nutrition. It is possible that other, possibly psychological, factors contribute to the cessation of periods. Similarly, the restoration of weight does not lead to reinstatement of periods immediately, and in severe cases the delay can be considerable. During the period of severe illness, depression often sets in and can contribute to reduction in sex drive. Those with bulimia nervosa tend to have significant levels of depression, and this may, at least at times, affect their sexuality, even at not very low weight. The effects of depression on libido are well known (Mathew and Weinman, 1982). Depressed mood can also affect sexual interest through the related effect of low self-esteem. A further consideration is that a good proportion of recovered anorexics report continuing sexual difficulties. Even when normal eating is established and the person's overall functioning is back to pre-morbid levels, sexuality may remain impaired. In some, this may be accompanied by a continuing rejection of femininity.

Perhaps the safest conclusion that one can draw from the diverse literature is that the occurrence of sexual problems in eating disorders is not open to a single or simple explanation (Hsu, 1990). It is clear that, whatever the pre-morbid psychological state, severe anorexia with its concomitant endocrine dysfunction does affect sexual behaviour and sexual desire. In addition, in a significant proportion of cases, psychological factors, such as conflicts and anxieties about sexual development and femininity, contribute to the impairment of sexual functioning. This impairment, usually originating prior to the onset of the illness, may get more severe during the illness itself, and is likely to continue in some form after recovery. These psychological factors can have a contributory role in the development of the illness itself.

The role of sexual abuse and other sexual traumata

Recent clinical and other evidence suggests that a major factor in this type of impairment may be traumatic sexual experiences, including sexual abuse in childhood or adolescence. The possible effects of sexual trauma, in the widest sense, on the development of eating disorders had been noted even by early writers. Rahman, Richardson, and Ripley (1939), for example, cite a case where problems began after she, at the age of 13, accidentally witnessed her parents engage in sexual intercourse, to which she reacted with disgust. Bliss and Branch (1960) refer to an immature adolescent girl who was touched on her genitals by a male companion while swimming, which led to her self-starvation. In her autobiographical account of anorexia, Liu (1979) recounts the experience of being raped by two boys while she was still a pre-adolescent; she developed anorexia a few years later. Oppenheimer *et al.* (1985) carried out a pioneering study of seventy-eight patients with eating disorders, in which sexual experiences were investigated with the help of a Sexual Life Events Questionnaire. For purposes of this enquiry, they defined coercive sexual events as (i) events occurring when the patient was under 13 and the other participant was over 16; or (ii) events occurring when the subject was between 13 and 16, and the other participant was five years or more older. A wide range of sexual experiences were included in the analysis. Of the total of seventy-eight patients, twenty-three (29.5 per cent) reported sexual events in childhood or adolescence as defined by the study. A further twenty-two (34.6 per cent) reported other adverse sexual experiences (e.g. rape by a same-age person). The perpetrators in these reported incidents were almost entirely male. The majority were not strangers, but those well known to the person. Thirty-six per cent were in fact family members, including six fathers, two grandfathers, two uncles, five brothers, two cousins, and a brother-in-law. The perpetrators were, on the whole, considerably older than the patient. The experiences included nine instances of full intercourse, seventeen instances of sexual fondling, and eighteen instances of genital exposure. The authors state that their figures are likely to be an underestimate. They write:

> Our work has persuaded us that there are often important links of meaning in the patient's mind between such [coercive sexual] experiences and subsequent eating disorder. Frequently the sexually molested subject has feelings of inferiority or disgust about her own femininity and sexuality. These may come to be entangled with concern about her body weight, shape and size.
>
> (Oppenheimer *et al.*, 1985: 359)

In an American study, Root and Fallon (1988) found that, out of a sample of 172 bulimics, 28 per cent had a history of childhood sexual abuse. There are other reports, too, that show an association between a history of sexual abuse and eating disorders (e.g. Courtois, 1988; Gil, 1988; Hambridge, 1988; Hsu, 1990), so there is an emerging picture of these experiences possibly being a contributing factor in the sexual impairment of these patients. Whether these experiences are also the chief causative factor of the eating disorder *per se* is a matter for speculation. It is likely that at least in some cases this is so.

Perhaps it is worth noting briefly that the overall evidence for traumatic sexual experiences leading, or at least contributing, to the development of sexual dysfunctions is increasingly impressive. In a study carried out in the United States over a decade ago (Tsai, Feldman-Summers, and Edgar, 1979), differential adjustment of women who had been sexually molested in childhood was investigated. Three groups of thirty women each were compared: (i) a clinical group, consisting of women who were seeking help for problems associated with childhood sexual molestation; (ii) a non-clinical group consisting of women sexually molested as children but who did not see themselves as needing help; and (iii) a control group of women with no history of such molestation. Findings showed that the clinical group was significantly less well adjusted than the other two groups in psycho-sexual functioning and on some other measures. The sexual variables on which the clinical group differed from the others significantly were: frequency of coital orgasms; number of sexual partners; sexual responsiveness; satisfaction with sexual relationships; and the quality of close relationships with males. The findings also suggested that the occurrence of sexual problems following sexual molestation was more likely if the experience had taken place in late childhood or early adolescence, the molestation took place relatively frequently over a long period of time, and the experience had powerful emotional impact at the time.

There are several, more recent, reports on the prevalence of sexual problems in those with a history of childhood sexual abuse (Baisden and Baisden, 1979; Briere and Runtz, 1987; Jehu, 1988). The most detailed and informative of these studies is that of Jehu (1988). He reported on a series of fifty-one previously sexually abused females seen and treated in a clinical research programme in Manitoba, Canada. Ninety-four per cent of these patients reported at least one sexual dysfunction. The commonest problems were sexual phobias/aversions (58.8 per cent), lack of satisfaction in sex (58.8 per cent), impaired interest (56.9 per cent), impaired arousal (49 per cent), and impaired orgasm (45.1 per cent).

A variety of psychiatric patient groups have also been reported as having including a proportion with a history of abuse (e.g. Zverina *et al.*, 1987). These have been reviewed in Jehu (1991).

Traumatic sexual experiences other than abuse in childhood or adolescence are also known to be associated with the development of sexual dysfunction. It is well established that sexual assault including rape can contribute to sexual difficulties (e.g. Becker *et al.*, 1982; Becker *et al.*, 1986; Feldman-Summers, Gordon, and Meagher, 1979).

In sum, there is no doubt at all about the high incidence of sexual problems in women with eating disorders. The existing evidence suggests that, in a significant sub-group of these patients, a history of sexual abuse or similar sexual trauma has contributed to the sexual difficulty and possibly to the development of the eating disorder itself.

The clinical presentation of sexual problems in eating disorders

The clinical presentation of the sexual problem may come as the initial complaint in a small proportion of cases. More commonly, the sexual disorder presents as a part of the overall clinical picture, and is not usually treated as a priority in the acute stage of anorexia. The priority is weight restoration and enhancement of overall functioning. However, the desirability of including intervention for the sexual difficulty in an overall treatment package in appropriate cases has been recognised. Guile, Horne, and Dunston (1978), for example, have reported a case where a programme of sex education and desensitisation was added to the treatment regime for anorexia nervosa. The patient was a 19-year-old anorexic woman whose problems included sexual guilt, which appeared to have contributed to the onset of her illness, and ignorance. The sexual education and desensitisation programme was undertaken after three weeks of in-patient stay, when she gradually began to talk about her sexual guilt and fears. The therapy involved an experienced female psychiatric nurse, and included education and instructions for graded behavioural exercises. She was desensitised to body touching, viewing her genitals, touching her genitals, and masturbating with the aid of a vibrator. The intervention was successful. Hemsley and Powell-Proctor (1979) have also reported a case where the intervention included sex education and sexual behaviour modification. More recently, Fichter (1991) has reported the inclusion of help with sexual problems in the treatment package of bulimic patients, as required, with significant success.

In clinical practice, the need for help with sexual problems is usually recognised fairly easily, but all too often the assumption is made that with overall improvement the sexual problem will be alleviated. This, however, is not often the case, and many patients need specific help. A considerable number remain affected by sexual problems even after achieving considerable improvement in the anorexia, and long after menstrual functioning has resumed.

Andersen (1985) has provided a list of sexual problems associated with anorexia nervosa and bulimia. He includes the following for anorexic females: decreased sexual interest, dyspareunia, infertility, decreased sexual attractiveness, prolonged amenorrhoea after weight recovery, and impoverished sex life. For bulimic women, he lists the following: decreased sexual interest, sexual life interfered with by strong negative emotions experienced by both partners, sexual promiscuity, inhibition of sex life by drug or alcohol dependence, and unwanted pregnancy. While this list is useful, in that it draws one's attention to specific problems that may arise in the two groups of patients, a simpler approach would be to use a general classification of female sexual dysfunctions (see pp. 85–6) as the initial framework, and to make additional comments where necessary.

Low libido is very common in anorexic women. This is part of the typical clinical picture, especially in the acute stage of the illness. In the early stages, when the body weight is still not dangerously low, this may present as a problem if the patient has a partner, as she would find the spouse's advances increasingly difficult to cope with. When the body weight is quite low, the emaciated woman is not usually found sexually attractive by the partner. The most common clinical presentation with regard to sex arises after recovery from the very low weight stage, when the sexual desire still remains low. Conflicts arise between the partners due to the mismatch of needs, and, even though the spouse may make many allowances for the wife's illness history, prolonged refusal of sex can lead to discord. In those without partners, who are the majority, low libido may cause concern to the patient in that she may see it as an impediment to developing normal relationships.

Lack of physiological responsiveness is only to be expected in the period of emaciation. The endocrine disorder would be expected to cause this (cf. Bancroft, 1989; Russell, 1983a). If sex is attempted during this phase, the lack of vaginal lubrication is likely to cause pain and discomfort in intercourse, leading to an aversive reaction and further loss of interest. In recovered anorexics, this in itself is rarely a presenting problem.

Anorgasmia is not uncommon in anorexics (e.g. Beumont, Abraham, and Simson, 1981; Raboch, 1986). Again, due to low libido this may not be a major problem that the patient complains about. However, even when the libido is recovered, some still remain anorgasmic. In fact, a proportion of anorexics have a history of never having had orgasmic experience.

Vaginismus, if present, is likely to be due to anxiety about sex and to lack of arousal, and could be secondary to dyspareunia. Dyspareunia itself would be due to attempts at coitus when there is no physiological responsiveness. Both of these presentations are rare on their own.

Aversion is probably the most widespread of sexual problems among women with anorexia nervosa. If not the main complaint, it is likely to be an associated problem in many. The aversion may be in some cases due to a basic attitudinal factor with regard to sex and sexuality, and/or is associated with the patient's negative view of her own body. In some, it may be secondary to the experience of unsatisfactory attempts to have coitus. It is also likely that, in those with a history of sexual assault or abuse, the aversion may be a direct result of the traumatic experience. A

history of sexual trauma may of course contribute to the other dysfunctions as well, e.g. vaginismus and lack of libido.

With regard to those with bulimia nervosa, the incidence of low libido
or lack of physiological responsiveness tends to be lower when compared
to anorexics, except during those phases, if any, when the body weight is
very low. Still, a significant proportion appears to be affected in this way
(e.g. Fichter, 1991). Further, orgasmic problems are not uncommon
among bulimics. Depression, low self-esteem, and the secrecy with regard
to bingeing and vomiting and/or purging may also contribute to
impaired sexual functioning in these women. In those bulimics who have
a multiplicity of disordered behaviours marked by impulse control difficulties, the sex life is likely to be as impaired as other areas of functioning.

TREATMENT ISSUES

The treatment of these problems requires careful assessment of the individual case and evaluation of how best to offer help. There is little to be
gained by attempting to impose sex therapy on a woman who is not
willing to consider it a priority. Thus, despite possible partner pressure in
those cases with partners, the therapist must not rush into a therapy
programme. Encouragement to talk about the sexual difficulties will help
and, as in the Guile, Horne, and Dunston (1978) case, a gradual approach
is likely to be productive. Often the therapy will need to include sex
education and work on attitudes. Self-exploration and self-stimulation
instructions, with carefully tailored guidelines, may be used. Even when
the patient has a partner, these early stages are best undertaken on an
individual basis; the joint work will be introduced as the next stage. The
individual work needs also to include attention to body image and self-
image, and the meaning of sex and sexuality, at least in those with clear
conflicts in this area. The role of cognitions in both eating disorders and
sexual problems is now well documented (e.g. Baker and de Silva, 1988)
and exploration of the patient's cognitions, and using strategies to modify
them as needed, will be a valuable part of therapy. In some of these
patients, underlying cognitions may specifically link the two areas. It is
important, too, to discuss with the patient her ideas and fears about
pregnancy. Fear of pregnancy and motherhood is a complicating factor in
many cases and it is necessary to explore this and, if required, offer advice
on contraception.

For those with partners, the joint work, which should be in addition to
at least a few individual sessions, should be based on the general
principles of sexual dysfunction therapy, as described for example by
Bancroft (1989), Cooper (1988), de Silva (1987b), and Hawton (1985, 1989).
These principles and procedures are fully described elsewhere in this
book (see Chapter 5) and will not be repeated here. The approach,

however, should be modified to fit the clinical presentation of each patient in terms of her history of eating disorder, and additional elements may need to be introduced.

For example, the touching (non-genital and genital sensate focus) exercises may need to be modified to take into account the patient's particular concerns about some parts of her body. A gradual and slow approach, where the patient does not feel under pressure to hurry along, is needed. If there is a clear aversion to genital fondling, this needs to be dealt with using a gradual desensitisation approach, including relaxation training where necessary. In some cases, the aversion may be so strong that the therapist may decide that it would be counterproductive to insist on genital sensate focus as an essential part of a therapy programme. The same applies to oral sex.

For those in whom the residual reluctance for sex is strong, a useful approach is the time-tabling procedure described by Crowe and Ridley (1990). The gist of this approach is that sexual intercourse, or indeed any other aspect of sex, is agreed to be undertaken on the basis of a mutually accepted time-table. If, for example, it is agreed that sexual intercourse should take place only on a given day of the week, then it will make it easier for the patient to relax in non-coital physical contact on other days, which in turn will contribute to her further improvement. If such a contract did not exist, she might avoid any physical contact altogether, out of the fear that all such contact would necessarily lead to her husband demanding intercourse.

A similar approach of contract and negotiation may profitably be used with regard to various other aspects related to sex. A not uncommon phenomenon is the reluctance of a woman with a history of anorexia to be fully naked, even in the marital bed. While the therapist may attempt to help her to accept nudity with the partner as a positive experience, there is not much point in making this a big issue if her reluctance is very strong. Problems with her body image and satisfaction or otherwise with her physique may well make full nudity in the presence of the partner particularly difficult for her, and this should be acknowledged, and the partner encouraged to accept it. Such a flexible and accommodating approach is more likely to help her eventually to get over this aspect of the problem than otherwise.

For bulimic women, the problems contributory to sexual difficulties such as depression will need to be dealt with, if necessary with specific therapy. If the patient has secretive behaviours, which affect her relationship with the partner, then the matter should be discussed in therapy. Generally, it is best to encourage the patient to take the partner into her confidence and tell him about her bingeing, vomiting, etc., but this is a decision that the therapist should not try to impose on the patient. With some bulimic women, the sexual behaviour may involve multiple partners despite a basic stable relationship; counselling in confidence may well be needed if this transpires to be the case. Work on self-esteem may also be needed with these patients. They may also need help with associated problems such as drug or alcohol abuse, or shop-lifting, and such help should be given or arranged.

If the patient has a history of sexual abuse in childhood or later, the present sexual difficulties may well be related to the effects of their experience (see pp. 91–4). It is important that this be fully taken into account in therapy. Individual sessions in which this is carefully dealt with may be needed. The techniques used in these sessions are manifold, and will need to be selected on the basis of each patient's trauma and current symptoms. Imaginal exposure, cognitive restructuring to deal with self-blame and guilt, general counselling and reassurance, coping statements, imaginal exposure with the content altered to include coping scenarios, strategies such as thought-stopping for intrusive images or thoughts, etc., may be considered. The principles of therapy for those with a history of abuse are described in Jehu (1988, 1991), Sanderson (1990), and elsewhere in this volume (see Chapter 5).

A key question with some of these cases with a history of sexual trauma is whether the partner should be told of the incidents concerned or not. In some cases, the partner may already have been told by the patient by the time therapy commences. In many others, however, the history is a dark and often guilty secret that she keeps within herself, and even the disclosure to the therapist is done with reluctance. Often the partner may have been told of some aspect of the traumatic experience, but not all the details that bother the patient. The advantage of disclosing these events in full to the partner need to be carefully discussed. The clear advantages of telling him include: (i) the removal of the burden of secrecy; (ii) greater understanding by him of the problems of the patient – for example, her reluctance for sex or 'freezing' during sex may be seen by him as a rejection of him, and disclosure of the past traumatic event/s will help him to appreciate that this is not the case; and (iii) the opportunity to involve him in active therapy for this aspect of the problem. It is, however, for the patient herself to decide whether disclosure to the partner should be made or not.

The point was made earlier that a few individual sessions may be necessary before conjoint therapy sessions when treating these patients. It must be stressed, however, that flexibility is needed with regard to this. Some of the issues that may need to be dealt with in individual sessions may not emerge in the initial meetings, and may come to light at a later stage. For example, once joint therapy has begun, persistent lack of progress or repeated difficulty in carrying out homework assignments may alert the therapist to the need to explore difficulties individually with the patient. A not uncommon situation is for a history of childhood abuse to be revealed at this later stage. The need may then arise to have a number of individual sessions with the patient. Joint sessions may either be suspended, or – if it is considered important not to do so – they may be held in addition to the individual sessions.

Should anorexic and bulimic females always be treated, for their sexual problems, by female therapists? In our experience, some of them ask to be seen by female therapists and, when this is the case, it is useful to arrange for this. Some of the individual sex-educational and attitudinal issues may best be handled in this way (cf. Guile, Horne, and Dunston, 1978). It is also not uncommon for a previously sexually abused woman to find it easier to confide in a female therapist with regard to the details of the experience. When joint therapy is undertaken, it is best if a male–female co-therapist team can be provided.

Treating sexual problems in the obese

This chapter has concentrated on the treatment of sexual problems in females with anorexia nervosa and bulimia nervosa, the two eating disorders most commonly encountered clinically. Women with obesity too sometimes present with sexual difficulties, although less frequently than in anorexia nervosa or bulimia. Gross body size can, obviously, cause mechanical difficulties in sex. Depression and low self-esteem can occur in obese patients, sometimes due to social stigmatisation and social isolation. Increasing weight and size can lead to a decrease in the attractiveness of the person to the partner, again causing the same effects. The depression and low self-esteem can, in turn, lead to sexual problems. When an obese woman with a sexual difficulty presents for treatment, use of the basic principles of sex therapy should be considered, with appropriate modifications and additional help with self-esteem, depression, etc. Counselling with regard to weight reduction by changing food habits and exercise may also form part of a treatment package (cf. Stunkard, 1989).

ILLUSTRATIVE CASES

Given below are three case examples. All presented with a major eating disorder, and all had sexual difficulties for which help was sought and given. They highlight some of the points made in the previous sections, both with regard to history and clinical presentation and with regard to treatment procedures. They also show the diversity of the problems and presentations.

Case I

Diane was referred for anorexia nervosa at the age of 26. She had had previous treatment, including an in-patient stay for several months at 18, in another hospital. She presented with rapid weight loss, and she feared that she might completely lose her ability to eat. Being a fairly successful professional woman, she did not want another period of severe illness.

Diane responded well to out-patient cognitive-behavioural treatment, including a package of target setting, coping strategies, relaxation, de-sensitisation to higher weights, and elicitation and challenging of dysfunctional cognitions (described in Channon *et al.*, 1989). After several sessions of therapy, Diane began to express concern about her sexuality. She had never had sexual intercourse nor had she had any close relationship. As a student she had gone out with one or two men and engaged in some kissing and cuddling, but nothing more. Her upbringing had been a strict one, in a Roman Catholic family and school, and she had been brought up to believe that sex was a duty and not a pleasure, and that premarital sex was unacceptable.

She had, in more recent years, wanted to break free from these inhibitions, and had tentatively begun to explore herself. She tried masturbation, rather tentatively and with some misgivings, but never achieved an orgasm. She 'did not know what an orgasm was like'. She increasingly felt despondent about her 'lack of normality'. The present episode of weight loss was closely associated with this phase.

Diane's treatment programme was expanded to include work on her sexuality. Some sessions were devoted entirely to this aspect. This included giving basic information on sex through books, slides, etc. – *The Book of Love* (Delvin, 1974) was recommended; encouragement to explore her body once again; instructions for self-stimulation; encouragement to develop sexual fantasies, including reading fantasies of women – Nancy Friday's *My Secret Garden* (1979) was recommended; and encouragement to give herself more opportunities to meet and go out with young men. She made slow progress initially, and needed a good deal of support and reassurance. After she achieved her first orgasm, her confidence in her sexuality considerably increased, and she made further rapid progress. She began to go out with a man, although this did not lead to sex.

Fourteen months after referral, Diane was at a healthy weight and had reasonable eating habits, although she still had some worries about becoming fat. She was sexually relaxed, and could masturbate to orgasm. She felt reasonably confident of developing a sexual relationship, and had a good social life.

Case II

Mary was hospitalised for anorexia nervosa at the age of 35, for the third time. She had been anorexic for over twelve years, with episodes of severe weight loss alternating with reasonably healthy phases. She married at 18 and had a child a year later. The illness developed two years later, following a period of severe illness of her child.

The in-patient treatment was followed by out-patient therapy. While she still struggled with eating some of the time, Mary was able to maintain a reasonable weight. She found a new job and began to function well in work.

Mary's sexual relationships with her husband, however, remained badly impaired. The couple had not had sex for several years, and physical contact was limited to holding hands and the occasional hug and superficial kiss. Ben, her husband, reported that any effort on his part to initiate sex led to a clear rebuff.

Therapy was focused on the sexual problem about a year after out-patient sessions began. As both agreed that an improvement in their sex life was a good thing to aim for, formal exploration of the sexual problem was commenced. Mary had, it transpired, a history of rape; she had been raped by several men when she was on holiday at the age of 17. The trauma, however, did not affect her own sexuality until many years later. She married and had her child, and cared for him when he was ill. She was 22 when her eating disorder started. Her sex drive declined with the progress of her anorexia nervosa. Periods of recovery from the illness, however, did not lead to a corresponding revival of her libido, and she became increasingly unwilling even to contemplate sex. Thoughts of sex began to bring back memories of the traumatic sexual experience she had as a teenager, and she felt sex to be dirty and unacceptable. Ben was most sympathetic and understanding, but was clearly not happy about the life of abstinence that had been imposed on him. Mary kept reassuring him that she was not rejecting him, which he accepted. However, both were deeply unhappy about the situation.

Conventional sex therapy was not possible for Mary and Ben, as Mary's aversion to all aspects of sex was very strong. Individual sessions that enabled Mary to express her anxieties, and to give vent to her feelings about the sexual trauma of many years ago, were offered. Mary asked to be seen on a one-to-one basis by a female therapist. This was arranged. She made some progress in talking about her feelings, but never found it easy. When joint sessions were resumed, Mary co-operated as best she could, but carrying out agreed instructions was almost totally impossible for her. An attempt was made to overcome this by negotiating a time-table, with little success. A further complication was that pressure to make progress in the sexual problem made it harder for her to eat reasonable meals.

It was then decided not to pursue the sexual problem as a focal issue, and to see the couple for supportive sessions in order to ensure that the anorexia was kept under control.

Case III

Liz, a 24-year-old nurse, was referred with bulimia nervosa. She had been going out with a young man, and all seemed to be going well. Then, at a party, she was seduced by another man, a work colleague, while she was drunk. This made her feel dirty and disgusted with herself, and she decided to break off with her boyfriend. She got depressed, and began to eat less and less. 'I did not want to be a woman any more', she said. Weight loss was followed by the development of craving for food, and Liz began to indulge in binge eating. She compulsively ate vast quantities of food, and – in order to get rid of the food – engaged in self-induced vomiting. This became the pattern of her eating behaviour. She continued to work, and had other relationships. The relationships, however, were unsuccessful, partly because she now found sex unenjoyable and she was unable to reach a climax, and partly because she had to go to great lengths to conceal her bingeing and vomiting from her partners. The need to prove to herself that she was normal led to her going out with many men, none of whom she saw more than a few times.

What led her to seek help was her bulimia, but she also talked about her sexual and relationship difficulties at assessment. In out-patient therapy, Liz gradually acquired some control over her bulimic behaviour, and individual counselling helped her to regain her sense of worth as a female. After over a year, she developed a stable relationship with a young man. Liz was encouraged to be open with him about her problems and they were then seen for conjoint therapy for several sessions. They reported considerable improvement in their relationship at discharge, and were engaged to be married.

A NOTE ON EATING DISORDERS AND SEXUAL PROBLEMS IN MALES

Although this chapter is about sexual problems in women with eating disorders, a brief note on male difficulties may be added for the sake of completeness. Anorexia nervosa in males is rare, and bulimia is even rarer (Andersen, 1985, 1990a, 1990b; Russell, 1983a). The clinical picture usually includes a marked decrease in libido, and impotence, associated with a disturbance of reproductive hormonal activity. Russell (1970, 1983a) includes loss of sexual interest and of potency among the diagnostic criteria for male anorexia nervosa. Sexual anxieties and sexual immaturity in the pre-morbid stage of male anorexia have been reported (e.g. Fichter and Daser, 1987). Some reports suggest that their sexual anxieties may be even greater than those of their female counterparts (e.g. Fichter, Daser, and Postpischil, 1985). Hormonal activity returns to normal levels with weight gain (e.g. Crisp *et al.*, 1982). Erectile function and libido also return with weight gain, but this may take time (Hall, Delahunt, and Ellis, 1985). Sexual anxieties and conflicts often need to be dealt with in therapy. Education about sexual development and sexual behaviours is a valuable part of this. Andersen (1990b) has given a comprehensive account of the treatment of males with eating disorders which includes sexual aspects.

An aspect of male eating disorders worth commenting on is the apparently relatively high incidence of gender dysphoria among these patients. Herzog *et al.* (1984) found significantly more anorexic and bulimic males presenting at an eating disorders unit to be homosexually orientated than comparable females. Herzog, Bradburn, and Newman (1990) make the observation that psycho-sexual and gender identity conflicts, as well as sociocultural pressures for homosexual men, may contribute to the development of eating disorders in men. The small numbers reported in the literature, however, do not permit a firm conclusion on whether there is a genuinely high level of homosexuality among anorexic and bulimic men. In clinical practice, if a patient has clear gender dysphoria or displays concern about his sexual orientation, then the treatment package should include some consideration of this.

CONCLUDING COMMENTS

In this chapter we have discussed the nature of the relationship between sexual problems in females with eating disorders. The large and growing body of relevant literature that has been reviewed here shows that many women with anorexia nervosa or bulimia nervosa, and other eating disorders, show impairment in their sexual functioning. Problems with regard to body image and femininity are clearly implicated in these problems for some patients. There is also evidence that, in a proportion of cases, traumatic sexual experiences including sexual abuse in childhood and adolescence may play a contributory role. As highlighted in the illustrative cases cited, a comprehensive approach is needed in the assessment and treatment of women with these problems. Assessment of women presenting with eating disorders should include specific but sensitive enquiry into sexual functioning and sexual history. Where sexual difficulties or conflicts are present, the therapeutic effort needs to include specific help towards these problems.

Finally, there is a pressing need for further research on the relationship between eating disorders and sexual problems. Such research should be geared towards identifying the relevant variables more systematically than at present. There is a clear need for rigorous methodology in research in this field, including the careful formulation and operationalisation of the questions asked (cf. Coovert, Kinder, and Thompson, 1989). Greater and more definitive knowledge would not only enhance our understanding of these problems; it would also enable clinicians to help those who are in need of such help more effectively.

ACKNOWLEDGEMENTS

The author wishes to express his thanks to Melanie Marks and David R. Hemsley for their comments on earlier drafts of this chapter, to Jane Ussher and Christine Baker for valuable editorial suggestions and to Jean Morgan, Moira Hall, and Hesha de Silva for their help in numerous ways.

REFERENCES

Abraham, S. and Beumont, P.J.V. (1982) 'Varieties of psychosexual experience in patients with anorexia nervosa', *International Journal of Eating Disorders* 1: 10–19.

American Psychiatric Association (1987) *Diagnostic and Statistical Manual of Mental Disorders, 3rd Edition, Revised (DSM-III-R)*, Washington, DC: APA

Andersen, A.E. (1985) *Practical Comprehensive Treatment of Anorexia Nervosa and Bulimia*, London: Edward Arnold.

Andersen, A.E. (ed.) (1990a) *Males with Eating Disorders*, New York: Brunner/Mazel,

Andersen, A.E. (1990b) 'Diagnosis and treatment of males with eating disorders', in A.E. Andersen (ed.) *Males with Eating Disorders*, New York: Brunner/Mazel.

Baisden, M.J. and Baisden, J.R. (1979) 'A profile of women who seek counselling for sexual dysfunctions', *American Journal of Family Therapy* 7: 68–76.

Baker, C.D. and de Silva, P. (1988) 'Zilbergeld's myths and male sexual dysfunctions: an empirical investigation', *Sexual and Marital Therapy*, 3: 229–38.

Bancroft, J. (1989) *Human Sexuality and Its Problems*, 2nd edition, Edinburgh: Churchill Livingstone.

Becker, J.V., Skinner, L.J., Abel, G.G., and Treacy, E.C. (1982) 'Incidents and types of sexual dysfunctions in rape and incest victims', *Journal of Sexual and Marital Therapy* 8: 65–74.

Becker, J.V., Skinner, L.J., Abel, G.G., and Cichon, J. (1986) 'Level of post assault sexual functioning in rape and incest victims', *Archives of Sexual Behaviour*, 15: 37–49.

Beumont, P.J.V., Abraham, S.F., and Simson, K. (1981) 'The psychosexual histories of adolescent girls and young women with anorexia nervosa', *Psychological Medicine* 11: 131–40.

Beumont, P.J.V., George, G.C.W., and Smart, D.E. (1976) '"Dieters" and "vomiters and purgers" in anorexia nervosa', *Psychological Medicine* 6: 617–22.

Bliss, G.L. and Branch, C.H. (1960) *Anorexia Nervosa: Its History, Psychology, and Biology*, New York: Hoeber.

Briere, J. and Runtz, M. (1987) 'Post sexual abuse trauma: data and implications for clinical practice', *Journal of Interpersonal Violence* 2: 367–79.

Bruch, H. (1962) 'Perceptual and conceptual disturbances in anorexia nervosa', *Psychosomatic Medicine* 24: 187–94.

Bruch, H. (1973) *Eating Disorders: Obesity, Anorexia Nervosa and the Person Within*, New York: Basic Books.

Buchan, T. and Gregory, L.D. (1984) 'Anorexia nervosa in a black Zimbabwean', *British Journal of Psychiatry* 145: 326–30.

Casper, R., Eckert, E., Halmi, K., Goldberg, S., and Davis, J. (1980) 'Bulimia: its incidence and clinical importance in patients with anorexia nervosa', *Archives of General Psychiatry* 37: 1030–5.

Channon, S., de Silva, P., Hemsley, D., and Perkins, R. (1989) 'A controlled trial of cognitive-behavioural treatment of anorexia nervosa', *Behaviour Research and Therapy* 27: 529–35.

Cole, M. and Dryden, W. (eds) (1988) *Sex Therapy in Britain*, Milton Keynes, Open University Press.

Cooper, G.F. (1988) 'The psychological methods of sex therapy', in M. Cole and W. Dryden (eds) *Sex Therapy in Britain*, Milton Keynes: Open University Press.

Cooper, P.J. and Fairburn, C. (1983) 'Binge eating and self-induced vomiting in the community: a preliminary study', *British Journal of Psychiatry* 142: 139–44.

Coovert, D.L., Kinder, B.N., and Thompson, J.K. (1989) 'The psychosexual aspects of anorexia nervosa and bulimia nervosa: a review of the literature', *Clinical Psychology Review* 9: 169–80.

Courtois, C.A. (1988) *Healing the Incest Wound: Adult Survivors in Therapy*, New York: Norton.

Crisp, A.H. (1965) 'Some aspects of the evolution, presentation and follow-up of anorexia nervosa', *Proceedings of the Royal Society of Medicine* 58: 814–20.

Crisp, A.H. (1980) *Anorexia Nervosa: Let Me Be*, London: Academic Press.

Crisp, A.H. (1984) 'The psychopathology of anorexia nervosa: getting the "heat" out of the system', in A.J. Stunkard and E. Stellar (eds) *Eating and Its Disorders*, New York: Raven.

Crisp, A.H. and Burns, T. (1983) 'The clinical presentation of anorexia nervosa in males', *International Journal of Eating Disorders* 2: 5–10.

Crisp, A.H. and Kalucy, R.S. (1974) 'Aspects of perceptual disorder in anorexia nervosa', *British Journal of Medical Psychology* 47: 349–60.

Crisp, A.H., Hsu, L.K.G., Chen, C.N., and Wheeler, M. (1982) 'Reproductive hormone profiles in male anorexia nervosa before, during and after restoration of body weight to normal: a study of twelve patients', *International Journal of Eating Disorders* 1: 3–9.

Crowe, M.J. and Ridley, J. (1990) *Therapy with Couples: A Behavioural-Systems Approach to Marital and Sexual Problems*, Oxford: Blackwell.

Dally, P. and Gomez, J. (1979) *Anorexia Nervosa*, London: Heinemann.

Delvin, D. (1974) *The Book of Love*, London: New English Library.

de Silva, P. (1987a) 'Sexual dysfunction: assessment', in S. Lindsay and G.E. Powell (eds) *Handbook of Clinical Adult Psychology*, Aldershot: Gower.

de Silva, P. (1987b) 'Sexual dysfunction: treatment', in S. Lindsay and G.E. Powell (eds) *Handbook of Clinical Adult Psychology*, Aldershot: Gower.

de Silva, P. and Eysenck, S.B.G. (1987) 'Personality and addictiveness in anorexic and bulimic patients', *Personality and Individual Differences* 8: 749–51.

Di Nicola, V.F. (1990a) 'Anorexia multiforme: self-starvation in historical and cultural context. Part I – Self-starvation as a historical chameleon', *Transcultural Psychiatric Research Review* 28: 165–96.

Di Nicola, V.F. (1990b) 'Anorexia multiforme: self-starvation in historical and cultural context. Part II – Anorexia nervosa as a culture-reactive syndrome', *Transcultural Psychiatric Research Review* 28: 245–86.

Duddle, M. (1977) 'Etiological factors in the unconsummated marriage', *Journal of Psychosomatic Research* 21: 157–60.

Fairburn, C. (1984) 'Bulimia: its epidemiology and management', in A.J. Stunkard and E. Stellar (eds) *Eating and Its Disorders*, New York: Raven.

Fairburn, C. and Belgin, S.J. (1990) 'The prevalence of bulimia nervosa', in C.N. Stefanis, A.D. Rabavilas, and C.R. Soldatos (eds) *Psychiatry: A World Perspective*, Vol. 1. Amsterdam: Elsevier.

Fairburn, C.G. and Cooper, P.J. (1985) 'The clinical features of bulimia nervosa', *British Journal of Psychiatry* 144: 238–46.

Feldman-Summers, S., Gordon, P., and Meagher, J. (1979) 'The impact of rape on sexual satisfaction', *Journal of Abnormal Psychology* 88: 101–5.

Fichter, M.M. (1991) 'Course and outcome of bulimia nervosa', paper presented at the International Symposium on Eating Disorders, Paris, April.

Fichter, M.M. and Daser, C. (1987) 'Symptomatology, psychosexual development and gender identity in 42 anorexic males', *Psychological Medicine* 17: 409–18.

Fichter, M.M., Daser, C., and Postpischil, F. (1985) 'Anorexic syndromes in the male', *Journal of Psychiatric Research* 19: 305–13.

Friday, N. (1978) *My Secret Garden*, London: Virago.

Garde, K. and Lunde, I. (1980) 'Female sexual behaviour: a study in a random sample of 40-year-old women', *Maturitas* 2: 225–240.

Garfinkel, P.E. and Garner, D.M. (1982) *Anorexia Nervosa: A Multidimensional Perspective*, New York: Brunner/Mazel.

Garner, D.M. and Bemis, K.M. (1982) 'A cognitive-behavioral approach to anorexia nervosa', *Cognitive Therapy and Research* 6: 123–50.

Garrow. J. (1988) *Obesity and Related Diseases*, Edinburgh: Churchill Livingstone.

Gil, E. (1988) *Treatment of Adult Survivors of Childhood Abuse*, Walnut Creek, CA: Launch Press.

Gordon, R.A. (1990) *Anorexia and Bulimia: Anatomy of a Social Epidemic*, Oxford: Blackwell.

Guile, L., Horne, M., and Dunston, E. (1978) 'Anorexia nervosa: sexual behaviour modification as an adjunct to an integrated treatment programme', *Australian and New Zealand Journal of Psychiatry* 12: 165–7.

Gull, W.W. (1874) 'Anorexia nervosa (apepsia hysterica, anorexia hysterica)', *Transactions of the Clinical Society of London* 7: 22–8.

Hall, A., Delahunt, J.W., and Ellis, P.M. (1985) 'Anorexia nervosa in the male: clinical features and follow-up of nine patients', *Journal of Psychiatric Research* 19: 315–21.

Halmi, K.A. (1985) 'Classification of the eating disorders', *Journal of Psychiatric Research* 19: 113–19.

Halmi, K.A., Falk, J.R., and Schwartz, G. (1981) 'Binge eating and vomiting: a survey of a college population', *Psychological Medicine* 11: 697–706.

Hambridge, D.M. (1988) 'Incest and anorexia nervosa: what is the link?', *British Journal of Psychiatry* 152: 145–6.

Hawton, K. (1985) *Sex Therapy: A Practical Guide*, Oxford: Oxford University Press.

Hawton, K. (1988) 'Sexual dysfunctions', in E. Miller and P.J. Cooper (eds) *Adult Abnormal Psychology*, Edinburgh: Churchill Livingstone.

Hawton, K. (1989) 'Sexual dysfunctions', in K. Hawton, P.M. Salkovskis, J. Kirk, and D.M. Clark (eds) *Cognitive Behaviour Therapy for Psychiatric Problems: A Practical Guide*, Oxford: Oxford University Press.

Hemsley, D.R. and Powell-Proctor, L. (1979) 'Modification of sexual behaviour in anorexia nervosa', *Australian and New Zealand Journal of Psychiatry* 13: 362.

Herzog, D.B., Bradburn, Z.S., and Newman, K. (1990) 'Sexuality in males with eating disorders', in A.E. Andersen (ed.) *Males with Eating Disorders*, New York: Brunner/Mazel.

Herzog, D.B., Norman, D.K., Gordon, C., and Pepose, N. (1984) 'Sexual conflict and eating disorders in 22 males', *American Journal of Psychiatry* 141: 989–90.

Hsu, G. (1990) *Eating Disorders*, New York: Guilford Press.

Jehu, D. (1988) *Sexual Abuse and Beyond*, Chichester: Wiley.

Jehu, D. (1991) 'Clinical work with adults who were sexually abused in childhood', in C.R. Hollin and K. Howells (eds) *Clinical Approaches to Sex Offenders and Their Victims*, Chichester: Wiley.

Kalucy, R.S., Crisp, A.H., and Harding, B. (1977) 'A study of 56 families with anorexia nervosa', *British Journal of Medical Psychology* 50: 381–95.

Kendell, R.E., Hall, D.J., Hailey, A., and Babigian, H.M. (1973) 'The epidemiology of anorexia nervosa', *Psychological Medicine* 3: 200–3.

Keys, A., Brozek, J., Henschel, A., Mickelson, O., and Taylor, H.L. (1950) *The Biology of Human Starvation*, Vol. I, Minneapolis: University of Minnesota Press.

King, M.B. (1989) 'Eating disorders in a general practice population: prevalence, characteristics and follow-up at 12 to 18 months', *Psychological Medicine*, Monograph Supplement, 14: 1–34.

Kolodny, R.C., Masters, W.H., and Johnson, V.E. (1979) *Textbook of Sexual Medicine*, Boston, MA: Little, Brown & Co.

Lasegue, C. (1873) 'De l'anorexie hysterique', *Archives Generale de Medicine* XXI: 385–403.

Lasegue, C. (1874) 'On hysterical anorexia', *Medical Times Gazette* 2: 367–9.

Liss-Levinson, N. (1988) 'Disorders of desire: women, sex and food', in E. Cole and E.D. Rothblum (eds) *Women and Sex Therapy*, New York: The Haworth Press.

Liu, A. (1979) *Solitaire*, New York: Harper and Row.

Mathew, R.J. and Weinman, M.L. (1982) 'Sexual dysfunctions in depression', *Archives of Sexual Behaviour* 11: 323–8.

McCann, I.L. and Pearlman, L.A. (1990) *Psychological Trauma and the Adult Survivor*, New York: Brunner/Mazel.

McCrea, C. and Yaffe, M. (1981) 'Sexuality in the obese', *British Journal of Sexual Medicine* 8: 24–37.

McGuire, L.A. and Wagner, N.N. (1978) 'Sexual dysfunction in women who were molested as children: one response pattern and suggestions for treatment', *Journal of Sexual and Marital Therapy* 4: 11–15.

Morton, R. (1694) *Phthisiologia: Or, a Treatise on Consumption*, London: Smith & Walford.

Moulton, R. (1942) 'A psychometric study of anorexia nervosa including the use of vaginal smears', *Psychosomatic Medicine* 4: 62–74.

Norton, K., Crisp, A.H., and Bhat, A.V. (1985) 'Why do some anorexics steal? Personal, social and illness factors', *Journal of Psychiatric Research* 19: 385–90.

Nylander, I. (1971) 'The feeling of being fat and dieting in a school population: epidemiologic interview investigation', *Acta Sociomedica Scandinavica* 3: 17–26.

Oppenheimer, R., Howells, K., Palmer, R.L., and Chaloner, D.A. (1985) 'Adverse sexual experience in childhood and clinical eating disorders: a preliminary description', *Journal of Psychiatric Research* 19: 357–61.

Orbach, S. (1979) *Fat is a Feminist Issue*, New York: Berkeley Books.

Patton, G.C. (1988) 'The spectrum of eating disorders in adolescence', *Journal of Psychometric Research* 32: 579–84.

Pyle, R.W., Mitchell, J.G., and Eckert, E.D. (1981) 'Bulimia: a report of 34 cases', *Journal of Clinical Psychiatry* 42: 60–4.

Raboch, J. (1986) 'Sexual development and life of psychiatric female patients', *Archives of Sexual Behavior* 15: 341–54.

Raboch, J. and Faltus, F. (1991) 'Sexuality of women with anorexia nervosa', *Acta Psychiatrica Scandinavica* 84: 9–11.

Rahman, L., Richardson, H.B., and Ripley, H.S. (1939) 'Anorexia nervosa with psychiatric observations', *Psychometric Medicine* 1: 335–65.

Robinson, P.H. (1986) 'The bulimic disorders', *Clinical Neuropharmacology* 9: 14–36.

Root, M.P.P. and Fallon, P. (1988) 'The incidence of victimization experiences in a bulimia sample', *Journal of Interpersonal Violence* 3: 161–73.

Russell, G.F.M. (1970) 'Anorexia nervosa: its identity as an illness and its treatment', in J.H. Price (ed.) *Modern Trends in Psychological Medicine*, Vol. 2, London: Butterworth.

Russell, G.F.M. (1979) 'Bulimia nervosa: an ominous variant of anorexia nervosa', *Psychological Medicine* 9: 429–48.

Russell, G.F.M. (1983a) 'Anorexia nervosa and bulimia nervosa', in G.F.M. Russell and L.A. Hersov (eds) *The Neuroses and Personality Disorders*, Cambridge: Cambridge University Press.

Russell, G.F.M. (1983b) 'Obesity', in G.F.M. Russell and L.A. Hersov (eds) *The Neuroses and Personality Disorders*, Cambridge: Cambridge University Press.

Russell, G.F.M. (1985) 'The changing nature of anorexia nervosa', *Journal of Psychiatric Research* 19: 101–9.

Ryle, J.A. (1936) 'Anorexia nervosa', *Lancet* ii: 893–9.

Sanderson, C. (1990) *Counselling Adult Survivors of Child Sex Abuse*, London: Jessica Kingsley.

Selvini-Palazzoli, M. (1974) *Self-Starvation: From the Intraphysic to the Transpersonal Approach*, London: Chaucer.

Sheldon, J.H. (1939) 'Anorexia nervosa', *Proceedings of the Royal Society of Medicine* 32: 738–41.

Silverman, J.A. (1983) 'Richard Morton, 1637–1698, limner of anorexia nervosa: his life and times', *Journal of the American Medical Association* 250: 2830–2.

Slade, P. (1985) 'A review of body image studies in anorexia nervosa and bulimia nervosa', *Journal of Psychiatric Research* 19: 255–65.

Slade, P.D. and Russell, G.F.M. (1973) 'Awareness of body dimensions in anorexia nervosa: cross-sectional and longitudinal studies', *Psychological Medicine* 3: 188–99.

Solyom, L., Freeman, R.J., and Miles, J.E. (1982) 'A comparative psychometric study of anorexia nervosa and obsessional neurosis', *Canadian Journal of Psychiatry* 27: 282–6.

Stunkard, A.J. (1959) 'Eating patterns and obesity', *Psychiatric Quarterly* 33: 284–92.

Stunkard, A.J. (1989) 'Perspectives on human obesity', in A.J. Stunkard and A. Baum (eds) *Perspectives in Behavioral Medicine: Eating, Sleeping and Sex*, Hillside, NJ: Erlbaum.

Szmukler, G.I. (1985) 'The epidemiology of anorexia nervosa and bulimia', *Journal of Psychiatric Research* 19: 143–53.

Szmukler, G.I. (1989) 'The psychopathology of eating disorders', in R. Shepherd (ed.) *Handbook of the Psychophysiology of Human Eating*, Chichester: Wiley.

Szmukler, G.I., McCance, C., McCrone, L., and Hunter, D. (1988) 'Anorexia nervosa: a psychiatric case register study from Aberdeen', *Psychological Medicine* 16: 49–58.

Szmukler, G.I., Slade, D.P., Harris, P., Benton, D., and Russell, G.F.M. (eds) (1986) *Anorexia Nervosa and Bulimic Disorders – Current Perspectives*, Oxford: Pergamon.

Theander, S. (1970) 'Anorexia nervosa: a psychiatric investigation of 44 female cases', *Acta Psychiatrica Scandinavica*, Supplement, 214: 1–94.

Thomas, J. and Szmukler, G.I. (1985) 'Anorexia nervosa in patients of Afro-Caribbean extraction', *British Journal of Psychiatry* 146: 653–6.

Tsai, M., Feldman-Summers, S., and Edgar, M. (1979) 'Childhood molestation: variables related to differential impacts on psychosexual functioning in adult women', *Journal of Abnormal Psychology* 88: 407–17.
Ussher, J. (1990) *The Psychology of the Female Body*, London: Routledge.
Waller, J.V., Kaufman, M.R., and Deutsch, F. (1940) 'Anorexia nervosa: a psychosomatic entity', *Psychosomatic Medicine* 2: 3–16.
Wardle, J. (1980) 'Dietary restraint and binge eating', *Behaviour Analysis and Modification* 4: 201–9.
Wyatt, G.E. and Powell, G.J. (eds) (1988) *Lasting Effects of Child Sexual Abuse*, Newbury Park: Sage.
Yager, J. (1982) 'Family issues in the pathogenesis of anorexia nervosa', *Psychosomatic Medicine* 44: 43–60.
Yager, J. and Strober, M. (1985) 'Family aspects of anorexia nervosa', in A. Frances and R. Hales (eds) *Psychiatric Update – IV*, Washington, DC: American Psychiatric Press.
Zverina, J., Lachman, M., Pondelickova, J., and Vanek, J. (1987) 'The occurrence of atypical sexual experience among various female patient groups', *Archives of Sexual Behavior* 16: 321–6.11.

Chapter 5

A cognitive-behavioural model for the formulation and treatment of sexual dysfunction

Christine D. Baker

INTRODUCTION

The role of cognitions, or an individual's thoughts, has been the focus of a great deal of empirical research in a number of psychological disorders, particularly depression and anxiety, in recent years (Beck *et al.*, 1979; Beck, Emery, and Greenberg, 1985). Other clinical areas where cognitions have been linked to the maintenance of psychological problems are: eating disorders (Garner and Bemis, 1985); obsessive compulsive disorders (Salkovskis and Warwick, 1988); and somatic problems (Salkovskis and Warwick, 1986). With respect to sexual problems, however, although patients' beliefs about their condition are invariably addressed during the course of therapy, there has been, thus far, limited empirical input in this area. In particular, the exploration of the specific relationship between the negative automatic thinking and faulty assumptions which can contribute to the maintenance of sexual problems has not been systematically addressed. More importantly, where therapeutic intervention is concerned, professionals involved in the field of sex therapy are becoming increasingly aware of a need to develop and expand the existing repertoire of treatment methods. This is particularly true in the presentation of sexual problems where a stable or willing partner is not available for the implementation of couple therapy or the more traditional Masters and Johnson treatment packages.

In this chapter, a cognitive/behavioural treatment approach for male sexual problems will be presented and discussed.[1] This approach is based on an empirical study by Baker and de Silva (1988), which revealed that males presenting with sexual dysfunction, namely, premature ejaculation and erectile problems, express belief in a number of sexual 'myths' or misconceptions, such as believing that 'good sex requires an erection'. These misconceptions relate to assumptions with regard to 'desirable' or expected male sexual behaviours, and are argued, by Zilbergeld (1983), to represent the fantasy model of sex. The results of Baker *et al.*'s study, confirmed that cognitive factors, at least in certain men, constitute a major area to be addressed in any therapeutic package. Indeed, there is indirect support for this argument from a number of other authors in the area of sexual dysfunction (Hawton, 1985, 1991; Gillan, 1987; Frachner and Kimmel, 1987; Masters and Johnson, 1970). For example, Bancroft (1989), in his eloquent 'psychosomatic circle of sex', describes how physical as well as psychological factors can affect the sexual system, at any point in the circle. Not only could cognitions set off a chain of negative factors within the system, they could also perpetuate and enhance pre-existing negative factors, even if these cognitions are themselves the result of such factors. Moreover, Barlow (1986) argues that cognitive interference acts as a maintaining factor in sexual dysfunction through its capacity to act as an inhibitor. For example, potentially sexual or erotic tactile stimuli are not perceived as such, and, therefore, either do not lead to or inhibit arousal. In other words, attending to anxiety-provoking thoughts can be argued to be incompatible with fully attending to tactile and sensual stimuli which are essential to arousal.

The cognitive approach is based on the assumption that belief in sexual myths reflects patients' basic core attributions about gender role and accompanying expected behaviour (Baker, 1987, 1989). Clinically, such assumptions are reflected in the reported automatic thoughts, 'My partner will leave me if I continue to lose my erections', or 'I can't be very masculine if I don't last long with a partner'. Once 'failure' is perceived, patients possibly become sensitised to messages available in the popular media, thereby activating the basic belief system which may not have been in operation up to now. The treatment approach which will be discussed aims to break the vicious circle whereby continued 'failure' gives further rise to negative thoughts which in turn reinforce the belief system. The chapter will focus mainly on sexual problems experienced by heterosexual males, using as reference the author's previous work in this area. However, the general principles of the treatment package can be equally applicable in appropriate cases of female sexual complaints, as well as other clinical groups (see George, Chapter 10, this volume). The next sections will outline the main male and female sexual dysfunctions. A brief discussion of the current approaches used in sex therapy will be included. The central section will discuss the cognitive/behavioural model proposed for the formulation and treatment of sexual problems. Illustrative case studies will then be presented.

SEXUAL DYSFUNCTIONS

Prevalence and definitions

In general, it is not very easy to classify or categorise sexual problems as there is no universally accepted manner of doing so (see Ussher; Nicolson, both this volume). To complicate matters further, it is very difficult to gain accurate figures in relation to prevalence or the extent to which sexual problems exist. The reason for this is that the topic of sexuality continues to represent a very sensitive area for many, and, consequently, the reliability of responses of various quantitative studies remains rather dubious. Other methodological difficulties in studies of sexuality relate to sample selection and definition of sexual problems. Having said this, the pioneering studies of Kinsey and his colleagues (1948, 1953) provided the first figures related to prevalence (in America) of sexual problems in men and women. Perhaps of more relevance to professionals involved in sex therapy is the nature and extent of incidence of sexual problems in various medical and psychological settings. Golombok, Rust, and Piccard (1984) interviewed a random selection of thirty men and thirty women attending their general practitioners for non-sexual problems (age 18–50). They found that 27 per cent of the men had difficulty becoming sexually aroused. Seven per cent of the women were totally anorgasmic with their partners and 20 per cent of the men had premature ejaculation. Some degree of erectile problem was experienced by 7 per cent of the men. In another study at a clinic for sexually transmitted diseases (Catalan *et al.*, 1981), semi-structured interviews were carried out with seventy male and seventy female clinic attenders. The study revealed that almost a quarter of the men and two-fifths of the women were experiencing sexual dysfunction. Among the men, 13 per cent reported premature ejaculation, 7 per cent reported erectile dysfunction, and 6 per cent loss of libido. Among the women, 37 per cent reported 'coital orgasmic dysfunction' and 13 per cent 'loss of libido'. The studies mentioned above are by no means the only ones in relation to incidence of sexual problems. They were included in order to give the reader some idea of the extent of sexual problems presented to clinics.[2] For a very good breakdown of studies in frequencies and incidences of normal and dysfunctional sexual behaviour, the reader is referred to Cole and Dryden (1988).

Categories of sexual problems

On the whole, sexual problems or dysfunctions can be classified in terms of three main categories: interest; arousal; and orgasm.

Men

There is an increasing number of male attenders who complain of loss of sexual interest or reduced libido. However, at least in Britain, the most commonly encountered male problem relates to erectile dysfunction, which falls into the arousal category of problems. Problems with orgasm constitute the next most common male problem, in particular, premature ejaculation. Other problems with orgasm include retarded or absent ejaculation and painful ejaculation.

Women

The most frequently encountered complaint in women is loss of sexual interest and/or loss of arousal. Inability to achieve orgasm (with or without a partner) is another commonly reported female complaint (see Chapter 1). In addition to the above there is a group of problems for men and women which do not fall into the above categories, but which are very distressing. These are dyspareunia or painful ejaculation in men and vaginismus and dyspareunia in women. Vaginismus refers to the tightening of the vaginal muscles to such a degree that penetration is literally impossible, while dyspareunia in women is experienced as painful intercourse.

Causes of sexual problems

Causes of sexual problems can be either physical or psychological or a combination of both. Whilst this chapter is more concerned with psychological factors, it is important that the reader has some appreciation of the contribution of organic factors to sexual problems. The elimination of these is crucial during the assessment of any person presenting for sex therapy.

Physical causes

Some physical causes of sexual problems in men are: cardiovascular disease, e.g., arteriosclerosis, hypertension; endocrinological conditions, e.g., Addison's disease, diabetes mellitus, thyroid disorders; genitourinary conditions, e.g. Peyronies disease; neurological conditions, e.g. multiple sclerosis. Such conditions are known to impair erectile and/or ejaculatory function as well as sexual interest (Bancroft, 1989).

   In women, some endocrinological conditions, such as thyroid dysfunction, can affect sexual interest and orgasmic capacity, whilst genitourinary problems can lead to painful intercourse or vaginismus. Neurological conditions, especially if they involve spinal cord damage, can affect orgasmic function. Various types of surgery, particularly of a gynaecological nature, can have a contribution in the predisposition of sexual problems because of the strong emotional component they involve (Kolodny, Masters, and Johnson, 1979; see also Chapter 1, this volume). Drugs are amongst physical factors which can contribute to dysfunction. In particular, psychotropic medications such as tricyclic antidepressants, MAOIs, lithium carbonate, antihypertensives, diuretics, hormone-based drugs, and major tranquillisers can all interfere with interest or level of libido, arousal (especially erectile dysfunction), and orgasm in men (Bancroft, 1989). In addition, excessive use of alcohol can have very negative effects in the male sexual response (Cole and Dryden, 1988).

It must be noted that, even in cases where a physical disorder has been established, there may still exist a psychological component associated with a sexual problem. For example, a person's attitude to a particular condition will have an important part to play in the aetiology and maintenance of a sexual dysfunction. In men, performance anxiety is a good example of the relationship between attitude to a physical condition (e.g. heart disease) and sexual behaviour.

Psychological causes

One of the best and most cohesive psychological models to use in the assessment and formulation of sexual problems is that developed by Hawton (1985). His model addresses the aetiology of sexual dysfunction in terms of: predisposing factors; precipitants; and maintaining factors. Amongst predisposing factors, early experiences such as restrictive upbringing, disturbed family relationships, inadequate sexual information, or any traumatic early experience can all play a part in later incidence of sexual difficulties (Kaplan, 1974). Precipitants relate to such factors as: unrealistic expectations, marital difficulties and/or dysfunction in one partner, ageing, reactions to organic factors, depression, anxiety, and childbirth.

Maintaining factors include a wide range of psychological as well as physical factors, which, together with accompanying life stressors (e.g. financial problems, work-related issues), can contribute to particular problems being perpetuated over time. Examples of such problems include: anticipation of sexual failure, poor communication or resentment in the relationship, and performance anxiety. The significance of the above maintaining factors will become clear in the discussion of the cognitive/behavioural model of therapy in the next section.

TREATMENT AND SEXUAL SATISFACTION

Planning and providing clinical intervention for people who have sexual problems is rather complex due to the multifactorial nature of human sexuality. One has to be aware not only of the interaction between psychological and physical factors contributing to a particular problem, but also of issues such as the individual's culture (d'Ardenne, 1988). Matters are further complicated by the tendency many professionals have to distinguish between sexual and marital problems. In the author's clinical experience, such a dichotomy has not proven to be very helpful because of the very close and intricate relationship between sexual and marital satisfaction (Crowe and Ridley, 1990). Indeed, a very large number of couples seen by the author expressed mainly a general dissatisfaction with the overall sexual relationship, rather than distress over a specific sexual complaint like premature ejaculation or vaginismus, even if such a complaint was present (Baker, in press). For example, several men and women seen by the author reported that their main dissatisfaction related to the fact that their partner was 'unavailable' at times of emotional or practical need. Moreover, they believed that the 'sexual problem' was the 'silent' expression of the overall problematic relationship.

In support of the above, agencies dealing with marital and psycho-sexual problems have seen a rapid increase in the number of individuals seeking help for relationship problems (Crowe and Ridley, 1990). Despite this, however, the repertoires currently available with which to assess and treat individuals who present sexual problems are not very sophisticated. Bancroft (1989) argues that, although there have been major changes in social and professional attitudes to the treatment of sexual problems, these stem from mainly emotive or ideological rather than rational influences. Moreover, he believes that the situation is still in a state of flux, without a rational approach currently being achieved.

Current approaches

Until the mid-1960s and before Masters and Johnson (1966) began pub-lishing their research findings and methods of sex therapy, the psycho-analytic approach was the dominant form of therapy for most presentations of male and female sexual complaints. There was, however, some behavioural input which was based on the work of Wolpe (1958), and which followed the principles of classical learning theory and con-ditioning. For example, orgasmic reconditioning and aversive therapy (for deviant sexual behaviour) was widely used and still is in certain settings. What Masters and Johnson succeeded in doing was to provide the first empirical observations of human sexual functioning with an understanding of the physiological factors involved during sexual arousal and response. From Masters and Johnson's early work evolved their treatment package, better known as couple therapy. This aimed to provide heterosexual couples with the types of conditions which would enhance communication and an appreciation of the importance of taking personal responsibility in sexual enjoyment.

Currently, Masters and Johnson techniques are still used and adapted to a variety of sexual problems. Yet, whilst these have been very valuable to sex therapists, they have not been superseded by more innovative and up to date techniques. The latter are needed in order to address the changing expression of sexuality and individual needs. For example, there are no available techniques which deal specifically with important minority groups such as gay couples or drug addicts. More importantly, Masters and Johnson approaches and their derivatives do inevitably exclude those who have no stable partners.

A potentially valuable addition to existing interventions is the cognitive/behavioural approach to therapy, as it precisely addresses the maintenance of a particular sexual problem at the individual level. However, it is also adaptable to the needs of couples as well as a variety of clinical groups (see Chapter 10). Cognitive/behavioural techniques have been adopted by professionals involved in the treatment of psycho-sexual problems; however, these have not constituted a discrete package. The next section will deal with the presentation and discussion of such a package, which is proposed as an additional and specific treatment approach.

At the behavioural level, the package incorporates and makes use of existing techniques which deal directly with specific problems, such as premature ejaculation, erectile problems, orgasmic dysfunction, and arousal problems. Such techniques are described in detail in sex therapy guides and manuals (Zilbergeld, 1983; Hawton, 1985; Gillan, 1987). The important thing to keep in mind regarding the cognitive/behavioural approach to sex therapy is that it is the cognitions (in terms of negative thoughts and basic beliefs) which are the primary focus of therapy rather than the 'putting right' of a specific sexual problem. In other words, it is the individual's attitude to their 'problem' which is considered to be instrumental in the maintenance of sexual dysfunction. Consequently, the goal of therapy is to focus on adjusting faulty or unrealistic assumptions about what constitutes sexual fulfilment.

COGNITIVE/BEHAVIOUR THERAPY

Rationale

Theoretically, cognitive/behaviour therapy aims to challenge and restructure dysfunctional assumptions and associated negative automatic thoughts which are considered to be maintaining symptomatology. A downward arrow model, adapted from that utilised for the formulation and treatment of depression (Beck et al., 1979; Fennell, 1991) is used to describe the development of symptoms (i.e. sexual dysfunction), and is illustrated in Figure 5.1.

Early experience

This is considered to lay the foundations for certain basic assumptions about sexual role, through the types of learned, reinforced, and observed

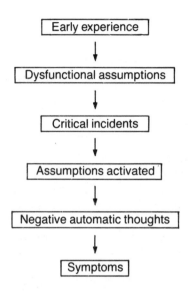

Figure 5.1 Cognitive model
Source: Adapted from Beck et al., 1979.

behaviour. Role models and exposure to particular behaviours (e.g. between parents), as well as education about sexual matters, will all have an input towards beliefs held. What was reinforced or, alternatively, punished for not being 'masculine' or 'feminine' behaviour, e.g. 'Little boys don't cry', or 'Girls should not take the lead', might have an important influence on the acquisition of response repertoires. More importantly, such early experience might predispose the maintenance of sexual difficulties later in life.

Sex education and what one learns about what constitutes a sexual relationship is of vital importance here. It is widely agreed that our educational establishments are still not ideal as conveyors of the appropriate and relevant sex information to young adults. More importantly, where some so-called sex education is available in schools, a global picture of sexual relationships, which should include notions of love, commitment, and mutual respect between two people, is rarely presented. In a study by Baker (1987), the overwhelming majority of subjects (in both the clinical and control samples) reported that they had received very poor sexual education. Most derived their knowledge about sex from talking to friends and reading magazines.

A haphazard collection of (mostly) erroneous facts about sexual behaviour can in some people lay very poor and misconceived foundations about how one is to behave sexually and what one should expect from a potential partner.

Dysfunctional assumptions

These refer to a held set of beliefs or assumptions about what is regarded as desirable behaviour. Assumptions are considered to be dysfunctional when they represent a rigid and stereotypical view of 'masculinity' or 'femininity', particularly when it provides a global blueprint for sexual behaviour. Some examples of dysfunctional assumptions are: 'In sex as elsewhere it's performance that counts'; 'Sex equals intercourse'; 'Sex should be natural and spontaneous', (Baker and de Silva, 1988). Assumptions such as the above were, amongst others, found to be significantly more prevalent in males receiving treatment for sexual dysfunction than in a group of controls (Baker and de Silva, 1988). The author's clinical experience has further supported this finding. It is possible that such assumptions form the basis of the sexual repertoire in a given person, even though they are not expressed consciously or verbally. Dysfunctional assumptions are particularly pertinent in the maintenance of individual distress in sexual relationships as they create unrealistic expectations about what is believed to be the 'ideal' sexual experience. More importantly, critical incidents can activate dysfunctional assumptions.

Negative automatic thoughts

These appear to be mainly related to sexual performance as well as negative consequences which might follow as a result of the dysfunction. Some examples of such thoughts are: 'I must be in some way different to other men'; 'My girlfriend will leave me if I continue to lose my erections'; 'I will never be able to enjoy sex as much as I used to' (Baker, 1989).

Clinical experience has shown that some men report such thoughts spontaneously whilst being assessed and, therefore, the treating therapist can gain a good deal of information regarding the patient's assumptions with respect to sexual roles as well as sexual myths. When negative automatic thoughts appear to be not only frequently expressed but also representative of a patient's general pattern of thinking and behaving, in such cases a cognitive/behavioural approach to treatment might be the most appropriate means of helping the patient.

Critical incidents

A critical incident constitutes a situation whereby a male perceives himself as having 'failed' sexually. An example of a critical incident is when a man feels he 'has come too early' or when he has lost his erection during lovemaking. How a male is able to deal with a critical incident would largely depend on what assumptions he holds about his role in the relationship, as well attitudes related to criteria for sexual fulfilment. It is possible that some males can accept a less than 'perfect' performance, at times, and view the loss of erection as 'something that just happens'. This will be further discussed in the next section. Generally, an ability to make use of as well as accept a wide repertoire of sexual activity within love-making protects the individual from catastrophising over one negative incident. If, however, a male holds 'black and white' attitudes over sexuality and construes performance in perfect or imperfect terms, such a male would be vulnerable at times of perceived failure.

A critical incident may also act to increase the discrepancy between what a 'vulnerable' male achieves and what he thinks he should achieve. In the study by Baker and de Silva, (1988), dysfunctional males were found to have greater discrepancy between 'ideal self' and 'real self' than non-dysfunctional males on variables relating to sexual attributes. It is argued that such a discrepancy acts as an important link factor between belief in myths and sexual dysfunction.

Maintenance of sexual dysfunction

Figure 5.2. below illustrates the author's model of maintenance of a sexual problem. As described above, a critical incident represents an event which could potentially lead to a person feeling that he has failed sexually. According to the model, two courses of development are possible following such an incident.

1. A person might be content that there has been no discrepancy between what he hoped to attain and what he has, in fact, received. For example, irrespective of the 'quality' of the sexual encounter experienced by a particular individual, the latter does not conceptualise his sexual performance in terms of failure and success. In other words, be it loss of erection or the ability to have 'lasted' for a relatively long time on any one occasion, both represent, for that individual, an accepted variation of events during lovemaking. Consequently, no personal conflict or vari- ation is perceived between 'ideal self' and 'real self' (Baker, 1987). 2. The second course of action is when a person does perceive a discrepancy between what he hoped to attain and what he actually feels he achieved sexually. If this is the case, two possibilities operate.

The first is positive, in that the person might feel that he attained something far more desirable than he expected. For example, a male expecting to 'fail', due to repeated past perceived 'failures', might in fact experience no such failure. In other words, there has been no perceived discrepancy between idealised sexual performance (if any) and actual performance. In such a situation, a 'critical incident' could, in fact, break the perpetuated negative self-fulfilling prophecy, e.g. 'I have failed before, therefore I can expect to fail again'. The second possible outcome, however, is potentially negative, in that the individual's experienced

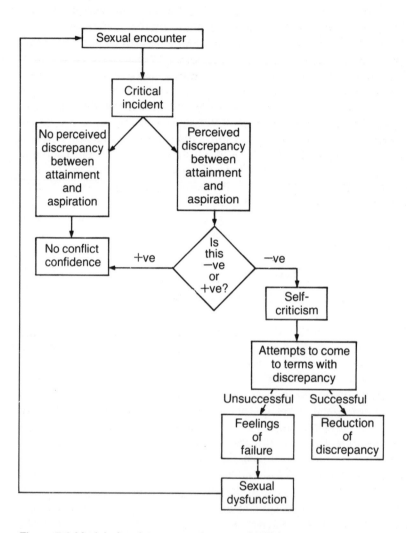

Figure 5.2 Model of maintenance of a sexual problem

discrepancy between what he hoped to attain and what he received is less than ideal. For example, a male hoping to 'set the record straight' by hoping at all costs to maintain an erection during a particular sexual encounter might be disappointed to find that in fact his erection has again 'failed him'. Clinically, this process is evident in patients' self-recriminations and expressed negative automatic thoughts. At this stage, two processes might operate in relation to attempts by the individual to come to terms with the 'negative' discrepancy.

1. The person might attempt to reduce this discrepancy by using various techniques, such as self-reasoning, seeking reassurance from partner, etc., which might prove successful and continue to maintain the person's confidence and sense of well-being.
2. A negative outcome occurs when attempts such as the above do not succeed, and thus feelings of failure are confirmed, since the gap between attainment and aspiration (or 'ideal self'/'real self') is not bridged. In such a situation, the more unrealistic an individual's expectations are, the more difficult it will prove for such an individual to adopt strategies which will successfully deal with the negative discrepancy. For individuals who find themselves in such a self-defeating situation, the model presented illustrates the maintenance of a particular perceived sexual problem within a vicious circle continuum.

Treatment package

The goal of cognitive behaviour therapy is: questioning/challenging + behaviour change, which will, hopefully, lead to the adoption of a new and more adaptive role. What characterises this approach is its emphasis, primarily, on the belief system the man holds about his 'masculinity' and sexuality (both in general and specific terms) as well as about his expected role in sexual relationships. The behavioural aspect of the therapy package makes use of traditional techniques directed specifically at dysfunctions, such as 'stop/start' (Zilbergeld, 1983), for premature ejaculation, or the ban on intercourse for appropriate cases of combined couple therapy. However, such exercises are introduced only when they are considered to be valid experiments and useful additions to the whole ethos of cognitive therapy. More importantly, specific exercises such as the 'stop/start' technique are incorporated only if the patient considers them to be relevant and acceptable.

In summary, therefore, the focus of cognitive behaviour therapy is, firstly, the person's belief system and, secondly, the specific 'dysfunction' problem. Collaboration between patient and therapist is considered to be as important to this therapy as it is in the treatment of depression (Beck *et al.*, 1979).

Strategies of cognitive behaviour therapy

To elicit negative automatic thoughts;
To identify myths or dysfunctional assumptions;
To identify faulty thinking;
To challenge all the above, whilst aiming for the adoption (by the patient) of a 'new', more adaptive role.

As mentioned above, negative automatic thoughts can give the clinician a good impression of the types of fears and anxieties the person holds about their dysfunction. It is particularly important to identify and address negative automatic thoughts, as they are often present during lovemaking and are argued to be very instrumental in disrupting the process of sexual arousal (Barlow, 1986; Bancroft, 1989). Negative automatic thoughts are often presented spontaneously by patients during treatment sessions, but they can also be elicited by encouraging the patient to think of the specific situation in which dysfunction or 'failure' last occurred, and what thoughts this situation triggered.

Identifying assumptions and sexual myths related to 'masculinity' and to the patient's expected sexual role in the relationship is very important. As discussed earlier, an individual's template for sexual behaviour is frequently based on unrealistic beliefs which encourage unrealistic expectations that are difficult to fulfil. If assumptions are, moreover, over-generalised and rigid they are considered to be dysfunctional as they help to perpetuate the presenting sexual problem. Assumptions can be identified by the types of value judgements a patient makes about himself or others with respect to sexual behaviour. In particular, 'should' or 'must' statements often indicate rigid assumptions, e.g. 'As a male it should be my responsibility to satisfy my female partner', or 'I must be in control during lovemaking'. A therapist can further identify assumptions by questioning following from a specific incident and by registering the types of sexual 'themes' which are volunteered by the patient.

It is very common for males presenting with dysfunction to express certain errors in thinking, such as: catastrophising; 'black and white' thinking; selective abstraction; jumping to conclusions (Beck et al., 1985). Statements like 'Nothing about my performance is good' or 'When I look back over the last few months all I see is failure' appear to be clinically very common, (Baker, 1989). Such statements can often act as self-fulfilling prophecies and increase the feelings of hopelessness and inadequacy.

The role of challenging in cognitive therapy

Challenging negative automatic thoughts, assumptions, and faulty thinking is an integral part of the therapy. The adoption of a 'new' sexual role by the patient can be realistically expected only if challenging incorporates not only cognitive elements within sessions, but also behavioural tasks the patient can experiment with between sessions. Only if the patient becomes convinced of the advantages and benefits of adopting a different sexual approach will he consider altering his basic belief system and current expectations. One very rewarding challenging technique is discussion of expectations within a sexual relationship between patient and partner (if applicable). Initially, many males find this a difficult thing to do, particularly if the relationship is recent. Some males seen by the author have been very surprised to know that their partners' needs and expectations with regard to lovemaking were very different to their own. For example, a common assumption is that, if 'performance' has been 'poor', the partner will inwardly feel resentful or critical and may compare the patient with previous 'better lovers'. Open discussion with the partner with regard to such anxieties can help to monitor faulty thinking such as 'mind reading'. It also challenges the frequently made assumption that the male in a relationship has the sole responsibility for creating and offering pleasure. The case examples below will further illustrate this point.

Encouraging the patient to experiment with different approaches in lovemaking is another challenging technique. A very commonly endorsed myth is that 'sex equals intercourse'. In addition, many males experiencing dysfunction tend to view every occasion of lovemaking as an opportunity to 'set the record straight'. Exploring the wide range of possible sexual behaviours with a partner, without focusing on penetration, is initially a great challenge to some men, but with willingness to experiment, the results can be rewarding. This exercise has as its aim the abolition of end products or goals, such as erections or orgasms. Instead, it aims to encourage the patient to learn how to focus on and derive pleasure from a number of different parts of the body, as a rewarding experience in itself and not as a preliminary to the 'real point' of the exercise, i.e. penetration and orgasm. Although this exercise bears some similarities to the Masters and Johnson couple therapy, it is also very different, in that it does not follow a specific progression of stages, nor is it prescribed for the ultimate resolution of the presenting complaint. Focused exercises which deal with specific dysfunctions can make a useful addition to homework assignments. Such exercises can be particularly useful for males with no current partner. Moreover, such exercises are encouraged to be a means of getting to relax with and to learn about one's body, but more importantly to get a better understanding about what creates the most favourable conditions for sexual enjoyment.

A very common approach for many males is to disregard conditions which are likely to interfere with sexual performance (Zilbergeld, 1983), e.g. anxiety about an unrelated issue, uncertainty about the relationship in general, too much alcohol, or an unrelaxed environment. Homework assignments which include focused exercises for impotence or premature ejaculation can be used as a means of becoming more in tune about which are the most favourable conditions for relaxation and enjoyment. With regard to homework assignments, the recording of negative automatic thoughts, as well as the reading of educational or relevant material are both very important additional elements in the challenging of beliefs and assumptions.

CASE STUDIES

Mike

Mike is a 34-year-old man who was referred by his general practitioner for a problem with maintaining erections. He had been given a physical examination and organic causes were excluded. His previous history was that he had been married for eight years to a woman with whom he shared an enjoyable and satisfactory sex life. They had no children and Mike ran his own catering business. When seen at the sex therapy clinic his current situation was that he had been amicably divorced and was living with a girl who was ten years his junior.

Problem as described by Mike

Mike was becoming increasingly anxious and unhappy because he felt he was letting down his girlfriend sexually. During the sessions he revealed that his sexual relationship with his girlfriend differed greatly from the one he had with his wife. He explained that his wife had always found it difficult to achieve orgasm, and this was something they both had adjusted to because she reported to be getting pleasurable feelings despite this. Mike, on the other hand, felt 'free to enjoy himself', having no pressure to provide her with an orgasm. His current girlfriend, however, felt that it was important for her to climax and was very experienced sexually. She frequently referred to previous boyfriends, and a number of them continued to maintain contact with her. Mike admitted to feeling insecure with this situation, particularly because of the age difference and also because of his girlfriend's previous sexual experience. He felt that he had to fulfil her expectation and there was an element of competition with respect to the other men. Mike would frequently have negative automatic thoughts, such as, 'I'm probably less good than her previous boyfriends' and 'She will get fed up and leave me'. He responded very well to a cognitive-behavioural approach and was seen alone as his girlfriend was unwilling to accompany him to the sessions. He was seen over a period of ten weeks.

The intervention consisted, initially, of keeping a record of negative automatic thoughts which were discussed and challenged during the sessions. About halfway through the therapy, it transpired that one of Mike's basic beliefs or assumptions about sexuality was that women tend to be passive in lovemaking and that it is up to a man to take the lead and to control events. This belief had its roots in adolescent discussions with friends on the topic of dating girls and 'what one was expected to do'. This assumption was later supported in his first marriage, in that his wife had assumed a passive role, which she had found satisfactory. Facing a girlfriend who was assertive and active in the sexual relationship was a challenging situation for Mike and one he was unfamiliar with. The behavioural component of the intervention consisted of encouraging Mike to be open with his girlfriend and test out his theory about being left by her. In addition, his fear that her other lovers were 'better than him' was an important one and was also addressed during frank discussions between the couple. Other 'experiments' involved Mike becoming aware of his own most favourable conditions for pleasurable sex. In addition, he experimented with initiating and responding to sex only when he felt happy and aroused enough to do so. In other words, he was training himself to become more attuned to his body's responses. Another important issue was to remove the focus from penetrative sex and encourage Mike to explore other ways of giving and receiving pleasure.

By the end of treatment, Mike was able to sustain an erection in approximately one in four attempts at intercourse. He felt that this constituted very good progress, but his main satisfaction was expressed as being a freedom from anxiety as having to be 'perfect' or the sole initiator and provider of sex. With respect to his girlfriend, Mike wrote to the author several months after the end of treatment saying that he had married her, and that the sexual relationship between them was very 'satisfactory'.

Andrew

Andrew is a 26-year-old man who was referred by his general practitioner for premature ejaculation. During the psychological assessment, he described feelings of anxiety related to having sexual relationships with women. At the time of the assessment he had no current partner and the picture he presented was that he believed that his premature ejaculation was to blame for his lack of a stable relationship. Moreover, he reported that, whilst he was able to attract members of the opposite sex, he felt that this was short-lived, in that his partners (he believed), lost interest in him following his 'failure' during the course of lovemaking. The first few sessions, in fact, revealed that the pattern was not as clear-cut as Andrew had presented it. Looking objectively at the order of events, it appeared that, indeed, Andrew had the type of personality and appearance which did not present him with difficulties in attracting members of the opposite sex. Andrew, in addition, had developed a particular style of behaving which included the belief that there was an expectation on his partners' side that 'intimacy' should take place without delay – provided both people were attracted to each other. Another very important factor, which became apparent during the discussions with Andrew was that his new-found partners did not in fact leave him immediately following what he had perceived as being a 'failure' (i.e. coming too early), but following behaviour on his part which was in response to his perceived failure. That is, he would behave in an aloof manner and as if he was no longer interested.

Explorations of Andrew's assumptions and beliefs revealed that he held a number of unrealistic expectations, in relation both to himself and to his partners. In addition, he focused on his own behaviour and performance to such an extent that he did not develop appropriate skills needed to judge the other person's needs as well as what constitutes the most favourable and appropriate setting for intimacy.

According to the author's maintenance model of sexual dysfunction, Andrew's perceived failure gave rise to behaviour which reinforced his belief that partners rejected him. More importantly, negative thoughts, such as 'no woman will ever want me . . . they just feel sorry for me' and 'there must be something physically wrong with me', helped to confirm the feeling of failure which was carried over to the next encounter. Treatment with Andrew consisted of eliciting negative automatic thoughts and later dysfunctional assumptions. These were used to formulate the types of beliefs Andrew had internalised which acted as blueprints in sexual encounters. The behavioural component of treatment involved giving Andrew educational material to read, as well as practising 'stop/start' masturbatory exercises to increase his 'lasting' threshold. These exercises also served to dispel his fear that there was something physically wrong with him.

The outcome was that, by the end of treatment, Andrew was able to adopt a more appropriate and realistic approach when interacting with members of the opposite sex. The behavioural aspects of the treatment helped to increase his confidence and to bring him more in tune with his own body and sexual needs.

CONCLUSION

This chapter reviewed the formulation of male sexual dysfunction using a structured cognitive-behavioural model. However, this approach is by no means confined to dealing with male problems. It could be equally applicable to female problems, as well as to other clinical populations such as gay couples (see Chapter 10). Indeed, the versatility of such an approach should make it a most valued tool when the presentation of sexual problems does not conform to the requirements made by more conventional approaches: for example, the necessity of having a partner (preferably heterosexual) for the application of the Masters and Johnson package.

This discussion focused mainly on men because this constituted a logical progression from the work already carried out in looking at male beliefs in sexual myths, (Baker and de Silva, 1988). Whilst the model presented here can be applied to female cases of sexual dissatisfaction, it is hoped that empirical work looking at corresponding beliefs held by women will be carried out. This would be most valuable in completing the picture and in offering a more objective understanding of the types of assumptions and unrealistic expectations which women hold. Certainly, in the author's clinical experience, a large number of women also held the types of male 'sexual myths' held by some of the men.

In aiming for a realistic degree of harmony and balance between couples, both sets of expectations should be looked into, otherwise one might fall into the trap of trying to mould an individual's experience into that expected by another. Possibly the most important innovative aspect of the approach discussed here is the emphasis on the acquisition by the individual of a global appreciation of the quality of a relationship. The main purpose of therapeutic sessions is to place the individual's current sexual experience within the context of acquired beliefs and behaviours as influenced by cultural and socialising factors. This approach, it is believed, is more appropriate within today's complex relationship dynamics. An important consideration, however, is that the cognitive/ behavioural therapeutic package described in this chapter, whilst having proved to be successful in clinical experience, has not yet been subjected to evaluation or outcome empirical enquiry. It is hoped that this contribution will provide the necessary impetus for these very necessary issues to be dealt with.

NOTES

1 This approach could equally be applied to work with women, but men will be the focus of attention in this chapter.
2 This chapter is concerned principally with sexual problems which have at their basis a largely psychological component, and therefore physical approaches to treatment will not be addressed.

REFERENCES

Baker, C.D. (1987) 'The fantasy model of sex: is there relationship between the extent of men's belief in sexual myths and sexual dysfunction?', University of London: MPhil Dissertation.
Baker, C.D. (1989) 'Cognitive therapy of male sexual dysfunction', paper presented to World Cognitive Therapy Congress, Oxford.
Baker, C.D. (1992) 'Female sexuality and health', in P. Nicolson and J. Ussher (eds) *The Psychology of Women's Health and Health Care*, London: Macmillan.
Baker, C.D. and de Silva, P. (1988) 'The relationship between male sexual dysfunction and belief in Zilbergeld's myths: an empirical investigation', *Sexual and Marital Therapy* 3(2): 229–38.
Bancroft, J. (1989) *Human Sexuality and its Problems*, 2dn edition, Edinburgh: Churchill Livingstone.
Barlow, D.H. (1986) 'Causes of sexual dysfunction: the role of anxiety and cognitive interference', *Journal of Consulting and Clinical Psychology* 54: 140–8.

Beck, A.T., Emery, G., and Greenberg, R. (1985) *Anxiety Disorders and Phobias: A Cognitive Perspective*, New York: Basic Books.

Beck, A.T., Rush, A., Shaw, B.F., and Emery, G. (1979) *Cognitive Therapy of Depression*, New York: Guilford Press.

Catalan, J., Bradley, M., Gallwey, J., and Hawton, K. (1981) 'Sexual dysfunction and psychiatric morbidity in patients attending a clinic for sexually transmitted disease', *British Journal of Psychiatry* 138: 292–6.

Cole, M. and Dryden, W. (eds) (1988) *Sex Therapy in Britain*, Milton Keynes: Open University Press.

Crowe, M. and Ridley, J. (1990) *Therapy with Couples: A Behavioural-Systems Approach for Marital and Sexual Problems*, Oxford: Blackwell.

d'Ardenne, P. (1988) 'Sexual dysfunction in a transcultural setting', in M. Cole and W. Dryden (eds) *Sex Therapy in Britain*, Milton Keynes: Open University Press.

Fennell, M.J.V. (1991) 'Depression', in K. Hawton, P.M. Salkouskis, J. Kirk, D.M. Clark (eds) *Cognitive Behaviour Therapy for Psychiatric Patients*, Oxford: Oxford University Press, pp. 169–234.

Frachner, J.C. and Kimmel, M.S. (1987) 'Hard issues and soft spots: counselling men about sexuality', in *Handbook of Counselling and Psychotherapy with Men*, Newbury Park: Sage.

Garner, D.M. and Bemis, K.M. (1985) 'Cognitive therapy for anorexia nervosa', in D.M. Garner and P.E. Garfinkel (eds) *Handbook of Psychotherapy for Anorexia Nervosa and Bulimia*, New York: Guilford Press, 107–46.

Gillan, P.W. (1987) *Sex Therapy Manual*, Oxford: Blackwell.

Golombok, S., Rust, J., and Piccard, C. (1984) 'Sexual problems encountered in general practice', *British Journal of Sexual Medicine* 11: 210–12.

Hawton, K. (1985) *Sex Therapy: A Practical Guide*, Oxford: Oxford University Press.

Hawton, K. (1991) 'Sexual dysfunctions', in K. Hawton, P.M. Salkouskis, J. Kirk and D.M. Clark (eds) *Cognitive Behaviour Therapy for Psychiatric Problems*, Oxford: Oxford University Press, pp. 370–405.

Kaplan, H.S. (1974) *The New Sex Therapy: Active Treatment of Sexual Dysfunctions* New York: Quadrangle.

Kinsey, A.C., Pomeroy, W.B., and Martin, C.E. (1948) *Sexual Behaviour in the Human Male*, Philadelphia and London: Saunders.

Kinsey, A.C., Pomeroy, W.B., Martin, C.E., and Gebhard, P.H. (1953) *Sexual Behaviour in the Human Female*, Philadelphia and London: Saunders.

Kolodny, R.C., Masters, W.H., and Johnson, V.E. (1979) *Textbook of Sexual Medicine*, Boston, MA: Little, Brown & Co.

Masters, W.H. and Johnson, V.E. (1966) *Human Sexual Response*, Boston, MA: Little, Brown & Co.

Masters, W.H. and Johnson, V.E. (1970) *Human Sexual Inadequacy*, London: Churchill.

Salkovskis, P.M. and Warwick, H.M.C. (1986) 'Morbid preoccupations, health anxiety and reassurance: a cognitive behavioural approach to hypochondriasis', *Behaviour Research and Therapy* 24: 597–602.

Salkovskis, P.M. and Warwick, H.M.C. (1988) 'Cognitive therapy of obsessive-compulsive disorder', in C. Perris, I.M. Blackburn, and H. Perris (eds) *The Theory and Practice of Cognitive Therapy*, Heidelberg: Springer Verlag, pp. 376–95.

Wolpe, J. (1958) *Psychotherapy by Reciprocal Inhibition*, Palo Alto, CA: Stanford University Press.

Zilbergeld, B. (1983) *Men and Sex*, London: Fontana.

Chapter 6

Sexuality, sexual problems, and people with learning difficulties

Jan Burns

INTRODUCTION

This chapter will examine the role sexuality has played in the care and provision of services to people with learning difficulties. Perspectives on the sexuality of this client group have echoed, often in an exaggerated fashion, the changing attitude of society towards people with learning difficulties. We have seen, with the demise of institutional care and the medical model, the growing acceptance that people with a disability both have and wish to express their sexuality – a sexuality that is as rich and varied as that of any other population.

When working with people with learning difficulties on sexual issues it is necessary to understand the heritage of oppression and misinformation that exists. Hence, this chapter will begin by describing the historical, psychological, and social origins of the acceptance of sexuality within the population of people with a learning difficulty. For reasons that will be explained later, much of the literature in the area concerns sex education, and there is little covering the identification, assessment, and treatment of what might be termed 'traditional' sexual problems within this client group. There are also wider issues that are unlikely to be raised in the general population, some of which have ethical implications, such as consent in the case of sterilisation. These issues will be discussed, and case examples provided to illustrate particular dilemmas. Finally, the identification, assessment, and treatment of sexual problems will be discussed in the context of working with this particular client group.

HISTORICAL PERSPECTIVE

Far from being ignored within the early writings on 'mental defectives', sexuality played a central role to their segregation and oppression. Indeed the term 'moral defective' was frequently used as synonymous with 'mental defective' to identify people with learning difficulties (Tredgold and Soddy, 1963). Indeed, the sexual behaviour of these individuals was used as one of the prime reasons for not only their removal from society, but also their possible annihilation through the eugenics movement, and certainly their mass sterilisation. The following extract comes from two respected and very influential writers of their time on the demise of certain aspects of the eugenics movement:

> It is our present civilization, however, which has proved the undoing of society in this respect, for the growth of humanitarian feeling has strongly reinforced the instinctive sanctions of the group against destroying life and has resulted in active measures to protect the unfit, who have not only been permitted to survive, but at times have been given opportunities for sexual indulgence which has simply provided more inadequate people, doomed by inheritance or environment to grow up as a charge on the more reasonable citizens, who limit their families to maintain their standard of living.
>
> (Tregold and Soddy, 1963: 469)

In the early nineteenth century it was believed that individuals with learning difficulties had an above average libido and that they engaged in sexual activity more frequently than the average population, in more 'perverted' ways, and were even more fertile than the average population, producing more offspring and of as inferior a nature as themselves, if not more so (Report of the Royal Commission, 1904–8). It is not hard to see how the medical profession at that time saw it as part of their responsibilities to contain and prevent such supposedly licentious behaviour and at all costs prevent such people from reproducing such problems. For example, the original draft of the Mental Defective Bill (1907) included a clause empowering the detention of those individuals 'in whose case it should be desirable that they should be deprived of the opportunity of procreating children'. This clause was dropped mainly through the pragmatic difficulties of actually providing services to detain such individuals (Tregold and Soddy, 1963).

Thus, much of the impetus for institutional care originated from fear related to the supposedly rampant sexuality of the person with learning difficulties. Tregold and Soddy point out in their text of 1963 that, if the rise of the eugenics movement within Nazism had not brought eugenics into ill-repute, the treatment of sexual problems within this client group might well have included both 'voluntary' and involuntary euthanasia. As it is, many people were removed from society, deprived of caring relationships, and supposedly denied any expression of sexuality.[1] A parallel can been seen here with the control of childbearing in the working classes in the late nineteenth century, prompted by the belief that they were more fertile and their rise in number would be the downfall of the upper classes (Littlewood and Lipsedge, 1982).

As a result, in an effort to protect society from such 'sexual reprobates', the ethos of the institutions was repression and denial of sexuality. Later, within North America especially, sterilisation became the fashionable expression of this attitude. For example, in the United States the first enacted sterilisation law occurred in Indiana in 1907. Although it was challenged in 1925, the Supreme Court upheld it and there then followed a flood of sterilisation laws in thirty States.

However, this authoritarian attitude began to shift in the early 1950s and 1960s, in both Britain and North America. There seemed to be three themes to these changing attitudes: a) new information appeared regarding the causes and genetics of learning difficulties, b) an interest in the upholding of civil rights began, and c) the legal profession became interested in defending the right of institutionalised patients. As a reflection of these new, more informed, and liberal attitudes about sexuality, legislation started to appear attempting to uphold and protect individuals' rights, especially the rights of those vulnerable to abuse.

Legislation

During the 1950s and 1960s legislation came into force in Britain which directly sought to control the sexuality of people with learning diffi- culties. However, this legislation also acknowledged the need to protect these individuals from sexual abuse. Hence, the 1956 and 1967 Sexual Offences Acts impose legal limitations on sexual behaviour, and some of these limitations apply specifically to individuals with learning difficulties. Gunn (1986) points out that there are six offences within the 1956 Act which make reference to a woman who is a 'defective':

a) unlawful sexual intercourse with a defective (section 7)
b) procurement of a defective to have unlawful sexual intercourse (section 9)
c) indecent assault on a defective, who cannot legally consent to pre- vent the assault (section 14)
d) abduction of a defective from the parent or guardian for the pur- poses of unlawful sexual intercourse (section 21)
e) permitting a defective to use premises under a person's control for the purpose of unlawful sexual intercourse (section 27)
f) causing or encouraging the prostitution of a defective (section 29)
(Gunn, 1986)

Interestingly, men are mentioned much less frequently. However, the 1956 Sexual Offences Act, Section 15, says that a 'defective' man is unable to provide consent to an indecent assault being committed upon him or to make a homosexual act lawful within the terms of the Sexual Offences

Act 1967 (Gunn, 1986). Obviously, terminology is of paramount importance here. The definition of 'defective' is very similar to that of severe
subnormality under the Mental Health Act of 1959. Gunn (1986) gives a
very clear and interesting account of this area, making some recommendations about how these laws could be altered. As they stand, it does
appear that the dominant emphasis lies upon the protection of people
with learning difficulties, at the cost of impinging upon the respect and
rights of individuals so defined. However, later in the 1970s the ideology
of normalisation arrived and started to have a major impact on the way
people with learning difficulties were seen and treated (Wolfensberger,
1972). No longer were they solely seen as people to be protected from, or
people to protect, but citizens in their own right.

A new consciousness of a sexually oppressed group

Since the advent of normalisation[2] and the growth in the ideological and
economic interests in community care, there has been a general raising of
interest in the identification and promotion of the previously denied
rights of individuals with learning difficulties.

However, that the issue of sexuality has lagged somewhat behind
interest in other issues in the campaigning for the expression of such
rights is perhaps not surprising (Craft and Craft, 1988). Nevertheless, the
expression of the individual's sexuality, as opposed to the repression of it,
has necessarily been put firmly on the agenda through the promotion of
self-advocacy (Irvine, 1988). This movement has encouraged the expression of individual rights, and, as a result of this encouragement, people
with learning difficulties have themselves raised and campaigned around
issues of sexuality. Here the view has been expressed that not only should
people with learning difficulties have a right to express their sexuality,
but they should receive the help they need to be able to do this. This is an
area within service provision that is fraught with anxiety, prejudice, and
caution. For example, the disclosure of abuse by the service staff and/or
other clients would have enormous ramifications for all concerned.
Hence, staff may be placed in very threatening and vulnerable positions
with little guidance except perhaps their own sexual practices, which they
may feel are of little use under such circumstances.

Undoubtedly, the issues at stake are very complex and with potentially
serious consequences; however, this has frequently led to passivity and
empty rhetoric. One avenue that people did feel that they could more
safely pursue in this area, and possibly as an antidote to such anxiety, was
that of sex education.

THE ARRIVAL OF SEX EDUCATION AND SOCIAL SKILLS TRAINING

Kempton in 1972 argued that it was unrealistic for society to expect and even demand 'responsible' sexual behaviour from people who had never been taught or had the opportunity to learn naturally about sexual development. Indeed, just as institutionalisation and segregation are now seen as being responsible for many of the atypical behaviours displayed by some people with learning difficulties, rather than these being seen as products of the impairment itself, the aetiology of sexual problems is also commonly attributed to the atypical and repressive environment rather than being seen as 'part and parcel' of the learning difficulty. For example, many adults with learning difficulties may have grown up and still remain in segregated environments, living in male and female dormitories. As Carson points out:

> Clients' experiences of this communal living can lead to them learning that their bodies are not private, not important. This leads to age-inappropriate (childish T-shirts on middle-aged people) and untidy dressing, and other forms of poor self-presentation. . . . They are daily presented with very false impressions of social standards and behaviour.
>
> (Carson, 1989: 360)

Yet these old paternal attitudes which dictate that these 'holy innocents' should be protected from the conflicts and dangers of sexuality have now been challenged on a variety of fronts. That people with learning difficulties do engage in sexual activities is now being recognised, together with an increasing acceptance of their right to a full sexual relationship should they so wish. However, with community care and the emphasis on integration not segregation, the potential dangers for abuse and exploitation had to be recognised. Thus, as far as many professionals involved were concerned, for the person with learning difficulties to be ignorant of sexual matters was no longer a desirable state, but a position of inherent danger (Craft and Craft, 1981).

Kempton was a forerunner in advocating the development of sex education for people with learning difficulties. She based her arguments on a number of research findings relating to the total lack of information or positive misinformation about sexual matters found in studies of people with learning difficulties. For example, in 1978 Kempton found that some married couples were totally ignorant about sexual intercourse and did not know how it took place. Others found that some women with learning difficulties believed that sexual intercourse would inevitably hurt the female (Watson and Rogers, 1980).

Yet, those advocating the development and promotion of sex education were not without their critics, and some, parents included, felt that the delivery of such information would only result in greater promiscuity, a greater number of sexual offences being committed, and unwanted pregnancies. Indeed, such ambivalence behind sex *education* resulted in courses on sex *negation*. Here the education focused on all the negative issues surrounding sexual activity, such as how to avoid sexual contact and sexually transmitted diseases, thus making the whole issue such a complex nightmare that individuals must have felt more inclined actively to avoid this side of life than to engage in it. There are still some sex-education packages available which include close-up slides of VD-smitten individuals supposedly to 'educate' others about the perils of sexual contact. Hopefully, these are now not used in this way.

However, apart from the explicit emphasis on teaching people to say 'no', there were less overt ways that early attempts at sex education served to discourage individuals from developing their sexuality. For example, there tended to be an emphasis on helping individuals to make themselves less vulnerable to exploitation, and to engage in the technical world of 'birth control', but little on how to actually express their emotions and relationships. It was more a case of 'don't do this', without much 'do do this'. There was also an adherence to a developmental model, as if individuals with learning difficulties had missed out a class in their developmental history, and were now skipping back to it. Syllabuses tended to make the assumption that individuals were completely naive and had not witnessed the changes in their own bodies nor been exposed to the portrayal of sexuality in the media. Such early teaching packages failed to capitalise on the sexual and relationship experiences of the participants and to integrate issues of sexuality into their own personal lives.

These days a more holistic approach is taken, where sex education is not just taken as a topic on the syllabus at, for example, the adult training centre, but an issue to be talked about at work, home, and during leisure, by a variety of people who may be involved with the individual. Indeed, as individuals are increasingly taking up their right to express themselves sexually, sex education is now not just a 'generic catch-all', including such things as menstruation for women and other aspects of health education, but is commonly more focused on relationships and specific sexual issues.[3.]

Indeed, today the area of sexuality that is most fraught with difficulties is not that of teaching people with learning difficulties about sex, but drawing the line between allowing them take up their rights and express themselves sexually, and protecting them from placing themselves at too great a risk of abuse and exploitation.

THE DIGNITY OF RISK

It is a complex and thin path to tread when trying to protect the freedom of others whilst protecting them from exploitation and consequences which they may not have had the opportunity to envisage. Indeed, this is all part of growing up, but, when this protection continues throughout the lifespan and includes the denial of experiences that contribute to achieving sexual maturity, then one important aspect of an individual's life has also been denied. At some point boundaries will have to be reached and lines drawn. This section will examine such issues using the specific example of sterilisation.

Sterilisation

Sterilisation within the arena of learning difficulties has a history which has resulted in the mass oppression and abuse of many people, particularly in the United States, which has been compared to Nazi Germany, where some 375,000 people were compulsorily sterilised (Irvine, 1988: 100). Indeed, by the early 1970s, thirty of the American States had sterilisation laws which had their basis in the early eugenics movement. As Irvine (1988) notes, 'most of these statutes did not provide such basic constitutional protection as notice of a hearing, a hearing itself, or the right to representation'.

Although, in Britain there have been no laws passed to promote sterilisation, as there have in the North America, the attitude has been similarly one of misguided overprotection and misinformation. Throughout the Western world such an attitude has resulted in many women having undergone sterilisation either without their informed consent or through coercive instruction. Many parents have requested that their offspring be sterilised believing that it will not only eliminate any chance of pregnancy but also erase any sexual feelings (Bass, 1967). Authorities and the medical profession have complied, believing that they will be adding to the quality of life for the individual by eliminating the chance of a possible pregnancy which is seen as having nothing but deleterious consequences, and also adding to the quality of life for 'mankind' by 'cleansing the most worthless one-tenth of our present population' (Irvine, 1988: 100).

It is not just that sterilisation has been used as an easy answer to a difficult, distressing problem, it is the way in which it has been done. This has included women not even being told what has been done to them, or given wrong information such as that they have had an appendectomy.

In Miriam's case, a tubal ligation was performed without her thoroughly understanding the procedure. She married a few years later and her husband had no knowledge of the procedure. During a general review of symptoms, she reported pain on intercourse. When presented with anatomically correct pictures to gain clarifications, she revealed that they were having anal intercourse because of the fear of injuring her tubes through vaginal intercourse.

For Beth, a misinterpretation of the doctor's informed consent prior to a tubal ligation led to a development of a phobic response to sex. It appears that having been told that if she ever wanted to try to have children, she would need to have another operation, she heard 'If you ever want to have sex you will need to have another operation'.

(Andron and Ventura, 1987: 31)

Submission to sterilisation has also been used as an exit criterion from institution to the community (Irvine, 1988). There are also many reports of women knowing quite clearly what has happened to them and feeling regret and resentment about their participation in that decision (Melton, 1984).

On the other side of the coin, there are cases where it is argued that the protection of the individual through sterilisation contributes more to the protection of their individual freedom, than the protection of their rights over their own body. The case of the sterilisation of 'Jeanette', which made headlines in British papers in 1987, is commonly used as an example of just such a situation. The *Independent*, (1 May 1987: 25) described the situation as follows:

[Jeanette] was unlikely to show any improvement in mental capacity beyond that of a six year old child.

She was beginning to show recognisable signs of sexual awareness and sexual drive exemplified by provocative approaches to a male member of the staff and other residents and by touching herself in the genital area. It was not thought right that she should be institutionalised all her life. She would inevitably be less susceptible to supervision when she went to an adult training centre. The risks involved in her becoming pregnant were formidable.

There was no prospect of her being capable of forming a long-term adult relationship. She has displayed no maternal feelings. There was no prospect of her being capable of raising or caring for a child of her own.

Nobody could for any minute doubt the agonising dilemmas in such a case, and even those who opposed such an outcome, such as Mencap and MIND, did not disagree that it would have serious, deleterious consequences for Jeanette should she become pregnant. The main area of disagreement was about whether sterilisation was the only solution to the problem. Interestingly, as mentioned earlier, the right of freedom to live in the community was used here as a reason for Jeanette to be sterilised.

The argument was that, once irreversible contraception was achieved through sterilisation, Jeanette would be free to move into the community without fear of pregnancy.

Such a stance was really missing the point, and served only partially to protect Jeanette from one of the consequences of her sexual vulnerability, whilst, incidentally, totally safeguarding those around her from the fears and consequences of an unplanned pregnancy. Firstly, the implication was that Jeanette would be more open to sexual abuse within the community than in the hostel. There is no evidence to suggest that this is the case, and evidence is emerging that it might be even more dangerous to be 'in care' (Elvik *et al.*, 1990). Thus, with the appropriate level of care for her needs, Jeanette might not have been any more vulnerable to pregnancy living in the community than in the hostel. Secondly, other methods of contraception should have been fully explored, with sterilisation being considered as a final option. Thirdly, and most importantly, it was unlikely that Jeanette would become pregnant by divine intervention. Clearly, all those involved in the case felt a pregnancy would be the result of sexual abuse, but no concern was given in the reporting of the court case and resulting moral dilemmas about who might commit the abuse and how abuse of others would be prevented in the future. The issue for Jeanette, and for other women in a whole variety of situations, is that it is always she, not he, who is expected to take precautions, unless she wishes to 'bear the consequences'. In situations like that of Jeanette it is that men do take such advantages that is the intractable problem in terms of prevention. This is a point that will be returned to in the discussion of sexual abuse, but it is sufficient here to let the media have the last word on perhaps the biggest fear which remains when compulsory sterilisation of an unconsenting woman is the 'final solution' arrived at by five Law Lords in modern day Britain.

> [T]he picture of B [Jeanette] which emerges from the accumulated legal judgements about her is not that of a hapless vegetable or an un-controllable animal. She is capable of finding her way around a limited area, of dressing and bathing herself, of performing simple household tasks under supervision and she has been taught to cope with menstru-ation. It is beyond dispute that she is very vulnerable. It is certain that she should be helped to avoid becoming pregnant. But there is still a hint of expediency about the Law Lords' collective judgements in favour of sterilisation. It is hard to rest easy that the courts have come up with the most humane solution to her problems.
>
> (*Guardian*, 1 May 1987: 14)

A very good review of this area is provided by Irvine (1988), who whilst examining American legislation, discusses some very interesting cases that highlight particular issues and major precedents that also have relevance to British practice.

Sexual abuse

There are no reliable national statistics available on the prevalence of sexual abuse of children or adults who have learning difficulties. However, there is no reason to doubt that this is any lower than the national average for children or adults with no learning difficulties, which is now thought to be between 20 per cent and 10 per cent (Brown, 1991). Indeed, there is some evidence to suggest the prevalence amongst those with mild learning difficulties may even be higher (Friedrich and Boriskin, 1976; Brooks, 1985). The following are some reasons why this might be so:

1. Some people with learning difficulties are more acquiescent and compliant. They are used to doing what others tell them, and accepting that that is the right course of events (Sigleman *et al.*, 1986).
2. Some people with learning difficulties may not understand the implications and potential consequences of certain situations or events, and thus find themselves without intention in vulnerable and dangerous circumstances (Kempton, 1972).
3. Some people with learning difficulties feel isolated and seek interaction in age and context inappropriate ways, making it possible for such affection and intimacy to be misunderstood (Craft and Craft, 1981).

Furthermore, the organisational situations in which people live and spend their time might allow sexual abuse to occur without detection. For example:

a) inadequate supervision;
b) lack of security, e.g. people can walk into a large hospital, usually without being noticed, and sometimes even onto wards;
c) exposure, in intimate and badly supervised situations, to a large number of different individuals;
d) inconsistent intimate carers, so that trust is not built up, mitigating against possible disclosure and increasing the chances of physical signs being missed or not reported;
e) abusive power relations between staff and/or other residents;
f) unclear lines of responsibility, so that nobody takes the first step in reporting any suggestion or allegation;
g) organisational inadequacies, e.g. low morale, negative attitudes, unclear policies, etc;
h) communication difficulties resulting in the individual not being understood or believed.

The serious effects of sexual abuse have been well documented elsewhere (Beezley and Kempe, 1981), but, once more, people with learning difficulties have been generally disregarded and separated from the issues of mainstream society, as there is little published information about how these individuals react to such abuse (Martin and Martin, 1990). However, it has not been unknown within clinical practice for 'carers' and professionals to assume that the effects are not as serious for the person with learning difficulties – 'they have not really understood' or 'they tend to forget faster', etc. Thankfully, awareness is growing, and services and professionals are beginning to be more conscious of the possible deleterious consequences for a person with learning difficulties who has been sexually abused (Hughson, 1991; Roth, 1991; Thomas and Mundy, 1991).[4]

The seriousness of such abuse is well documented through both the theorising and the clinical examples of Valerie Sinason's work. This can especially be seen in her work implicating early childhood trauma, such as sexual abuse, as being a contributing factor to the individual 'developing' a learning difficulty. Sinason defines 'secondary mental handicap' as that which results from the emotional awareness of difference in terms of intellectual and emotional capacity, and further subclassifies this into three varieties, including 'handicap as a defence against trauma'.

> This is the group where handicap is in the service of the self to protect it from unbearable memory of trauma; of a breakdown in the protective shield (Freud, 1920).
>
> (Sinason, 1986: 135)

Sinason, through her elegant case presentations, shows how some individuals have adopted unique, but not especially adaptive methods of dealing with sexual abuse in early life, and thrown over themselves 'a cloak of incompetence' as opposed to the 'cloak of competence' Edgerton (1967) talked about. The following extract refers to two case studies of Barry and Ali, which she presented in a paper entitled 'Secondary mental handicap and its relationship to trauma':

> Ali and Barry did not use the words 'mentally handicapped', 'learning impaired', 'special needs'. They had the freedom to use the old colloquial word 'stupid'; not because it had been said to them and was parroted back; but because very deeply they knew the meaning of that word. And they could only precisely and beautifully know the meaning of it and follow its laws of speech, facial expression and cut-off ears and eyes and feelings if somewhere they were not stupid.
>
> (Sinason, 1986: 152)

Hence, Sinason is suggesting that Ali and Barry have in some way chosen 'stupidity' as a way of absenting themselves from a frightening and hurtful world, and have become 'clever' at being 'stupid'.

Clearly, it is at a point like this that the division between 'learning difficulty' and mental illness becomes blurred, and being 'stupid' might indeed really mean being 'mad' (Spensley, 1985). Such work places a very different and important light on the existence of a learning difficulty and strongly prompts us to see 'all signs of learning difficulty and emotional and behavioural difficulty as possible sequelae to abuse' (Sinason, 1988: 109).

This is perhaps one of the most important, and possibly one of the most contentious, messages to hit practitioners working in the field of learning difficulties this decade. This stance has vital implications for working with people with learning difficulties, especially around issues of sexuality. For example, it suggests that the starting point should be the acknowledgement of abuse and how this has contributed to the learning difficulties, and not perhaps the naive assumption that people with learning difficulties know nothing about sexuality. The influx of psychodynamic theorising within this area should help us to challenge the assumptions made and give us greater understanding of issues of sexuality as applied to people with learning difficulties. For example, such theories should help us to understand individuals' problems in a framework that gives emphasis to the effects of past and present interpersonal dynamics, without concentrating solely upon the sequelae of cognitive-processing deficits.

Potentially, there is much to understand about the part sexual abuse can play in the manifestation of a learning difficulty, but also those working in the field of learning difficulties are now recognising that the prevention of sexual abuse is also an issue that needs to be taken on board quickly and seriously. In some ways, sex education has to re-focus on 'saying no', but in a more sophisticated and balanced way than previously. For example, Martin and Martin (1990) provide a useful review of a sex-education programme that examines issues of sexual abuse, for use with children with learning difficulties.

WORKING WITHIN SYSTEMS ON ISSUES OF SEXUALITY

Working with people with learning difficulties on sexual problems frequently means working other than on a one-to-one basis, and thus differs from work in the mainstream population. It is often the case that the person with a learning difficulty will be enmeshed in a complex system of services and professionals, all with their own interests, mechanisms, and policies. For example, the individual with a learning difficulty may attend a local authority adult training centre during the day, whilst living in a health service group home, have an allocated social worker, a key worker at both day and residential services, specialised services from speech therapy, a neurologist, and a physiotherapist, as well as being part of a family. All may have different knowledge of, attitudes towards, and wish to be involved, or uninvolved, in the sexual problems of that individual.

Effective case management should help to co-ordinate and

communicate service input, but it is still likely that the problems faced, and the ways of intervening, may well differ from working with people without learning difficulties. For example, the following is a case example where the intervention occurred at a systems level rather than at an individual level.

A referral was received at the Psychology Dept from a group home worker expressing concern about the behaviour of one of the male residents, suggesting that it might be time that he thought about moving on to more independent living circumstances. On investigation it is found that this man has formed a sexual relationship and his girlfriend has started to stay overnight at the group home. Hence, the real 'problem' might be that of sexual activity between two residents. The group home worker feared that the man's girlfriend would become pregnant, and consequently the worker would then face a lot of anger from both sets of parents, and also from management who might feel that she has been irresponsible in letting this happen.

The intervention involved some staff training exploring sexual issues, risk and responsibilities, and using the local operational policy on sexual issues as a reference point. Education about contraception was also offered to the couple, and the staff member was offered assistance in counselling her client about his relationship, especially telling his parents about his girlfriend.

One of the areas where working with people with learning difficulties who have sexual issues is exceptional is that the parents might well be involved. Usually, by the time sexual maturity has been reached, the individual is also at a stage of development where they are independent of their parents and the expression of their sexuality is their own business. Often this is not the case with people with learning difficulties. Sexual maturity is reached, but they may still be heavily dependent upon their parents for both their functional needs and emotional needs. In turn, the parents might have much greater influence over the way in which their offspring live their lives.

Within the area of learning difficulties it has almost become a tradition to see parents as 'overprotective'. However, when working with parents it is important to acknowledge that to be 'protective' is an entirely natural and appropriate response for parents. What is and what is not 'overprotective' is a matter of individual values and opinions. The sexuality of their offspring is a particularly delicate area for all parents, and it has to be acknowledged that generally parents are not especially adept at helping their children reach or deal with the issues that arrive at psychosexual maturity (Farrell, 1978). The problems may be even larger for those with offspring who have learning difficulties, possibly to the extent where they would ideally prefer them to be 'innocent to the ways of the world' (Alcorn, 1974). For those who hold steadfastly to this opinion the existence of sex-education programmes in schools, day services, and residential establishments may cause conflict between staff and parents, with young staff championing the rights of the individual and labelling the parents as over-protective and the parents losing confidence in the responsibility of the services to look after the best interests of their 'child'.

Certainly, the first step when working with parents is actually to work with them as opposed to against them. It is likely that both staff and parents share one basic common interest – the best welfare of the individual. This must be recognised and used as the base upon which to work and establish where opinions differ. There may well be religious, cultural, and age-related differences between parents and key staff, which again must be recognised and hopefully incorporated into any solutions.

The professional attitudes of staff may vary considerably from the 'old school' protective paternalism to the younger 'liberal' champion of individual rights. However, in terms of management of services there is a natural tendency to err on the side of caution in an attempt to avoid contention and even possible 'scandal'. Hence, there may be a tendency for the managerial organisational culture to adopt rather higher moral standards than would be expected in the wider society. For example, sex without marriage, or at least without formal commitment, may be discouraged and divorce might be a thing that is never considered. This may be further fuelled by staff wishing to bury their heads in the sand and ignore the whole issue, frequently as a result of their own wish to remain private about sexual issues. The resulting atmosphere may well be one where sexuality is repressed and where any such expression is seen as a 'problem' (Craft and Craft, 1988).

The other side of the coin is the tendency of the staff to make the sex lives of their clients their business and the business of other staff with little regard to privacy or appropriateness (Geraghty, 1979). Clearly, training with regard to the expression of sexuality and people with learning difficulties should be an integral part of training any service professionals, and be part of continuing in-service training.

One other vital link to promoting positive attitudes towards sexual issues in services for people with learning difficulties, whilst also developing adequate protection against exploitation, is that of operational policies. To prevent *ad hoc* decisions being made about clients' behaviour on the basis of staff's personal attitudes about sex and their subjective appraisal of the individual and situation, operational policies need to be developed which can then be invoked when decisions are to be reached. Operational policies may be developed for whole districts or regions, but each individual unit should have one; and, whilst incorporating district or regional policies, they should be in fine enough detail to cover those aspects that particularly apply to the work of the unit. The aim of such policies should be to provide information that will help staff to resolve situations, whilst maintaining agreed principles, avoiding any contraventions of legislation, and ensuring fair and equal treatment of each case.

There are especially tricky areas in terms of legislation, where staff may wish to, or be required to, assist couples. For example, s27 of the Sexual Offences Act 1956, states it is an offence if

> the owner or occupier of any premises who has, or acts or assists in, the management or control of any premises, to induce or knowingly suffer a woman who is a defective to resort to or be on the premises for the purposes of having unlawful sexual intercourse with men or a particular man.

Clearly, according to this section of the Act, if the manager of a hostel or day centre is on the premises when a woman with severe learning difficulties is having sex he may be committing an offence. Obviously, many barriers will lie in the way of such a prosecution, but the example highlights the need for the employing authority to have clear guidelines regarding such activities.

A second example is that of indecent assault. Under the strict application of the law should a member of staff endeavour to teach a client how to masturbate and physically assist him in some way, an indecent assault could be said to have taken place. Rationally, 'consent' would be used as defence to prevent this law being invoked. However, under the law, 'defective' men and women cannot provide consent to sexual acts, and hence consent cannot be used as a defence in such a situation. Another way around this issue is the defence of possessing a 'decent motive', which is the defence commonly used to allow medical professionals to carry out care such as genital examinations.

For either of the above two examples to be brought to court would be an unlikely event, but they do serve to highlight very serious reasons for having a clear and comprehensive policy statement. Perhaps a more ambiguous, and therefore more likely, example for potential prosecution would be in the case of a member of staff teaching an individual to masturbate.[5]

However, it is not enough just to have a policy statement on sexuality – staff must know it exists, know what it says and know how to use it. Research has shown that this is rarely the case, and, although much work may have gone into developing the policy, the work is lost because the information is not disseminated and used adequately (Saunders, 1979; Koheeallee and Dustin, 1989).

THE PRESENT POSITION CONCERNING SEXUAL PROBLEMS AND PEOPLE WITH LEARNING DIFFICULTIES

Clearly, from what has already been said, the issues concerning the expression of sexuality amongst people with learning difficulties differ somewhat from those of the general population. There is a heritage of repression, ignorance, and misinformation that has to be overcome. This heritage has, and continues to have, important effects on the sexual lives not only of those people with learning difficulties, but also of those who work with them.

As always when working with people with learning difficulties, there is a delicate balance to achieve between acknowledging the 'ordinariness' of their relationships, problems, and situations and recognising the 'special' issues that they have to face as a consequence of their learning difficulties. Most of this chapter has concentrated on those issues which arise directly as a consequence of the label 'learning difficulty'. However, this is only one side of it, and to finish this chapter an example will be presented of a problem that is commonly found in mainstream society, but in this case happens to affect couples who have learning difficulties, and so demands greater understanding both in terms of the development of the problem and in the intervention.

Sexual dysfunction in couples with learning difficulties

The Developmental Disabilities Program at the University of California identified seventeen couples over four years who had sexual dysfunctional problems, though only two had actually been referred for this reason. The range of problems was wide and not dissimilar to that found in the average population, with the exception of environmental factors, such as living in residential care. The following is a case example first presented by Andron and Ventura (1987).

> Caroline and Bill were one of the two couples who had listed sexual difficulties as a presenting complaint. They had been seen by a counselor with no expertise in the area of developmental disabilities and reached no resolution. While involved in a couples group, the issues resurfaced. Caroline reported pain on intercourse since the beginning of their marriage. She reported an inability to lubricate which she felt was related to the pill. After discontinuing the pill, lubrication had improved, but by then other problems developed. As advice for Caroline's complaints of pain, her mother-in-law insisted that she let Bill ejaculate or he would 'go crazy'. He usually masturbated behind closed doors because he believed that sperm was 'pus' and should go in the toilet. Caroline came to accept this view of semen as well, and became phobic to the sight of it, or the thought of it being

ejaculated within her. She allowed Bill to ejaculate inside her only once, in order to become pregnant. Over the years, Bill has developed secondary erectile and ejaculatory difficulties. While it could hardly be said that sexual intercourse was not important to them, they have substituted cuddling and touching as a way of relating.

(Andron and Ventura, 1987: 30)

From this study Andron and Ventura found it not uncommon for phobic responses to be presented by the couples, and these and issues of nudity appeared to be related to the negative messages the couples had received about their bodies and sexuality whilst growing up. Interestingly, erectile problems were reported by several of the men in the study, four of whom reported that this had increased following vasectomy. It was reported that all such vasectomies had been carried out at the request of others than the men themselves.

For women in this study sterilisation again was a concern, and a variety of examples were given showing the operations had been carried out without the full understanding of the women. Four of the women in the sample had been sexually abused, and all of these saw 'lack of pleasurable intercourse as their punishment for past behaviour'.

Physical problems and medical issues affected several couples in the study, ranging from muscle weakness, epilepsy, to lack of secondary sex characteristics due to Turner's Syndrome. As Andron and Ventura point out:

It is interesting to note that in contrast to the lack of resources for the learning handicapped, there exists a tremendous support, acceptance and availability of resources for sexual dysfunctions amongst the physically disabled, especially spinal cord injured.

(Andron and Ventura, 1987: 32)

Hence the types of sexual problems that Andron and Ventura came across in this study were not dissimilar to those of the general population; however, they did differ in their aetiology, and this had implications for their treatment. There are a number of lessons to be learnt from such information:

1. It is unlikely that many people with learning difficulties will complain about sexual dysfunction as what might usually be subjectively labelled as dysfunction is discounted because expectations of sex might be extraordinarily low (Craft and Craft, 1983). Hence, individuals or couples suffering from these problems may well go unnoticed and not referred.
2. Individuals with learning difficulties may hold particularly negative images of themselves and their bodies. They may have been exposed to years of social conditioning telling them that their bodies are 'dirty'

and if they do 'that' something particularly nasty will happen to them. This may itself lead directly to sexual dysfunction in later years, or may certainly contribute to it. Hence, when intervening, sensitivity needs to be paid to this area. For example, more time may have to be spent on developing positive attitudes about one's body and it may be necessary to include some preliminary sex education.

3. It is highly likely that the couple will be experiencing problems other than sexual, for example, they are likely to be on a low income, possibly with neither employed and living in not very comfortable surroundings (Flynn, 1989). Hence, it may be important to remember, as with all individuals, to see the sexual issue not in isolation, but as part of the context in which they live.

4. They may live in circumstances that prohibit or mitigate against a full sexual existence, for example, they may live in a hostel for twenty other people and not even have their own rooms or be able to share a room together. In this case it would be important to maximise the privacy available to the couple whilst maintaining some confidentiality. This would require working sensitively with both the couple and the staff at the hostel.

In conclusion, inherent within sexual relationships lie the concepts of power and dependency. We are only just beginning to understand the complex interplay between these concepts in mature, adult relationships, and how both power and dependency can contribute to the continuum of fulfilling to damaging relationships. As with other groups such as children and women, the concepts of power and dependency are central to the life experience of people with learning difficulties. Their experience is that of usually being placed in a position of disempowerment and dependence. As such, any understanding of the sexual relationships that people with learning difficulties develop must include an understanding of their societal context.

NOTES

1 It is worth noting at this point that hospitals were not at all the celibate places suggested and, as research is now revealing, many people have suffered much sexual abuse whilst under the care of such places.

2 Normalisation concerns a wish to create an existence for people with learning difficulties as close to ordinary living as possible.

3 For a complete review of sex-education packages and resources, one might consult Craft and Craft (1983) and, for a sample syllabus, the 'Policy and Guidelines' 1986 document produced by the Borough of Camden.

4 For an excellent review of this area, readers are advised to refer to Brown and Craft, 1989.

5 Dixon and Gunn (1985) provide an excellent guide to the application of the law in this area.

REFERENCES

Alcorn, D.A. (1974) 'Parental views on sexual development and education of the trainable mentally retarded', *Journal of Special Education* 8: 119–30.

Andron, L. and Ventura, J. (1987) 'Sexual dysfunction in couples with learning handicaps', *Sexuality and Disability* 8(1): 25–35.

Bass, M.S. (1967) 'Attitudes of parents of retarded children toward voluntary sterilization', *Eugenics Quarterly* 14(1): 45–53.

Beezley, M. and Kempe, M. (eds) (1981) *Sexually Abused Children and Their Families*, London: Pergamon.

Brooks, B. (1985) 'Sexually abused children and adolescent identity development', *American Journal of Psychotherapy* 39: 401–9.

Brown, H. (1991) 'Facing facts', *Nursing Times* 87(6): 65–6.

Brown, H. and Craft, A. (1989) *Thinking the Unthinkable: Papers on Sexual Abuse and People with Learning Difficulties*, London: Family Planning Association.

Carson, D. (1989) 'The sexuality of people with learning difficulties', *Journal of Social Welfare Law*, 355–73.

Craft, A. (1982) *A List of Audio/Visual Resources on Sexuality for Use with Mentally Handicapped People*, London: Family Planning Association.

Craft, A. and Craft, M. (1981) 'Sexuality and mental handicap: a review', *British Journal of Psychiatry* 139: 494–505.

Craft, A. and Craft, M. (1883) *Sex Education and Counselling for Mentally Handicapped People*, London: Costello.

Craft, A. and Craft, M. (1988) *Sex and the Mentally Handicapped*, revised edition, London: Routledge.

Dixon, H. (1986) *Sexuality and Mental Handicap: An Educator's Resource Book*, Wisbech: LDA.

Dixon, H. and Gunn, M. (1985) *Sex and the Law: A Brief Guide for Staff Working in the Mental Handicap Field (England and Wales only)*, London: Family Planning Association.

Edgerton, R.B. (1967) *The Cloak of Competence*, London: Cambridge University Press.

Elvik, S., Berkowitz, C., Nicholas, E., Lipman, L., and Inkelis, S. (1990) 'Sexual abuse in the developmentally disabled: dilemmas of diagnosis', *Child Abuse and Neglect* 14: 497–502.

Farrell, C. (1978) *My Mother Said. . . .*, London: Routledge & Kegan Paul.

Flynn, M. (1989) *Independent Living for Adults with Mental Handicap*, London: Cassell.

Friedrich, W.N. and Boriskin, J.A. (1976) 'The role of the child in abuse', *American Journal of Orthopsychiatry* 46: 580–90.

Freud, S. (1920) *Beyond the Pleasure Principle*, S.E. 18.

Geraghty, P. (1979) 'The joy of love', *Community Care* 5 April: 24–5.

Gunn, M.J. (1985) 'The law and mental handicap: consent to treatment', *Mental Handicap* 13: 70–2.

Gunn, M.J. (1986) 'Sexual rights of the mentally handicapped', Division of Legal and Criminological Psychology of the BPS.

Hughson, A. (1991) 'Working with women who have learning difficulties and have been sexually abused', Workshop given at the Dept of Psychiatry, Leeds University, July 1991.

Irvine, A.C. (1988) 'Balancing the right of the mentally retarded to obtain a therapeutic sterilization against the potential for abuse', *Law and Psychology Review* 12: 95–122.

Kempton, W. (1972) *Guidelines for Planning a Training Course on Human Sexuality and the Handicapped*, Philadelphia: Planned Parenthood Association of South Eastern Pennsylvania.

Kempton, W. (1978) 'Sex education for the mentally handicapped', *Sexuality and Disability* 1: 137–46.

Koheeallee, G. and Dustin, G. (1989) 'Everything you always wanted to know about sex policies but were afraid to ask', *Clinical Psychology Forum* 24 (December): 4–7.

Littlewood, R. and Lipsedge, M. (1982) *Aliens and Alienists: Ethnic Minorities and Psychiatry*, Harmondsworth: Penguin.

Martin, N. and Martin, B. (1990) 'Sexual abuse: special considerations when teaching children who have severe learning difficulties', *Mental Handicap* 18: 69–73.

Melton, G. (1984) 'Evaluation of mentally retarded persons for sterilization: contributions and limitations of psychological consultation', *Professional Psychology: Research and Practice* 15(1): 34–48.

Policy and Guidelines for Staff Working in the London Borough of Camden Establishments (1986) *The Sexuality of People with a Mental Handicap*, London: Camden Social Services.

Report of the Royal Commission on the Care of the Feeble Minded, 1904–1908, London: British Parlimentary Papers.

Roth, S. (1991) 'Silent pain', *Nursing Times* 87(6): 62–5.

Saunders, E.J. (1979) 'Staff members' attitudes towards the sexual behaviour of mentally retarded residents', *American Journal of Mental Deficiency* 84: 206–8.

Sigleman, C., Budd, E., Spantel, C., and Schoenrock, C. (1981) 'When in doubt say Yes: acquiescence in interviews with mentally retarded persons', *Mental Retardation* 19: 53–8.

Sinason, V. (1986) 'Secondary mental handicap and its relationship to trauma', *Psychoanalytic Psychotherapy* 2(2): 131–54.

Sinason, V. (1988) 'Richard III, Echo and Hephaestus: sexuality and mental/ multiple handicap', *Journal of Child Psychotherapy* 14(2): 93–105.

Spensley, S. (1985) 'Mentally ill or mentally handicapped? A longitudinal study of severe learning difficulty', *Psychoanalytical Psychotherapy* 1(3): 55–70.

Thomas, B. and Mundy, P. (1991) 'Speaking out', *Nursing Times* 87(6): 67–8.

Tredgold, R. and Soddy, K. (1963) *Tredgold's Textbook of Mental Deficiency*, London: Bailliere Tindall & Cox.

Watson, G. and Rogers, R.S. (1980) 'Sexual instruction for the mildly handicapped and normal adolescent', *Health Education Journal* 39: 88–95.

Wolfensberger, W. (1972) *The Principle of Normalization in Human Services*, Toronto: NIMR.

Chapter 7

Sexuality and disability

Chris Williams

INTRODUCTION

Until 1980 the terminology describing people with disabilities was ambiguous and unclear. The terms disability, handicap, impairment tended to be used interchangeably and led to difficulties of communication and understanding with respect to the specific difficulties and specific solutions relating to a topic that impinges on a large section of society. It is rare for any individual, at some time during their life, not to experience the difficulties of having a disability albeit temporarily. The greater problems arise when these disabilities exist for long periods of time and impinge on everyday activity including sexuality. This chapter will explore the recent clarification of disability terminology and attempt to develop a psycho-social interpretation of handicap in parallel with identifying how handicap and sexuality coexist.

The World Health Organisation in 1980 described, in their *International Classification of Impairments, Disabilities and Handicap*, a three-category understanding of disability which clarified each of these terminologies in such a way that the biological, the functional, and the psycho-social elements could be separately identified and extended in understanding whilst at the same time recognising the overlap between any two and ultimately overlap between all three. The three elements refer to impairment as a biological dysfunction of system or organ of the body, leading to lowered function of that system or organ. The lowered function of the system or organ is the disability experienced by the individual where their ability to perform actions is lowered below the level considered generally to be within the normal range. These disabilities are then impinged upon by the socio-cultural environment in which the disabled person lives. This environment will more or less handicap that individual. It is the social element of handicap that creates the greater difficulty for disabled people and it is in this arena that aspects of sexuality have to be considered. Sexuality is viewed as an aspect of human relationships and the human biological state which exists as a natural phenomenon within all humans across the full range of biological and psychological statuses. There has been no indication that any individual, however disabled, lacks sexual aspects to their life. In many cases it is easier to appreciate the full range if the term sensuality is substituted and it then becomes clear that there is no way that sensuality and humanity can be separated, and, in order that a disabled person can live and experience a full life, that disabled person has to experience sensuality and consequently sexuality.

REHABILITATION

It is only comparatively recently that health care and rehabilitation professionals have considered seriously aspects of sexuality in enabling disabled people to enjoy and experience those elements of life which had been denied through ignorance, distaste, and prejudice, particularly in those situations where the power relationship between the able-bodied and the disabled person existed to the detriment of the disabled individual and prejudice, stigma, segregation, and isolation were common practices in the so-called care of people with disabilities. More recently it has become clear that such a situation is intolerable and the circumstances to enable disabled people to enjoy their sexuality have been enabled and brought into existence. Early studies on rehabilitation (Frankel, 1967) indicated that disabled individuals' sexuality was primarily considered as problematic and that treatment and therapy were the appropriate reactions. Thankfully this concept of problems associated with sexuality has diminished and health-care professionals would now consider their contribution to be more along the lines of a partnership with the disabled individual in creating opportunities for companionship and sexual experience. Hohmann (1972) prepared an extensive review of psychological and psycho-social aspects of sexual functioning of men with spinal-cord injury in which he discussed the suitability of counselling and the limitations of sexuality consequent upon a spinal-cord injury. Of note at this time is the emphasis on the sexuality of men and the absence of reference to women. This is not fully accounted for by the differential incidence of spinal-cord injury. It is more likely accounted for by the cultural perspectives on sexuality and their relative emphasis on men and intercourse (see Ussher; Baker, both this volume). The gender-specific concentration was continued by Comarr (1973) when writing about individuals, again with spinal-cord injuries, and discussing the neurological and physiological aspects of their sexual functioning. He presents data derived from interviews with 530 young men and in the whole text he provides one single paragraph in which these are discussed in relationship to women with spinal-cord injury. This anomaly can begin to be understood when in 1975 Singh and Magner asserted that for men an intact spinal cord was a necessary component for 'full sexual activity' in other words penetrative intercourse, the inference being that the physical aspect of sexuality was only necessary to a lesser degree in women. They point out that, although up to 70 per cent of all spinal-cord victims are capable of some degree of sexual activity, many do not practise their sexuality because of psychological factors relating to body image, increased dependency, and feelings of inferiority. It is these latter aspects of psycho-social functioning in disabled individuals that have to be attended to in order that full expression of sexuality can be created.

ATTITUDES TO SEXUALITY

The critical importance of beliefs and attitudes associated with sexuality is clearly relevant in determining whether or not a continued active sexual life is available to individuals after disabilities such as spinal-cord injury (Isaacson and Delgado, 1974). The important element of early counselling in the areas of sexual functioning and in the acceptance of the nature of the disabling consequences of impairment of injury are crucial elements in psycho-sexual adjustment. These beliefs and attitudes however do not exist in isolation and are impinged upon by social and cultural attitudes. These have been thoroughly explored by Wada and Brodwin (1975) who surveyed 104 individuals to explore with them their knowledge and attitude as non-handicapped individuals concerning the sexual functioning of men with spinal-cord injury. The results of their interviews confirmed the existence of a belief that once an individual takes to a wheelchair their sexual activity is at an end, although the medical evidence is clearly contrary to this belief. Unfortunately, their study went on to show that, at the time, the medical practitioners attending to individuals with spinal injury invariably shared that opinion.

Miller (1975) demonstrated that spinal-cord-injured individuals themselves had many fears and misapprehensions about their own sexual functioning. In a study whereby they were encouraged to express and explore their fantasies and belief system of sexuality it was discovered that many men with disabilities believed that they would be incapable of having sexual intercourse and that those individuals with any form of spinal-cord injury would be thereby unable to provide sexual satisfaction for able-bodied women. Neither of these belief systems has any validity, arising, as they do, from the common myth that sex equates to intercourse (a myth challenged by both evolving critiques and by the cognitive approach to sexuality, as is illustrated in this volume). Miller stresses the need for a clear and accurate picture of the facts to be made available particularly for newly disabled individuals. He strongly asserts that the fact that spinal-cord injury does not mean sexual incapacity has to be imparted at an early stage in the rehabilitation process. The individual and his or her partner needs to know that a continuing and satisfying sex life remains available to them.

A more sophisticated investigation into the beliefs and attitudes of disabled individuals in comparison to their able-bodied peers was reported by Ferro and Allen (1976) in which they carried out in-depth interviews, in conjunction with a semantic differential scale, with twenty-three physically disabled college students and forty-seven non-disabled college students on attitudes about various sexual behaviours and their own feelings on sexuality. Seven concepts associated with sexuality were judged using twelve bipolar adjective pairs. The concepts were sexual intercourse, masturbation, oral sex, sexual fantasy, petting, orgasm, and an item entitled 'my sexuality'. They found that the groups were not significantly different in their attitudes towards sexual behaviour but that the disabled group scored significantly lower in regard to their own feelings of sexuality. In other words, the practice of sexuality remained identical irrespective of physical status. It is the internal belief systems and psychological components of sexuality that differ markedly between able-bodied and disabled people. It is not a necessary consequence of the physical impairment that this should be so. It is more likely to be the result of psycho-social constraints that form the elements underpinning the handicap experienced by disabled people. This has significant importance when considering the role of rehabilitation professionals and Sidman (1977) indicated the importance of appropriate post-injury counselling with respect to sexual readjustment and in her study showed how this element of rehabilitation was most likely to be ignored rather than attended to in any systematic fashion. This necessarily further handicaps the disabled person. Fear and ignorance would appear to be the chief psychological factors which prevent individuals with severe disability from attaining their optimum sexual functioning (Sandowski, 1976). The willingness to experiment and adapt is a necessary feature for satisfactory adjustment to disability and would form an early component of the helping process towards re-establishment of a positive sexual identity and an active sexual life.

This relationship between self-concept and sexuality has been explored by Fitting et al. (1978), who showed a clear relationship between the two in the twenty-four women they interviewed. Most of the women who had experienced spinal-cord injury viewed themselves as attractive and viewed sexual relationships as enjoyable. They nevertheless had inhibited sexual expression and their opportunity to put into practice their belief was severely impaired by their self-concept as disabled individuals. This was particularly manifested in their perceived relationship between sexuality and bowel and bladder function and, where this had not been satisfactorily resolved, there remained difficulties in expressing sexuality.

This is in some ways an unusual study, as it is only more recently that there appears in the literature a fuller recognition of the sexuality and sexual needs of disabled women. Mary Romano (1978) published an extensive discussion considering disabled women and stressed the importance of communication and cueing between partners and their preparedness for sexuality by knowledge and attitude change. She stressed the need to recognise that the sexuality of disabled women has more commonality with 'normal sex' than with the previously considered 'abnormality' or problematic sexuality of disabled people. This was further explored at a personal level by Davidson and Venditti (1979) who described in full their own disabilities and the problems they encountered in expressing their own sexuality. In a fuller exploration of the range of disabling conditions and the effects they have on individual sexuality, Bullard and Knight (1981) reported a collection of personal experiences gathered from a wide range of individuals with physical disabilities. This text covers areas of work from those individuals with congenital disorders such as cerebral palsy through acquired disabilities consequent upon head injury, as well as the effect that such disabilities have on family perspectives and professional issues. This is one of the few texts in which particular emphasis is placed upon difficulties of disabled women and the implications for professional care and sexuality where a whole range of moral and ethical dilemmas can impinge.

Despite what appeared to be the beginnings of a developing and maturing perspective on sexuality and disability in the academic and professional literature, there nevertheless remained widespread ignorance and prejudice against such explorations, perpetuating the notion that sexuality and disability were contradictions in terms. For example, MacDougall *et al.* (1979) conducted a series of three-hour personal interviews with forty-five young physically disabled adults, in which they discussed attitudes towards pornography, masturbation, and other aspects of sexuality. They also investigated the degree of personal interest in sexuality and the extent and form of the individuals' own sexual behaviour and experience. The results indicated that, while the majority of the people with whom they carried out discussions tended to express liberal attitudes towards sexuality, they did not indicate a high degree of personal interest in sexual activity. Nearly all of the people interviewed were single and over half had never had *any* form of intimate relationship with another person, including any sexual contact or experience. This level of absence of sexual experience stands in sharp contrast to the sexual experience of non-disabled young adults. They further demonstrated that the negative attitudes felt towards sexual activity could largely be attributed to the restrictive living conditions and lack of sex education and guidance received by these young people. They further noted that the young women expressed more conservative attitudes towards sexuality than did the men and they asserted that, while the knowledge of and belief concerning sexuality appeared to be no different between able-bodied and disabled young people, the opportunities for expression were severely curtailed and a major shift in social and cultural attitudes of the non-disabled population towards recognising and accepting the emotional and sexual needs of disabled fellow citizens was needed before any progress could be made.

CHANGING ATTITUDES, CHANGING BEHAVIOUR

One approach which has been successfully adopted in an attempt to develop a more positive perspective on sexuality and disability is assertiveness training. Dunn, Lloyd, and Phelps (1979) have shown that training in assertiveness, particularly with the emphasis on sexuality, can significantly enhance communication between individuals with respect to how sexual desires and needs may be expressed. They did recognise that there could well be differences in the form of assertiveness related to the individual disabilities. Nevertheless there was still an emphasis on the physical component of sexuality, at the expense of psychological and emotional aspects. This is further emphasised by Geiger (1979) who published an extensive investigation into the neurophysiology of sexual responses; although presenting in detail the biology and anatomy of sexual activity, he ultimately acknowledges that it is more than a biological event and in conclusion argues that it is necessary to stress that, while sexual activity may or may not involve genital stimulation and sensation, it remains primarily a cerebral and therefore psychological event.

Further work on the recognition of the importance of psychological factors was identified by Thornton (1979) in her study of women where she found that the sexuality of women with spinal-cord injury was primarily a function of their psychological perspectives rather than of any physical limitations experienced by them. The conceptualisation of sexuality as a psychological event further highlights the nonsense of denying the sexuality of disabled individuals, for in the majority of cases of physically disabling conditions the ability to experience at a psychological and emotional level is unimpaired. This should be a major consideration which facilitates the elimination of any action which would limit sexual expression on the part of those whose responsibility is to provide care and intervention.

The role of professional care workers in enhancing full expression of sexuality in individuals with disabilities has been progressively emphasised with the development of appropriate forms of sex education and sexual therapy in which partnership with disabled people can be formed. In this vein, Narum and Rodolfa (1984) have reviewed the literature on sex therapy and spinal-cord injury and include discussions of a range of support systems, the education input that is appropriate, and the modifications in behaviour that are achievable in order that clients express their sexuality in a mutually satisfying manner. Robbins (1985) further explores this issue in her study of the role of counselling in assisting a newly injured person to incorporate their physically altered appearance into a revised body image, emphasising that sexual assertiveness and sexual alternatives can be explored and appreciated. Although this enlightened view is clearly enhanced by appropriate training of professional staff, Dunn (1983) has shown that it is one of the areas that staff invariably avoid when working in rehabilitation (a parallel to the situation in other areas of work, such as that described by Mulleady, this volume, in her discussion of drug work). Dunn surveyed fifty-one staff members in a rehabilitation setting and indicated that aspects of sexuality were kept to a minimum in their discussions with clients and that the clients had to particularly assert themselves if they wished to have information relating to their future possibilities of sexual experience. In order to address this issue, Dunn emphasised the necessity for staff training in interpersonal skills as much as in factual knowledge, for many staff feel anxious themselves about discussing sexuality, and will consequently avoid it.

Additional support in favour of a psycho-social model was provided by Willmuth (1987) in her literature review on sexuality after spinal-cord injury. She described the growing body of information about sexual adjustment and presented a discussion of the methodological problems for future research in this area, stressing the importance of consideration of gender issues and appropriate sexual counselling for those striving to achieve full rehabilitation.

Rehabilitation

This issue of reintegration of newly disabled individuals into the open community has a particular relevance when considering the rehabilitation of individuals recovering from severe head injury. As a consequence of a severe head injury a common phenomenon reported is that of disinhibition where sexual activity and sexual expressions may no longer be so adequately socialised and individuals are more prepared to express themselves in both words and behaviour to a point where they are vulnerable to misunderstanding by the community at large. For example, Valentich and Gripton (1984) described the problems experienced by a 29-year-old man recovering from a head injury, whose major residual manifestation of disability was inappropriate sexual behaviour. Their treatment techniques involved cognitive restructuring, assertiveness training, and social skills training to great effect. Acquired as opposed to congenital disability is clearly an important dichotomy. Those individuals whose disabling condition has been a characteristic of their life from birth have had a considerable period of time to develop their abilities in spite of the impairments, whereas individuals whose developmental period has been as an unimpaired individual, and who now find themselves disabled as a result of disease or accident, may have markedly different adjustment agenda. In one study which illustrates this, DeHaan and Wallander (1988) studied three groups of college women where the physically disabling conditions were of early onset, that is before the age of 3, or of late onset, occurring after the age of 18. They compared these two physically disabled groups with a group of thirty women with no disability. Their findings indicated that the early onset group had considerably fewer current sexual experiences than did the non-disabled group and that this early group was dissatisfied with this low frequency of sexual behaviour. Both disabled groups believed that they could enjoy sexual experiences but that their current circumstances precluded them from so doing in many cases. Again, this inability to express a normal range of sexuality has to be seen in the context of a culture which views sexuality in disabled people as inappropriate and in many cases to be prevented by institutional practices both explicit and implicit. Chandani et al. (1989) further extended this view by inviting undergraduate students to discuss their views of sexuality and disability. The results showed significantly more non-acceptance of the sexuality of disabled women than of women in general, and in addition that men were particularly guilty of holding negative attitudes towards the sexuality of people with disabilities, attitudes which were greatly magnified in their belief about disabled women, where they considered that sexuality was the most unacceptable. This astonishing study further underlines the critical importance of a wider sex education programme with respect to disability and sexuality, one which does not merely target disabled people themselves.

Moving forwards

To summarise, there have clearly been two parallel strands of development with respect to sexuality and disability. The first strand has been a consequence of the empowerment of disabled people, through their adoption of more political strategies, where active engagement with the non-disabled population has enabled both a dramatic change in attitude and in resources and facilities to be created. This empowerment movement is ably represented by Oliver (1989) in his cogently argued text on the politics of disablement where he puts a very powerful case for the recognition of disability not as a problem but as an opportunity for unique experiences, and challenges and charges non-disabled individuals to recognise this aspect of disability rather than the 'problem' aspect of disability. This shift of opinion is very clearly represented by developments in opportunities for the expression of sexuality and the creation of organisations specifically for the continued empowerment of disabled people, the organisation SPOD being a clear example in point. This organisation originally began as a consequence of research by Stewart (1975) cataloguing the difficulties experienced by people with physical disabilities in expressing sexuality. He drew together a number of like-minded but able-bodied people and formed a registered charity under the title of Sexual Problems of the Disabled. This title contains within it evidence of this former style of thinking whereby sexuality in disability was viewed as problematic and disabled people were considered to be homogeneous. More recently, the organisation SPOD has altered its *modus operandi* and is now known as the 'Association to Aid the Sexual and Personal Relationships of People with a Disability' and has deliberately enabled its management at executive level to be the responsibility of people with disabilities. Mike Oliver clearly picks up this empowerment point when he says 'I have never denied some people experience disability as loss but that seems to me to be a distortion of the experience of disability for myself and for most disabled people I have met over the years'. He emphasises the solidarity of disability and the unique belonging to a community having a common identity and ideology and it is this strength that has enabled disabled people to create a climate of opinion in which sexual expression becomes the accepted norm rather than the unique consequence of a struggle.

The second thread over the past two decades has been the recognition of the gender bias in discussions of disability and sexuality. In the initial stages it was rarely recognised that disabled women would want or be able to experience a continued sexual life or even had any wishes so to do. As the empowerment movement in disability developed so did the women's movement, and this in parallel has led to the equalising of recognition of sexuality and disability needs. There could now be no distinction drawn between men and women with respect to the importance of sexuality and sexual need. (This area of work is more expertly developed and in greater depth in the chapter on women's issues in Bullard and Knight (1981).)

Finally, these two parallel threads of empowerment and enablement have had significant influences in contemporary care practices, with the direct employment of care attenders by disabled people, and in increasing access to ordinary housing in the open community. This stands in direct contrast to the previously dominant institutionalised care which took place in segregated settings, at the hands of paid professional carers who had no requirement for any more intimate or close relationship than any other professional care worker would have.

VARIETIES OF DISABILITY AND THEIR EFFECT ON SEXUALITY

Many of the arguments rehearsed above are applicable to individuals with a wide range of physical disabilities, yet there is still need for specific distinctions to be drawn between the particular needs of those with specific disabilities. In this light, and in order to illustrate a range of issues arising from disability and its impact on sexuality, a number of case histories from ongoing clinical work will be presented. Each will consider the impact of one of the major forms of disability, describing the particular effects on sexuality and the solution developed jointly between the client and the psychologist.

Head injury

There is a virtual epidemic of head injury at present, with the increasing incidence of road-traffic accidents and subsequent survival following implementation of seat-belt legislation and the wearing of motor-cycle head protection. Prior to these legally enforced innovations, a severe road accident involving a motor car or motor cycle would most likely have led to the death of the person involved, and so consequently the survival of people is now much greater. However, the morbidity of their survival has dramatically increased. The peak period for head injury is between 17 years and 24 years, and these ages capture a wide range of young people whose sexuality is beginning to emerge and become an important part of their lives.

The head injury does not in itself affect the normal manifestations of sexuality. It is the major personality changes that occur as a consequence of damage to areas of the brain, particularly the frontal lobes, which are of significance. Although individuals recovering from severe brain trauma will have no difficulty in functioning biologically as sexual beings, their psychosocial functioning can be severely impaired. This is particularly the case where the phenomenon of disinhibition is commonly experienced. Normal social controls learnt through the development period become loosened and the individual can feel able to express themselves sexually without regard to the consequences of their acts. Alongside the disinhibition in many cases is irritability and shortness of temper. The individual may become less tolerant of others, which may then lead to outbursts of verbal or physical abuse. This again can be disconcerting to the partner and requires careful explanation and counselling with respect to understanding its origin and managing its consequences. The opposite effect, a depression of sexual interest, may also occur, and again this can be disconcerting where an active and developing relationship with a partner is suddenly ceased as a consequence of an accident from which it would appear the individual has fully recovered.

A further characteristic of head injury is the long period of time over which recovery occurs. Although there is initially rapid improvement, in most cases this rate of recovery diminishes over time, yet still continues over decades. It is inappropriate to consider that the stage reached within the first twelve months is indicative of the complete recovery process, and opportunities for continued rehabilitation and psychological therapy must be made available to such individuals and their partners. In a number of cases where the victim of the head injury is a young male it may be that his original partner feels no longer able to deal with the difficulties imposed upon their relationship and this young man may return home to his mother who finds herself reassuming a maternal role. This can cause great distress and strain in the family, particularly if a physically active but disinhibited adult male attempts to maintain an active sexual life in circumstances where such behaviour is inappropriate.

Virtually all individuals with a severe head injury will have some memory impairment, and this is particularly so concerning the circumstances of the accident or injury, but these amnesias can remain and cause difficulties in relationships with partners. It may be that the individual fails to recall their partner's name and uses alternative names unwittingly. It may be that the individual fails to recall any recent sexual experience and behaves in a way likely to cause distress by insistence on repeated sexual activity even though only recently engaged upon. For example, a study conducted by Rosenbaum and Najenson (1976) concerning changes in mood and behaviour among wives of severely brain-injured soldiers in Israel indicated that significant sexual difficulties and the development of sexual aversion to the partner were not uncommon.

Although the main effect of head injury on sexuality will manifest itself through the secondary aspects, there are elements of primary dysfunction that are attributable to organic causes consequent upon head injury. If damage occurs to the hypothalamus there may be disorders arising from endocrine imbalance which affects testicular and ovarian function and which can result in infertility and loss of secondary sexual characteristics, or a failure to achieve puberty in young adolescents. In some children precocious puberty has been reported in association with temporal lobe injuries. There may also be altered motor or sensory function as a direct result of the brain trauma and various states of altered tonicity and movement disorders have been described which can interfere with pre-parations for or participation in sexual activity to varying degrees. The individual may find full sexual expression to be uncomfortable or difficult and the possibility exists of precipitating epileptic seizures which can be distressing and cause fearfulness and avoidance of repetition. In addition to these direct effects, there are effects which follow from medication, particularly sedative and anti-convulsant treatments, which may be prescribed as a continuous prophylactic pharmacotherapy regime.

However, it is the secondary sexual dysfunctions that have the major impact. These are very often exaggerations of pre-injury psycho-social sexual adjustment or dysfunction and it is important when counselling such individuals to take a full history of sexual knowledge and sexual experience prior to the injury in order that the content and pace of post-injury sexual counselling can be appropriately judged. These effects can have quite wide-ranging consequences in disturbing the family or partnership dynamic and the non-injured member should similarly receive sensitive counselling in order to facilitate understanding of the altered relationships, and to allow the partner to play an active part in the rehabilitation of their partner or family member.

The head-injured person may make excessive or inappropriate sexual demands on their partner and their partner begins to feel trapped in this situation, unable to satisfy either the emotional or intellectual demands of the brain-injured person whilst at the same time being unable to develop alternative relationships in compensation. Staff reactions to the expression of sexuality by individuals recovering from head injury are therefore important in order to enable the readjustment to a more acceptable level of sexuality and expression. It is important that staff develop a consistent and constructive response to such expressions, at the same time avoiding shock or withdrawal. Emphasis on the normality of disinhibition in the early stages can be helpful, particularly to staff who may not have extensive experience in head-injury rehabilitation. This can be conveyed to relatives and partners in order to alleviate some of their distress. In some cases it will be necessary to enable the individual to develop new styles of self-control, particularly with respect to identifying private as opposed to public places for the expression of sexuality. Aspects of sexuality should be included early in the rehabilitation programme and should form an integral component of such programmes. Griffiths *et al.* (1990) have developed a comprehensive sexuality rehabilitation programme for young people recovering from head injury and their work is recommended.

Case history – Martin

Martin is 28 years old and six years ago was involved in a severe traffic accident when he came off his motor cycle whilst he was being pursued by the police. He was well known to the police, having committed a number of prior offences related to taking cars and driving away. He was also known to consume large quantities of alcohol and to have an active sexual life. The head injury caused severe brain damage and Martin was comatose for a period of two months after the accident. Although he has recovered to some extent intellectually, he remains with quite major residual physical problems, having a paraplegia and dysphasia. He is a wheelchair user and lives in his own adapted flat. He continues to abuse alcohol, drinking up to three bottles of whisky each week. More recently he has begun to express an attraction to a female rehabilitation worker and he is expressing delusions relating to the closeness of their relationship. These delusions involve elaboration upon innocent interactions which Martin misconstrues as evidence of physical and emotional attachment. He is becoming increasingly distressed by the apparent unwillingness of his object of affection to respond and, although the situation has been clearly described to him, he remains convinced that all but he are misconstruing the situation. He is beginning to become verbally and physically aggressive as a result of this misapprehension and it is increasingly difficult to maintain his rehabilitation programme as it invariably involves the member of staff with whom he has formed this imaginary attachment. Martin does have some opportunity for sexual expression through meeting female 'companions' in local public houses. These one-night stands provide immediate gratification but no long-term satisfaction for him. He recognises the difficulty of his situation but cannot reconcile a previously active and satisfactory sexual life with his now severely restricted opportunities. Part of the therapeutic endeavour with Martin is exploring reality testing so that he can begin to recognise that opportunities for sexual expression are not denied him but they have to be reciprocated. He will not be denied access to the rehabilitation programme but he has to adapt his delusional belief system such that it can accommodate a fantasy which is harmless, without it spilling over into practice which is potentially harmful. In circumstances such as these it would not be inappropriate for the therapeutic regime to discuss with the client the involvement of surrogate partners. Unfortunately, Martin lives in a rural setting where such opportunities are extremely restricted. A further alternative, where partners are not readily met and relationships established, is the incorporation of prosthetic sexual aids as a means of sexual satisfaction. This latter strategy clearly raises a number of aesthetic as well as individual moral and ethical considerations as does the potential use of surrogate partners.

Spinal injury

Spinal injuries are invariably the result of traumatic interruption of the spinal cord by accident or injury. The level and the extent of damage will determine the disability experienced by the person concerned. The spinal cord may be completely severed, in which case sensation and function at levels below the transection are completely lost. The spinal cord may be only partially severed, in which case a variety of lower sensations and functions are maintained. Reflex arc function that does not depend upon central nervous system control is mostly retained in spite of complete transection. Fortunately, a component of the sexual arousal cycle depends upon such low-level reflex arcs and can consequently be maintained in spite of complete transection of the spinal cord. In men erection and ejaculation can occur and in women lubrication will occur and sexual intercourse is possible. However, in both cases the cerebral components of orgasm will be absent. Coupled with this altered sexual arousal capacity there is invariably some form of lower-limb paralysis making positioning an important consideration when counselling sexual partners. In addition to the paralysis there can be bowel and bladder difficulties causing reflex incontinence and advice on emptying bowel and bladder prior to sexual activity is important. The use of indwelling catheters as a means of permanently overcoming incontinence does not physically interfere with the capacity for sexual intercourse in either men or women but the presence of a catheter can have a profound psychological effect and must be included in any discussion of self-image when preparing individuals for a resumption of their sexual activity following spinal-cord injury. In cases where spinal-cord injury has occurred, the involvement of the partner becomes crucial in enabling a satisfactory sexual relationship to become re-established. There will need to be discussions concerning the use of positioning and the possible inclusion of prosthetic aids as a means of stimulation to arousal. One particular area of difficulty that can affect men involves the occurrence of retrograde ejaculation whereby the semen, instead of being externally ejaculated, passes via the urethra into the bladder during orgasm. Although this has no deleterious effects it can alter the perception of orgasm and sexual satisfaction. It also clearly affects the possibility of pregnancy. The exact physiological capabilities of any particular spinal-cord-injured person regarding sexual activity can be discovered only by their own exploration of varieties of position and persistence. No assumptions should be made about sexual functioning strictly on the basis of the site of lesion. Matters such as previous sexual experience and willingness to explore new methods of sexual and sensual satisfaction are important elements to introduce to the couple.

Case history – Paul and Jane

Paul received his spinal-cord injury as a result of a motor-car accident. The level of damage is such that he has lost the use of his lower limbs but has full use of both arms. He can achieve reflex erection and has some sensation. He is overweight and needs help to move position from his wheelchair to bed. He and Jane have moved their bed downstairs in their house to their living room which has been adapted with a hoist in order to enable him to transfer with ease. They were referred for sexual counselling as a result of continued difficulty in achieving satisfactory sexual encounters. The presenting problem was one of an incomplete erection and subsequent non-penetration. Discussions centred on the range of sensual encounters that the couple were employing without the demand for full sexual intercourse. They were encouraged to explore each others' bodies by touch and taste to a greater extent than they had prior to Paul's accident. They were also introduced to a variety of prosthetic aids which would enable Jane to stimulate both herself and Paul and to maintain Paul's erection once achieved by reflex stimulation. They found these prosthetic aids to be both fun and productive and, although not using them on every occasion, they found that the occasional introduction of variety enabled a more regular and satisfying sexual relationship to be maintained. One of the crucial elements in helping Paul and Jane resume a satisfactory sexual life was to decouple the notion of satisfaction being solely from orgasm. Their perception of a sexual life as being equivalent to penetration and ejaculation needed readjustment and the employment of the entire body as a source of sexual and sensual pleasure was brought to their attention. This revelation appeared to free up their concern that following Paul's injury he would not be capable of sexual activity and the realisation that novel activities could become sensually satisfying, in some cases to a greater extent than their previous rather mechanical sexual encounters, was some compensation for loss in other areas.

Multiple sclerosis

This progressive disorder whose cause remains unknown affects young people at a point in their lives when they are beginning to achieve a full expression of their sexuality. It has a higher incidence of occurrence in women and is progressively debilitating. Once the diagnosis is made it is possible for the individual to recollect a whole series of prior disturbances which can now be accounted for by their disease but which were previously puzzling. These early symptoms can very often lead to an increasing difficulty in sexual expression and are often misinterpreted as having psychological origins when in fact they are based in the physiological changes occurring during the demyelinisation process of MS. Nevertheless, they have profound psychological consequences which are increasingly difficult to remedy following the definitive diagnosis. The most prominent symptoms of MS are a loss of motor control throughout the body, with increased weakness, coupled with blurring of vision, particularly in the early stages although these visual effects very often resolve themselves as the motor disturbances become more apparent. Men with MS often experience difficulties in establishing and maintaining erections and subsequently require extended stimulation in order to achieve ejaculation and orgasm. In women the manifestation of MS produces a reduced level of lubrication and difficulties in controlling movements and at times bladder disorders. The major change is one of self-perception and self-image with respect to attractiveness and the defence adopted is very often one of a withdrawal from sexual encounters with partners. A characteristic of MS is its cyclical nature. The disease process goes through a series of relapses and remissions. It is important that the couple recognise the onset of remission and use that time to reaffirm their relationship. During periods of relapse a great strain can be placed upon the relationship in that it can often be construed as a final debilitating process from which recovery is unlikely. The counselling necessary at this point is one of goal-directed target setting to enable a realistic understanding of the limitations of the relapse whilst retaining in mind the potentialities of the remission to come. Nevertheless, even during this period of time it is possible to maintain an active sexual life, in particular using prosthetic aids and continued stimulation in order to achieve orgasm.

Case history – Richard

Richard was formerly a hairdresser and was married. Over a period of time he had begun to recognise a developing weakness in his arms and hands, making his work progressively difficult. He was 38 at the time of coming into treatment and his MS had been diagnosed five years previously. The rate of deterioration had accelerated more recently and he required a wheelchair for mobility and was living alone in an adapted flat. His wife had found the complications of MS to be excessive and they had parted amicably. Richard made a request for help on the grounds of difficulty he was experiencing in achieving orgasms through masturbation. The progressive weakness that he had experienced at work had reached the point where he was unable to maintain any manual stimulation for longer than a few seconds at a time. Although this enabled him to achieve an erection he became exhausted before achieving orgasm. The complete satisfaction of sexual activity for him was important and a prosthetic aid (artificial vagina) was made available that he could use in order to aid his own action in masturbation. This has proved to be perfectly satisfactory for him and achieves one end for his sexual requirements. However, this has to be balanced against the difficulty he has in establishing and maintaining the partnership relationship. As a man approaching his middle age he has found it increasingly difficult, given his condition, to meet potential partners and when that situation does arise he has found himself to be over-keen on exploring whether or not an immediate sexual relationship can be established. This is clearly disadvantageous to such relationships and he has found no success to date. A more systematic element in his treatment was to explore ways and means of forming relationships that did not so overtly express a sexual need and where the goal was companionship rather than sexual satisfaction. Sadly in Richard's case his condition has deteriorated to the point where he now requires full physical care and this poses for him a major dilemma. He is the recipient of close physical contact with a number of care attenders, but with whom he cannot progress towards a sexual relationship. He finds this ambiguity and contradiction a source of physical strain and without recourse to periodic sexual relief through the use of a prosthetic device he claims that life would be for him intolerable. It is likely that this unsatisfactory situation will continue unless he can meet a sympathetic partner willing to see beyond his disability. In his present circumstances this is impossible although recent contact has been made through a specialist agency.

CONCLUSION

Sexuality is no less a consideration for the individual with a disability than it is for an able-bodied individual. It is an element of their social and personal relationships as well as a source of personal and sensual pleasure. In the setting of a relationship sexual activity can confirm the closeness of the couple and act as a means of communicating love and concern for each other. When the physical or intellectual capabilities of either or both are impaired it does not necessarily follow that these psychological needs or desires are similarly impaired. It is the responsibility of the appropriately trained rehabilitation worker in conjunction with the individual to construct a means whereby emotional and sensual experiences can be maintained and used in the same fashion as if the individual were not disabled. It is not the achievement of orgasm through sexual intercourse that is the purpose of a developed sexuality, but the expression of a sexuality involving a total body and mind combination that satisfies an individual and their partner. What takes place during this encounter is no business of the rehabilitation worker apart from affirming with the individuals concerned that no harm or coercion is involved. When a third party is necessary in order that sexual activity can be performed, the third person has to maintain their professional role, a situation which is possible when a mature and sexually adjusted rehabilitation worker chooses to help in this way. When someone with a disability has come to believe that their self-worth is so diminished that they no longer hold any attractiveness it is unfortunate if the rehabilitation staff collude with this self-image by providing access only to self-stimulation. If an individual fails to find their body acceptable then there is the very real possibility that they will find relationships with other people unacceptable and become reclusive and isolated as a consequence. The rebuilding of a positive self-image and sexual identity should therefore be the primary purpose of therapy rather than the physical relief of sexual frustration.

Underpinning these developments in sexuality and disability are the concepts of dignity and freedom. The dignity of an individual to act and feel in a way that is self-determined and the freedom to put into practice these thoughts and feelings to enable independence and self-determination to be achieved have to be paramount in rehabilitation. All staff who offer services in the arena of disability rehabilitation must be themselves prepared to acknowledge aspects of their own sexuality and recognise that these impinge upon the way they will be dealing with disabled individuals for whom sexuality can become a primary source of concern. The staff member must recognise that their intent is to uphold and promote human characteristics in addition to physical components and that the measure of a successful rehabilitation will be in psychological as well as motoric parameters. Sex as fun can be a major driving force behind such help. All too often in the past there has been an implicit assumption that nothing existed between a full sexual life or a platonic and asexual life. Since it is clear that these are points on a continuum there is no reason to suppose that a disabled individual could not also explore the full range of sexual activity, sexual opportunities, and sexual experiences, albeit there will exist times when a helping hand is necessary.

REFERENCES

Bullard, D.G. and Knight, S.E. (1981) *Sexuality and Physical Disability – Personal Perspectives*, St. Louis: Mosby.

Chandani, A.T., McKenna, K.T., and Maas, F. (1981) 'Attitudes of university students towards the sexuality of physically disabled people', *British Journal of Occupational Therapy* 52(6): 233–6.

Commarr, A.E. (1973) 'Sex among patients with spinal cord and/or cauda equina injuries', *Medical Aspects of Human Sexuality* 7(3): 222–38.

Davidson, A. and Venditti, V. (1979) 'Two clients' views', *Sexuality and Disability* 2(1): 23–7.

DeHaan, C.B. and Wallander, J.L. (1988) 'Self-concept, sexual knowledge and attitudes, and parental support in the sexual adjustment of women with early- and late-onset physical disability', *Archives of Sexual Behaviour* 17(2): 145–61.

Dunn, N. (1983) 'Sexual questions and comments on a spinal cord injury service', *Sexuality and Disability* 6(3–4): 126–34.

Dunn, M., Lloyd, E., and Phelps, G. (1979) 'Sexual assertiveness in spinal cord injury', *Sexuality and Disability* 2(4): 293–300.

Ferro, J.M. and Allen, H.A. (1976) 'Sexuality: the effects of physical impairment', *Rehabilitation Counseling Bulletin* 20(2): 148–51.

Fitting, M.D., Salisbury, S., Davies, N.H., and Mayclin, D.K. (1978) 'Self-concept and sexuality of spinal cord injured women', *Archives of Sexual Behaviour* 7(2): 143–56.

Frankel, A. (1967) 'Sexual problems in rehabilitation', *Journal of Rehabilitation* 33(5): 19–20.

Geiger, R.C. (1979) 'Neurophysiology of sexual response in spinal cord injury', *Sexuality and Disability* 2(4): 257–66.

Griffiths, E.R., Cole, S., and Cole, T.M. (1990) 'Sexuality and sexual dysfunction', in M. Rosenthal, E.R. Griffith, M.R. Bond, and J.D. Miller (eds) *Rehabilitation of the Adult and Child with Traumatic Brain Injury*, second edition, Philadelphia: F.A. Davis, pp. 206–24.

Hohmann, G.W. (1972) 'Considerations in management of psychosexual readjustment in the cord injured male', *Rehabilitation Psychology* 19(2): 50–8.

Isaacson, J. and Delgado, H.E. (1974) 'Sex counselling for those with spinal cord injuries', *Social Casework* 55(10): 622–7.

MacDougall, J.C., Morin, S., and McGill, U. (1979) 'Sexual attitudes and self-reported behaviour of congenitally disabled adults', *Canadian Journal of Behavioural Science* 11(3): 189–204.

Miller, D.K. (1975) 'Sexual counseling with spinal cord-injured clients', *Journal of Sexual & Marital Therapy* 1(4): 312–18.

Narum, G.D. and Rodolfa, E.R. (1984) 'Sex therapy for the spinal cord injury client: suggestions for professionals', *Professional Psychology: Research and Practice* 15(6): 775–84.

Oliver, M. (1989) 'A very positive perspective', in *The Politics of Disablement*, London: Macmillan.

Romano, M.D. (1978) 'Sexuality and the disabled female', *Sexuality and Disability* 1(1): 27–33.

Robbins, K.H. (1985) 'Traumatic spinal cord injury and its impact upon sexuality', *Journal of Applied Rehabilitation Counseling* 16(1): 24–7, 31.

Rosenbaum, N. and Najenson, T. (1976) 'Changes in life pattern and symptoms of low mood as reported by wives of severely brain injured soldiers', *Journal of Consulting Clinical Psychologists* 44: 881–94.

Sandowski, C.L. (1976) 'Sexuality and the paraplegic', *Rehabilitation Literature* 37(11–12): 322–7.

Sidman, J.M. (1977) 'Sexual functioning and the physically disabled adult', *American Journal of Occupational Therapy* 31(2): 81–5.

Singh, S.P. and Magner, T. (1975) 'Sex and self: the spinal cord-injured', *Rehabilitation Literature* 36(1): 2–10.

Stewart, W.F.R. (1975) *Sex and the Physically Handicapped Person*, London: National Fund for Research into Crippling Diseases.

Thornton, C.E. (1979) 'Sexuality counseling of women with spinal cord injuries', *Sexuality and Disability* 2(4): 267–77.

Valentich, M. and Gripton, J. (1984–6) 'Facilitating the sexual integration of the head-injured person in the community', *Sexuality and Disability* 7(1–2): 28–42.

Wada, M.A. and Brodwin, M.G. (1975) 'Attitudes of society towards sexual functioning of male individuals with spinal cord injury', *Psychology* 12(4): 18–22.

Willmuth, M.E. (1987) 'Sexuality after spinal cord injury: a critical review', *Clinical Psychology Review* 7(4): 389–412.

World Health Organisation (1980) *International Classification of Impairments, Disabilities and Handicaps: A Manual of Classification Relating to the Consequences of Disease*, Geneva: WHO.

Chapter 8

Psychological perspectives on working with sex offenders

Derek Perkins

INTRODUCTION

To discuss sexuality in the context of sex offenders is to conceive of a problem: their sexuality is the very thing that has marked them as outsiders in society, as deviant. Sexual offending in itself raises many difficult issues for society. Should convicted offenders be locked away for as long as the law allows in order to protect the public, or is this a short-sighted and ultimately counter-productive reaction based primarily on a desire to punish the offender whatever the effect might be on future victimisation? Might not offenders incarcerated without hope of treatment or rehabilitation be even more bitter and dangerous when they are eventually released? Before any question of intervention for sex offenders can be addressed, these issues have to be confronted.

The present law requires all imprisoned sex offenders, apart from the minority subject to indeterminate sentences, to be released at fixed dates irrespective of their dangerousness to the public. Should offenders in custody not therefore be offered treatment with the aim of minimising the risk of re-offending after release? What, though, of evidence about the treatability of sex offenders? Can they be successfully treated? Is treatment likely to be successful or would it simply put the public at unjustifiable risk by implying that a 'cure' is possible and placing offenders more quickly than would otherwise be the case into situations where they might be tempted to re-offend?

All of these questions become charged with the many emotions – anger, disgust, despair, sympathy, fear – which the topic arouses. It is often difficult to distinguish facts from assertions, but it is important to try to do so if the problem is to be effectively tackled for the benefit of all. With this aim in mind, this chapter will examine our current knowledge about sex offenders, look to the different explanations of motivational factors behind different types of offence, then examine a number of current treatment approaches positioned within a cognitive-behavioural framework, illustrated by a detailed case example.

CLASSIFYING SEX OFFENDERS

Information about sex offenders comes from three main sources. First, the official statistics of sexual offences known to the police give an indication of the rates at which members of the public report different classes of sexual offence. Secondly, surveys of the general population, including groups who have recently been victimised, such as those attending rape crisis centres, provide a better and generally higher estimate of actual levels of sex offending within society. Thirdly, sex offenders themselves, within assessment or treatment, can provide information about the levels at which they had been offending, possibly over many years of an offending career.

Official statistics

Contrary to popular misconception, sexual offences comprise less than 1 per cent of all offences known to the police (Criminal Statistics, 1990). Figure 8.1 illustrates the eight most prevalent offences of (in decreasing frequency known to police) indecent assault on female, rape, indecent assault on male, unlawful sexual intercourse with girl under 16, indecency between males, buggery, gross indecency with a child, and incest.

Figure 8.2 illustrates the way in which sexual offences known to the police have increased over the last ten years for which figures are available, namely at 3.8 per cent per annum. Offences of violence known to the police, in contrast, display a rapid escalation from year to year at a rate of approximately 8.8 per cent per annum. The categories of sexual

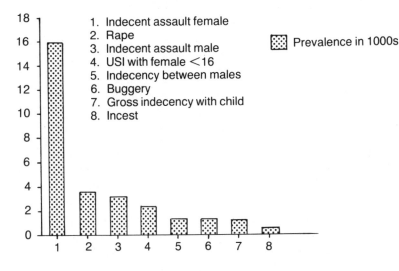

Figure 8.1 Sex offences known to police, 1990

Percentage change

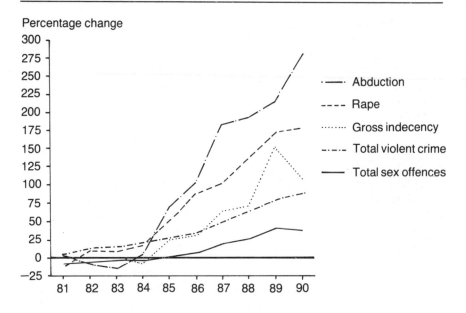

Figure 8.2 Cumulative percentage increases in sex offences known to police, 1981–90

offences known to the police which show rates of increase comparable with or in excess of rates for violent offences are rape, with rates of reported rape increasing at about 18 per cent per annum over the last ten years, and reported gross indecency with children, at 11 per cent per annum over the last six years that this has been recorded, and abduction at 27 per cent per annum.

There have been dramatic changes in public attitudes towards sexual offending over the last ten years or so. These have arisen through a combination of the influence of feminism and the women's movement (e.g. Brownmiller, 1975; Sanday, 1981; Herman, 1990) and as a result of increasing public awareness of, and rejection of, past practices of discrimination and minimisation concerning sexual offending within the police and judicial systems. Rapid recent increases in offences known to the police, as in the case of rape, reflect a combination of two factors – actual levels of offending in society and the reporting of offences to the police.

Victim reports

As far as surveys of the general population are concerned, evidence from this country and the USA suggests that something like one in ten children will be likely to have experienced some form of sexual abuse during childhood (Finkelhor, 1986). Recent findings highlight the possibility that sexual abuse, although more prevalent against girls than boys, may be very dramatically under-reported against boys, with much abuse against boys having come to light with even greater difficulty than that against girls (Jehu, 1991). Not only may agencies be differentially receptive to male and female abuse but also boys and girls may psychologically process this experience differently.

There are many possible reasons for this, including the predatory nature of much sexual abuse against boys outside family situations, perhaps related to the greater freedom which boys may have had to roam away from home, together with the high level of stigma for boys in complaining about having been sexually abused. Being the victim of a sexual assault may be seen as not 'macho' and may for this reason have deterred some young male victims reporting incidents of abuse.

The suggestion has been made that male victims may not only feel less able to report abuse than females, attacking as this does notions of male control over the environment and interpersonal relationships, but may also then go on to integrate in some way the experience of being abused into later patterns of abuse or violence against others. This may relate to findings that about 23–57 per cent of convicted sex offenders have themselves been sexually abused during childhood (Jehu, 1991). This is not of course to imply that all male victims of sexual abuse are likely to offend, but simply that the experience of having been abused is statistically more frequent than expected in offender samples. In contrast, there is no evidence to suggest that women who are sexually abused in childhood go on themselves to abuse.

Rape statistics are also contentious. Lifetime prevalence rates of rape are reported by Resnick and Markaway (1991) to range from about 5 per cent (George and Winfield-Laird, 1986) to 44 per cent (Russell, 1982). However, the work of Koss and colleagues in the USA in surveying members of non-officially recorded offender and victim samples has indicated that sexual offending may not be as easily differentiated from consenting sexual activity as may at first be supposed (Koss and Oros, 1980; Koss et al., 1988). The notion that there is some clear-cut dichotomy between, on the one hand, consenting sexual activity, taking place in the majority of male–female sexual encounters, and, in contrast, a rare and categorically different act, rape, perpetrated by only a minority of men, is challenged by these researchers' findings based upon interviews with both men and women.

The results indicated that women have experienced sexual activity with males across a broad spectrum, from clear-cut assaultative rape by strangers at one end of the continuum, through uses of threats, blackmail, or financial power wielded by men in order to achieve sexual activity, to truly consenting sexual activity freely engaged in by equally powerful partners at the other end of the continuum. Reports from women correspond to a large degree with those obtained from men, who report having used a wide range of coercive techniques during sex. Equally, recent research on both acquaintance rape and marital rape (Koss, 1990) demonstrates once and for all that the notion of the rapist as a dangerous stranger is certainly a myth. This all suggests that reports of rape may be just the tip of the iceberg as far as male sexual aggression against females is concerned.

Offender reports

Turning to the sex offenders themselves, most studies are carried out with incarcerated offenders and are therefore unrepresentative for this reason. Most offenders are not caught and, of those who are, most do not end up in custody. Based upon the victimisation studies, there must be many sex offenders within the community who have not been processed by the legal system. Notwithstanding this, information provided by sex offenders in custody or proceeding through clinical assessment and treatment provides an insight into the very high levels with which some sexual offenders have persisted in their offending. In a study by Abel *et al.* (1987) for example, 561 rapists and child molesters reported having carried out over 200,000 sexual assaults on over 195,000 victims. Clearly, with such high levels of self-reported offending, even minimally effective intervention schemes may well have a significant effect on levels of sexual victimisation within society.

POLICIES AND PERCEPTIONS

The idea of sex offender treatment is one which invariably arouses controversy on many levels.

> 'Why should we provide treatment for offenders after what they have done to victims?'
> 'Sex offenders can never be cured so why should we waste resources on providing treatment for them?'
> 'Treatment just gives sex offenders a lot of excuses for their inexcusable behaviour'.

These are all common 'gut reactions' when sex-offender treatment is discussed within the arenas of public or professional debate. Contained within such questions and statements are a whole range of legitimate concerns which need to be addressed so that informed public debate can occur and coherent and logically consistent public action can be taken.

We should perhaps begin by looking at some key points of principle in working therapeutically with sex offenders. First, it is suggested, a central purpose of sex-offender treatment should be to reduce levels of victimisation in society. Any treatment programme which fails to achieve or jeopardises this principle should be considered a failure. Secondly, treatment should aim to undermine false moral or legal excuses for sex offending. From a moral and legal perspective, the offender alone is responsible for his actions except (as the law stands at present) in those relatively few cases where the offender is categorised under the Mental Health Act (1983) as being mentally disordered, in which case sectioning under the Mental Health Act with appropriate detention and treatment would follow.

Within these two broad principles some more specific questions can be asked. Can we set up treatment initiatives in those various parts of the system through which sex offenders pass – the police, courts, prison, probation and social services, as well as the psychiatric/psychological services which are increasingly called upon to become involved in such cases – such that their offending will be reduced without jeopardy to other legal and social principles? To take an extreme example, society cannot legally execute sex offenders or incarcerate them without review even though such actions may well have an effect on reducing levels of sex offending in society.

In considering the question of the effectiveness of sex-offender treatment programmes, we need to examine two issues: firstly, the context in which treatment occurs and, secondly, the nature and effectiveness of particular forms of intervention. The context of treatment within the United Kingdom, for example, is rather different from that within other countries. In some respects our system works towards effective treatment but in other respects it works against (Howard League, 1985).

Cultural factors

It may be helpful from the point of view of maximising treatment effectiveness to consider those aspects of our system which collude with sex offending or undermine the effectiveness of treatment. A number of themes might be identified, summarised as follows:

a) Sociological studies (e.g. Sanday, 1981) indicate that societies in which rape is most prevalent are characterised by a social legitimisation of violence as a means of problem solving and by male domination, with related negative attitudes towards women. It is left to the reader to judge how far contemporary British society might still be characterised as falling within this general description.

b) There is considerable scope for improvement in the communication and co-ordination between the various agencies which deal with sex offending. Good practice reported from various other countries highlights the way in which a much greater co-ordination between the police, courts, prison, probation, social and medical services could be achieved to secure more comprehensive and valid information about sex offending within society and more effectively engage sex offenders in treatment which does not simply end when the offender passes from one system (e.g. prison) to another (e.g. community).

c) Perhaps related to the above point is the question of the resources, support, and morale of those working in the area of sexual offending. It is a potentially stressful and traumatic area of work in which workers from all disciplines have regularly reported (within training and consultation groups run by the author) feelings of hopelessness, being overwhelmed by the size of the problem, lack of support from management, and an absence of adequate interpersonal support. Under these circumstances, 'burn-out' of staff and associated inefficiency and ineffectiveness of treatment programmes becomes a risk.

d) Although still subject to considerable public and scientific debate, a line of thought with supporting evidence now exists which indicates that depictions of men, women, children, and sexuality within the media generally and within the media sub-set characterised as pornography may well be implicated in some forms of sexual offending (Murrin and Laws, 1990) even though more general, society-wide studies have in the past failed to find a direct link between pornography availability and sexual offence rates (Kutchinsky, 1971).

It is quite likely that the cultural factors outlined in (a) and (d) above have a significant if not major part to play in accounting for the most striking statistic within the area of sexual offending, namely that it is mainly perpetrated by males. As society changes for the better or worse, according to the various criteria that might be applied to this, there will be corresponding changes in the nature and pattern of sex offending. Curtis (1976) some years ago pointed to the possibility that high reported rates of black perpetrators raping white women was a manifestation of the increasing emancipation of both groups within American society and their correspondingly higher levels of mutual interaction within a predominantly white justice system.

Within British society as it exists at present, treatment programmes for sex offenders tend to be directed primarily towards male abusers of children, both within and outside family settings, and male sexual aggressors against women. Reconviction studies indicate that homosexual paedophiles exhibit one of the highest rates of re-offending and this adds weight to their inclusion in any treatment programme (Finkelhor, 1986). An even more highly recidivistic group are indecent exposers who, although rarely subject to the more stringent sanctions of imprisonment or hospitalisation, nevertheless represent a further target group for treatment because of their high levels of offending and their potential, albeit in a small number of cases, to escalate to more violent sexual offending. Rapists form a third target group in that, although reconviction levels are less than for the other two groups, the levels of violence involved and victim trauma are extremely high.

The showing on British television of a documentary series on the work of the Thames Valley Police some years ago is a further example of changing public attitudes and practices. In one episode male officers were seen interrogating a woman reporting having been raped to the point that she became distressed and tearful. This apparently resulted in such an outcry that police procedures were re-examined with national consequences, including improved facilities for, and sensitivity with which police now deal with members of the public reporting sexual victimisation, who are mainly women and children. These changes include the greater availability of specially trained female officers to deal with sex-offence complaints and special suites in which victim interviews are carried out.

Also within the last twenty years, some of the more extreme and unjustifiable public statements made in sex-offence cases have aroused a level of public opposition not previously experienced, and now seem to be less frequently in evidence. Within the judicial arena, phrases such as 'contributory negligence' and 'in the true sense asking for it' (referring to rape victims) hopefully become rarer as public opinion is increasingly sensitised to their inappropriateness.

The changing public climate towards sex offences is also manifested in the massive increase in publicity and information about child sexual abuse. Programmes of anti-abuse education and training have been introduced into many schools (Elliott, 1985). Subtle, but no less important, are the ways in which public attitudes and statements about sexual offending against women and children are gradually changing. For example, it was only twenty years ago that the Paedophile Information Exchange, a group advocating sex with children, almost seemed to have a respectable platform within public debate.

Most first convictions for sex offending are not repeated. The probability of reconvicton for a sexual offence after a first sexual conviction is statistically very low. However, once two or more sexual convictions are recorded against an offender, the probability of his continuing to offend increases dramatically. Long-term follow-up studies of sexual offenders indicate that follow-up periods of twenty-five years or more are needed in order to make realistic estimates about changes in sexual-offending patterns (Furby et al., 1989).

TYPOLOGICAL RESEARCH

One of the important issues in working with sex offenders is the question

of determining underlying causes and motivations for their sexual behaviour, and in this light sex-offender typologies which aim to establish
sub-groups based on clusters of shared characteristics between offenders
have evolved. Descriptive or typological research is of relevance not only
in terms of knowing what might be expected from particular offender
groups but also in designing appropriate treatment programmes. The
results of research on large samples of sex offenders provide what are in
effect checklists of potentially relevant points to cover in working therapeutically with the individual offender.

Child sexual abuse

One of the most accepted views is that of Finkelhor (1984), who proposed
a model of child sexual abuse which involved a sequential system of four
pre-conditions for offending to occur, each pre-condition representing a
characteristic of the offender or offender–victim relationship. These four
pre-conditions, which may also prove to have relevance to the process of
rape, might be summarised as:

a) some motivation to abuse a child sexually
b) overcoming internal inhibitions against acting on that motivation
c) overcoming external impediments to committing sexual abuse
d) undermining or overcoming the child's resistance to the sexual abuse.

(A more psychoanalytically orientated account of sexual abuse is
presented by Stephen Frosh, Chapter 2, this volume.)

Rape

Typological studies of rapists have tended to emphasise the importance
of sexual, social, and aggressive (power- or anger-related) motives in the
generation of rapist 'types' (e.g. Cohen *et al.*, 1971; Seghorn and Cohen,
1980; Groth and Birnbaum, 1979). Typically, three, four, or five rapist
'types' are generated.

Groth and Birnbaum (1979) distinguished between anger-motivated,
power-motivated, and sadistically motivated offences. A similar typological classification, described by Cohen *et al.* (1971) and Seghorn and
Cohen (1980), proposed the following motivational types:

a) *Compensatory*
   Here the motivation for the offence is primarily sexual. The offender is
   seeking sexual gratification from the victim and generally only uses as
   much force as is necessary to achieve this. Such offenders typically
   have social/sexual relationship difficulties which have resulted in
   normal sexual relationships being difficult for them to achieve.

b) *Displaced aggression*

Here the offender is motivated by anger or hatred, the sexual aspect of the offence being simply one means of hurting or degrading the victim. Typically more force than is needed to commit the sexual act will be used and it may be directed towards a particular type of victim, e.g. prostitutes, older women, or those perceived to be of higher social status. These offenders typically have histories of poor relationships with women and offending may be preceded by conflicts with females in their lives.

c) *Sadistic*

Here the motivation for the offence is sexual but the offender derives sexual gratification by inflicting pain and fear on the victim. As with the 'displaced aggression' offender, the sadistic offender will use more violence than necessary to achieve sexual acts, but, unlike the displaced aggression offender, the violence will appear more cold and deliberate and may culminate in sexually motivated murder.

d) *Impulsive/opportunistic*

These offenders typically have histories of various forms of anti-social behaviour and obtaining sex by force is yet another example of a generally impulsive and delinquent life-style. Sex offences are often committed in the course of some other activity such as burglary or non-sexual violence.

The work of Knight and Prentky (1987) has attempted to extend such classifications by developing a sub-classification system based on a sequential consideration of the following questions for each offence:

a) What is the meaning of the aggression in the offence?
Is it 'instrumental' (e.g. for controlling victim resistance) or 'expressive' (e.g. satisfying a desire for power)?

b) What is the meaning of the sexuality in the offence?
For the 'instrumentally aggressive' offenders, is it 'compensatory' (e.g. making the offender feel better about his own sexual identity) or 'exploitative' (e.g. delinquent and predatory)?
For the 'expressively aggressive' offenders, is it 'displaced anger' (e.g. from a girlfriend to a stranger) or 'sadistic' (e.g. deriving sexual pleasure from others' fear and pain)?

c) Finally, for the four above sub-classifications, is the impulsivity in the offender's history and life-style 'high' or 'low'?

This then produces eight sub-types.

Prentky *et al.*'s (1987) validation study had not at that stage confirmed the validity of these sub-groups, but did report relationships between some groupings and certain childhood factors. For example, 'exploitative rapists' typically used physical aggression after rape, had been drinking, committed offences around conventional social settings (e.g. bars), tended to have histories of non-intact parental marriages, childhood physical abuse, and juvenile crime.

Other studies have yielded complementary or overlapping motivational systems to those described above. Scully and Marolla (1985), for example, suggested five types of rape motivation, the first four of which might be summarised as sexually motivated, power motivated, revenge motivated, or rape incidental to other offences, and are therefore similar to a number of other classification systems. The fifth motive was described as 'recreational' and based largely on adventure seeking, often in groups.

Sexual homicide

Burgess *et al.* (1986) proposed a social-developmental and fantasy-based motivational model for sexual homicide consisting of five interacting components. These were impaired development of attachments in early life, formative traumatic events, patterned responses that serve to generate fantasies, a private internal world consumed by violent thoughts which leave the person isolated and self-preoccupied, and a feedback filter that sustains repetitive patterns of thinking.

Prentky *et al.* (1989) examined the role of fantasy as an internal drive mechanism for repetitive acts of sexual violence. They obtained information from official records on twenty-five serial sexual murderers in the USA with more than three known victims each, compared with seventeen single sexual murderers. They found that the serial murderers had a higher incidence of paraphilias (i.e. sexual deviations), higher incidence of documented or self-reported violent fantasies, as well as an organised rather than disorganised pattern of crime. MacCulloch *et al.* (1983) in the UK also studied the role of fantasy among a group of sexual sadists, and suggested that fantasy rehearsal of offences is a common and important component in the escalation of offending.

Similarly, Leyton (1983) identified certain sociological features that he felt to be characteristic of sexual mass murderers. He found that their families were characterised by extreme disruption, for example, adoption, illegitimacy, institutionalisation, having a brother or father charged with violence, and having a mother who had married three or more times. He found that these variables occurred in 20 per cent of the normal population but in 90 per cent of sexual mass murderers.

Ressler *et al.* (1988) in their group of sexual homicides again found a long-standing preoccupation and preference for an active fantasy life involving thoughts and fantasies of sexualised violence. They found that most of the fantasies prior to the first murder focused on killing, whereas fantasies subsequent to the murder focused on perfecting various aspects of the offence.

ANALYSIS OF SEX OFFENDING

Approaches to sex-offender assessment have changed over time. Early work with sex offenders tended to emphasise the need to understand how the sex offender's behaviour had developed and gave therapeutic predominance to insight-developing psychotherapy. Later work, recognising the limitations in this approach, focused more on breaking current cycles of offending. Each approach on its own is unlikely to be the full solution to helping sex offenders change. A comprehensive system of data gathering and analysis which incorporates both approaches is the most likely path to success.

Feldman (1977) drew attention to the distinction between *offence acquisition* – the accumulation of factors from early childhood onwards which set the scene for later offending patterns – and *offence maintenance* – those factors in the offender's contemporary environment which trigger off and which reinforce the tendency to continue offending. Factors which lead to the acquisition of sex offending may be quite different from those factors which maintain the offending within the offender's current cycle of behaviour. Effective treatment for sex offenders depends on obtaining as full an understanding as possible of their offending, on both the *acquisition* and *maintenance* phases of their offending.

Sex-offence acquisition

Typical of factors related to sex-offending acquisition are sexual incidents which result in the subsequent sexualisation of normally non-sexual stimuli (e.g. young children) or acts (e.g. violence). For some offenders these early sexual incidents might involve being the victim of sexual abuse but this is not always the case. Only a small proportion of individuals sexually abused as children go on to abuse others. Most sexual abuse results in a heightened risk of subsequent abuse and suffering for the victim (Finkelhor, 1986).

For other offenders, these childhood sexual incidents do not involve having been abused, but involve a whole variety of other early sexual memories which appear to have preceded the development of sexual deviations associated with subsequent offending. These range from the chance exposure to sexual imagery or activities through to the development of a whole philosophy of interpersonal relationships in which sexual offending is seen as normal, harmless, or justifiable.

Sex-offence maintenance

For an understanding of the factors maintaining an offender's behaviour, the procedure of functional analysis is particularly relevant. The offender's offence behaviour (B) is examined in terms of its antecedents (A) and its consequences (C). This analysis can yield information on various levels of the offender's functioning, along the lines of Lazarus's (1976) *'multi-modal analysis'*. For sex offenders, particularly relevant levels of analysis which might be proposed are:

behavioural, i.e. what the offender and others within the immediate circumstances of the offence were doing at the time

cognitive, i.e. what was going through the offender's mind before, during, and after the offending – the kind of 'self talk' in which he was engaging

attitudinal, i.e. what attitudes held by the offender were particularly in the forefront of his thinking around the time of his offending

emotional, i.e. how the offender was feeling prior to and after his offending – angry, depressed, etc.

physical condition, i.e. the physical state of the offender at the time of his offending, for example, effects of drink or drugs, hunger or lack of sleep

personal relationships, i.e. how the offender was relating to other people before and after his offending

sexual interests, i.e. the extent to which the offender is sexually aroused by material or fantasies related to offence behaviour as opposed to consenting adult sexual behaviour, as well as

opportunities for offending in which the offender might find himself or create for himself through, in Laws' (1990) terms, the 'apparently irrelevant decisions' he makes.

In addition to its use within a functional analysis, multi-modal analysis can also be used as a linking system between information about the offender's development (acquisition phase) and the behavioural analysis of his offending (maintenance phase). Some themes in the history, e.g. poor temper control (at the level of emotions) or distorted beliefs about women (at the cognitive level), may also become relevant in the maintenance of offending.

Antecedents and consequences on the various levels of multi-modal analysis each represent a potential focus for therapeutic input. 'Vicious circles' in the cycle of offending can also be identified. For example, alcohol (which might precede offending as a result of its disinhibiting effects) might also become a consequence (with the offender using alcohol to cope with anxiety or guilt). Breaking into such vicious circles can be effective therapeutically.

Use of multi-modal functional analysis yields a number of advantages for assessment and treatment. This system:

a) provides a baseline for reassessment, in that the factors associated with the maintenance of offending are clearly set out within the framework and their subsequent presence or absence is an index of how far the offender has changed in ways which are relevant to his likely future offending.

b) identifies treatment objectives, in that each antecedent and each consequence is in effect a treatment target.

c) splits treatment between institution and community. Those working with sex offenders in the community and in custody often debate what and how much can be done in these different settings. The functional analysis provides a kind of shared agenda for action in the two settings, e.g. deviant sexual interests might be best tackled while the offender is in custody whereas the most potent ingredient of therapy for marital relationship or alcohol abuse problems might occur when the offender is back in the community.

d) provides a rationale for group therapy. Often sex offender groups are set up on the basis that it is somehow a good idea to get groups of similar offenders together, perhaps using as the main criterion for group membership the legal offence category, e.g. a rapists' group or an incest offenders' group. Not only does this beg the question of the relevance of these legal categories to defining group membership, it also fails to address the question of the purpose of such groups. From the functional analysis of a group of potential treatment candidates, themes such as a need for anger control, social skills, sex education, etc., can be identified. These can then form the basis of a series of parallel, thematically distinct and relevant groups.

e) helps overcome denial and hopelessness by encouraging client participation in the process of assessment and treatment. Unlike some other systems, multi-modal functional analysis is at its best an explicit contract of interaction between therapist and client in which the *therapy benefits* from sharing of information about the processes of offending and behaviour change have a major part to play.

In summary, there are two main advantages to this system of analysis:

comprehensiveness – the approach enables the systematic bringing together of information about the offender's behaviour which also enables gaps in that information set to be identified, e.g. cognitive antecedent to offending not known, emotional consequence of offending not known, etc.

relevance – the data assembled in this way are relevant to offending behaviour. One danger in setting up treatment programmes is to make the false assumption that, because an offender displays a particular deficiency, e.g. lack of social skills, this deficiency necessarily requires treatment. If the lack of social skills is not instrumental in his offending (e.g. an antecedent), as would be ascertained by the behavioural analysis, then it may not only be irrelevant to treat it but may even be counter-productive. A socially inadequate exhibitionist could conceivably become a more socially confident rapist if social skills training were the only therapeutic intervention.

THE CONTEXT OF TREATMENT

The extent to which society deals with sex offenders by custody varies according to the offence committed. Most men convicted of rape can expect to receive a custodial sentence, whilst most of those convicted for indecent exposure will receive a non-custodial disposal. However, if sexual offending which would not normally receive a custodial disposal persists, the courts may eventually turn to custodial disposals in order to try and deal with the problem (Howard League, 1985).

Most convicted sexual offenders are not mentally disordered under the terms of the Mental Health Act 1983 and for these a custodial disposal will mean imprisonment. Approximately 5 per cent of the prison population are sex offenders. A small minority of convicted sexual offenders are, however, deemed to be suffering from mental disorder (usually psychopathic disorder) and may as a result be hospitalised in a regional secure unit or indeterminately in a special hospital. In these cases, the offender will not be discharged into the community until the authorities are satisfied that the mental disorder (psychopathic disorder) has ameliorated and the offender's dangerousness has declined to a degree that the public is no longer at risk.

In general terms, incarcerated sexual offenders comprise those sent to prison, where there was until recently no formal or systematic requirement for treatment to be carried out. There are and have been over the years a number of local initiatives on the treatment of sex offenders in prison but these have tended to come and go with the individuals responsible for setting them up. Until recently, the Prison Service position on this was that, whilst not actively seeking to set up sex-offender treatment programmes nationally, it nevertheless supported such local initiatives as had been developed.

At the time of writing, it looks possible that the currently higher public profile in support of treating sex offenders for the purpose of reducing victimisation in society may have influenced the Home Office and the Prison Service to place sex-offender treatment higher on the agenda of priorities. A comprehensive programme of sex-offender assessment with subsequent allocation to brief or more complex treatment programmes, according to risk and to need, is currently being set up within the Prison Service. (Outcome evaluation built into this programme commenced in 1991.)

The context in which treatment occurs can be as important in determining outcome as the treatment itself. Much within the current British justice system inadvertently fosters offender denial. Upon apprehension, offenders will typically attempt to deny or minimise their offending in the hope of gaining non-custodial disposals. Such denial or minimisation is again reinforced at the stage of imprisonment where sex offenders in custody are typically subjected to verbal or physical abuse from other inmates.

Even the prison system's own management of sex offenders has in the past inadvertently encouraged offenders to deny or minimise their offending by moving them to more distant prisons where the true nature of their offences can more easily be denied. Whilst this had a positive function in avoiding victimisation from fellow prisoners, it also had a negative effect on treatment, a key element of which must be at least some acknowledgement by the offender of what he has done and that it is wrong.

The prison context to the treatment of sex offenders stands in contrast to that of the special hospitals and regional secure units. The function of these hospitals is to contain dangerous, mentally disordered individuals, including sex offenders, in the case of the special hospitals without limit of time, and to provide appropriate treatments until it is safe for them to be discharged. Valid information about the sex offender/patient's needs, problems and past offending is central to his/her successful movement through the hospital and out into the community. There are three such special hospitals in England and Wales, Broadmoor in Berkshire, Ashworth in Liverpool, and Rampton in Nottinghamshire.

The facts (a) that hospitalisation has treatment as one of its primary aims and (b) that the length of hospitalisation can be indeterminate, depending on response to treatment, are major contextual differences from the prison system. Even the most uncooperative sex offender in a secure psychiatric hospital will generally come to see that unless his problems are addressed he will not move on. Coming to realise this eventually results in co-operation and attitude/behaviour change for most sex offender patients.

APPROACHES TO TREATMENT

Literature on the treatment of sex offenders can be broadly divided into:

a) that concerned with helping the offender gain insight into the origins his offending, and

b) that helping him to control or remove those influences which maintain the offending.

Given the complex nature of sexual offences, interventions focused on both the acquisition and maintenance phases of offending are likely to be needed if treatment is to be effective and the offender is to control his offending. It may be that prior to the commencement of treatment, insufficient is known about what precisely happens during and around the time of offending. A comprehensive analysis might only be established after integrating within a preliminary analysis additional data from many more interviews with the offender as well as from other sources, including information which unfolds during the course of psychotherapy. Multi-modal functional analysis can be a useful framework for this process.

Traditionally, approaches to sex-offender treatment tended to follow the course of a broadly dynamic psychotherapeutic model with its roots in Freudian psychoanalysis. Offenders would recount aspects of their past history including incidents which may have precipitated them into a sex-offending life-style. Insight-developing psychotherapy, it was hoped, would help offenders understand the origins of their offending and through this come to control their behaviour.

Research evidence shows that the effectiveness of dynamic psychotherapy alone with sex offenders is poor, however, and such approaches have increasingly given way to cognitive-behavioural approaches to the problem. Within this alternative framework, attention is focused primarily on the sex offender's contemporary patterns of offending behaviour. Specific antecedents to sexual offending are identified through a combination of interview and official report information. So too are the precise offence acts committed and the subsequent actions of the offender together with the consequences for him of having offended. From this, the precise patterns of reinforcement (rewards and punishments) maintaining the offender's behaviour can be identified.

From this identification of 'triggering' antecedents of the sex offending and its maintaining contingencies, specific interventions can be designed to address each particular antecedent and consequence of a particular offender's offences.

Early work in applying behavioural approaches to sex offenders tended to be rather simplistic, often focusing exclusively on deviant sexual fantasies and their manifestation in the sexual offence, or perhaps on inadequate social skills and their role in preventing the offender from achieving consenting adult legal alternatives to offence behaviour. Whilst both of these themes are clearly relevant to many offenders, these alone may well be insufficient to form a comprehensive behavioural analysis of the offender's behaviour.

Treatment techniques used with sex offenders can, like those for other behaviour problems, be categorised in various ways, notably:

a) by treatment goals – e.g. modify deviant sexual interests, improve appropriate social skills, etc.;
b) by the type of therapeutic model being employed – e.g. psychodynamic, behavioural, environmental, etc.;
c) by the levels of functioning which may need to be addressed, along the lines of Lazarus's (1976) above-mentioned multi-modal analysis.

TREATMENT TECHNIQUES

The ultimate aim of most reported work on sex-offender treatment is a reduction in the dangerousness or frequency of sex offending after treatment compared with what it would have been without treatment. Of the specific treatment techniques employed with sex offenders a broad distinction can be drawn between treatment goals related to:

a) deviant sexual interests,
b) socio-sexual behaviour,
c) attitudes, beliefs, and thinking,
d) motivation and denial,
e) relapse prevention.

Deviant sexual interests

Where offenders are sexually aroused by deviant acts (e.g. sadism) or by other than consenting adult partners (e.g. children), these deviant interests can be assessed by a combination of self-report, behavioural and psychophysiological assessment. Abel *et al.* (1985) reported how self-reported sexual interest and penile plethysmograph (PPG) results coincided in only 30 per cent of offenders assessed even when complete confidentiality was assured. When the remaining 70 per cent of the offenders were confronted with this discrepancy, 70 per cent of these (i.e. 49 per cent of the total sample) revised their self-reports in the direction of the PPG assessment.

Psychophysiological assessment at Broadmoor special hospital involves a combination of penile plethysmograhic (PPG), heart-rate (HR), and galvanic skin responses (GSR). Penile plethysmography has an important part to play in assessing sadistic, paedophilic, and other deviant sexual interests with many sex offenders. As well as helping the patient accept his sexual interest patterns prior to treatment, such PPG assessments can also be useful in monitoring treatment and, in combination with other data, provide some pointers to possible future risk factors.

At Broadmoor, we have been involved in assessing many patients who have at the time of assessment denied the presence of current deviant sexual interests. In some of these cases, PPG results have indicated the presence of sexual interest in the deviant material and this has been very helpful in encouraging the patient to acknowledge this aspect of his problems. In some cases the acknowledgement has occurred with very little discussion once the PPG has been completed. This has then enabled therapeutic work to be carried out.

In addition to this, the very process of discussing with patients the implications of PPG assessments has unlocked various facts, ideas, and feelings relevant to the therapeutic process. This has proved of value over and above the PPG results themselves. For example, some patients mention current deviant interests which they had hitherto not disclosed, others refer to concerns about possible re-offending after transfer, and so on.

Not all patients consent to PPG assessment and not all will respond to this form of assessment, due to anxiety, low sexual drive, or other factors. Our policy has been to explain as fully as possible to patients the options open to them and the likely range of consequences flowing from these options, with the final decision about participating being left to the patient. Agreement to participate is recorded on a consent form.

It is very important for PPG results to be seen in the context of other relevant assessment information and not viewed simply on their own. PPG only measures physiological sexual reactions to stimuli and cannot necessarily be generalised beyond this to imply whether or not the patient would act upon these sexual interests. Acting out sexual interests has as much to do with attitudes, self-controls, personality style, etc. There is a danger of PPG results being over-emphasised in decision making, possibly because they appear to be a very 'technical' kind of output. Like other clinical data they are subject to error but nevertheless have an important part to play in a total assessment.

Some research attention has been focused on the issue of faking, which appears to be easier for subjects to achieve with less 'powerful' stimuli such as slides. Video material is generally more likely to elicit sexual responses but there are also potential problems with video material, including (a) the problem of obtaining stimulus material specific enough (whilst yet being ethically acceptable) for the offence behaviour being assessed and (b) the danger of showing subjects material of greater deviance than that to which they had previously been exposed (with corresponding risks of 'corruption' or claims of corruption). We take these factors into account in conducting assessments.

PPGs have been carried out on males who have not been convicted of sexual offences, and there is some evidence that a minority of non-offender males are sexually responsive to deviant material, such as paedophilic and rape scenarios, without their necessarily acting upon such interests. This reinforces the notion that PPG results alone cannot indicate likelihood of offending. However, the presence of deviant sexual interests in a proportion of the general male population does not invalidate the use of the procedure with offenders in that the presence of deviant sexual interests, albeit along with other factors, is likely to be an important factor contributing to whether or not re-offending will occur.

Treatment at the level of sexual interests involves decreasing deviant, and increasing non-deviant interests. Available evidence points to the relevance of orgasmic reconditioning, covert sensitisation, and (electrical or olfactory) aversion therapy (Marshall et al., 1990). Not all offenders will require this, however, and the distinction between those offenders who require such interventions in order to avoid future offending and those who do not is one of the most important distinctions in designing therapy programmes.

Of the techniques used for treating deviant sexual interests, the literature reports successful outcomes for:

Aversion therapy

Aversion therapy, in which material depicting deviant imagery or prompting deviant thoughts is paired with unpleasant consequences, has been used in many treatment programmes for sex offenders. Developed originally from conditioning principles, the procedure has varied by paradigm (types and schedules of reinforcement), by stimulus materials used (slides, video depictions, or audio descriptions for example), and by aversive stimuli used (electric shock, unpleasant smells, etc.).

Covert sensitisation

Unpleasant imagery has also been used, as in the covert sensitisation procedure pioneered by Cautela (1967). Here the offender is helped to imagine a scene of relevance to his offending (e.g. walking to a school with the intention of finding a child to assault), following which he imagines some unpleasant consequence such as being arrested.

Recent reports on the use of covert sensitisation have tended to emphasise the use of both negative imagined consequences for imagined offence behaviour and also positive consequences for imagined alternatives to the offending (Salter, 1988). Salter describes how these positive imagined consequences of non-offending can be cognitive (e.g. 'I made it. I can be in control'), social ('I'm home with my wife and family. I'm not afraid of anyone knocking on the door with something to tell them. I don't have anything to hide'), or material ('I'm having dinner in a restaurant and thinking "no more prison food for me"').

Orgasmic reconditioning

Marquis (1970) successfully introduced a procedure termed orgasmic reconditioning, also referred to as masturbatory conditioning, in which the offender replaces deviant with non-deviant masturbation fantasies. This positive reinforcement procedure was based on the association between early masturbatory imagery and subsequent sexual behaviour, as reported by McGuire *et al.* (1965).

Successful results with the procedure have been reported by Abel *et al.* (1973) with a patient with sadistic fantasies, Marshall (1973), using a combination of aversion therapy and orgasmic reconditioning with a group of child molesters, and Marshall *et al.* (1977) with a group of incarcerated sex offenders.

Socio-sexual behaviour

Social skills

In addition to the deviant sexual interests which sex offenders may exhibit, they may also present with problems of social and sexual relationships and attitudes. Many offenders are either anxious in, or lack, the skills to function satisfactorily with other adults, or they may possess attitudes and modes of thinking about relationships which propel them towards further offending and away from legal alternatives (Overholser and Beck, 1986; Lipton *et al.*, 1987; Baxter *et al.*, 1986).

Both group and individual social-skills training for sexual offenders has been reported. Rehearsal and feedback on role-played interactions relevant to the offender's behaviour patterns are the central feature of the approach, this often being supplemented by coaching and modelling by the therapists, other offenders undergoing the training, or specially prepared training material.

Sexual skills and knowledge

Other more direct approaches to developing appropriate sexual behaviour have been reported. Cole (1982), for example, reported how 'surrogate therapy', in which sexually inexperienced males were guided to successful sexual intercourse with therapist aides, resulted in improved social skills and confidence which was maintained if the experiences were reinforced by real-life successes after treatment. Cole's sample was not by and large sexually deviant or sexual offenders, and there would remain reservations about this procedure with offenders who may be disordered on many more levels of a multi-modal analysis than Cole's subjects.

Sex education has been an issue addressed by a number of workers who have noted the lack of sexual knowledge of many sex offenders in prison (Woodward, 1980) and other residential settings (Wyre, 1989). It is also one of the major themes of assessment and treatment now addressed with sex offenders in special hospitals (Grounds *et al.*, 1987).

Attitudes, beliefs, and thinking

Group therapy

There have been various reports on the use of group therapy with sex offenders. Some groups in the USA have involved offenders being pressurised into attending to avoid police prosecution – e.g. Matthis and Collins (1970) with indecent exposers and Hartman (1965a, 1965b) with paedophiles. Hartman's approach emphasised group support, reality testing, and controlling deviant sexual urges. Resnick and Peters (1967) carried out group work with child molesters referred by the courts. Therapeutic elements in their approach again included peer support together with exploration of relationships with women, attitudes towards authority, and self-esteem.

Costell and Yalom (1972) reported a group programme directed towards impulse control for sex offenders in a maximum security hospital. Reference was made to the problems involving the morale of long-term patients in treatment and the dual role of staff as therapists and agents of control, issues which are common to many treatment programmes in long-term custodial settings.

Quayle (1989), at Broadmoor special hospital, reported on the use of a series of groups for young adult male patients diagnosed as suffering from 'psychopathic disorder', many of whom had committed sex offences or sexually motivated acts of violence. Patients progress from basic social-skills-training groups into groups within which they take part in 'family sculpting' (to uncover and work on past family relationships) and reverse role playing, in which they come to see their past offending through the eyes of their victims.

Motivation and denial

Offenders' motivation to change well-established patterns of behaviour may be mixed. There may be denial of facts ('I didn't do it'), of implications of those facts ('It did no harm') and of responsibility for what happened ('It was her fault'). Offenders may perceive various advantages, in addition to the obvious disadvantages, for persisting in their offence behaviour.

In any form of psychotherapy it is generally accepted that the client should give his/her informed consent to what takes place, i.e. that the therapist should:

a) be clear that the client is physically and mentally competent to give informed consent, and
b) make the client aware of the advantages and disadvantages of the proposed treatment, including its risks and alternatives.

Perkins (1991), in working with sex offenders in prison, community, and special hospital settings, distinguished between the processes of *negotiation* and of *persuasion* in addressing sex-offender motivation and co-operation in treatment. Negotiation is defined as that process of interaction with the offender (about the need for treatment, sticking with a particular treatment initiative, etc.) in which the therapist has some potential control over outcomes within the offender's life. Examples here might be where the therapist is preparing a report for the court (in cases where the offender is in the community), for the Parole Board (in cases where the offender is in prison), or for the information of the Home Office (in cases where a mentally disordered offender is indeterminately hospitalised).

The process of persuasion is defined in terms of interactions with the offender, devoid of these negotiating possibilities, in which the therapist seeks to discuss with the offender the benefits of treatment and disadvantages of non-treatment given the offender's goals for his life. Controversy can arise as to whether this is a legitimate or an illegitimate process for the therapist to use. Those who claim that it is illegitimate point to dangers of the therapist coercing the offender into treatments in which he would otherwise not wish to be participate and thereby violating his right freely to give or withhold consent to treatment. Those who claim that the use of persuasion as defined above is legitimate point to the fact that truly *informed* consent should involve a full appraisal by the offender of all options surrounding both treatment and non-treatment, and that it is not only legitimate but highly desirable for the therapist to ensure that the offender has fully considered *all* implications of *all* options before him. In doing this, and in addressing the barriers of denial and minimisation with which sex offenders often present, the therapist may have to draw on a range of techniques in order to 'get the message across' to the offender so that he may make a truly informed choice.

With these potential difficulties in mind, the question arises next as to what strategies and skills are necessary to break through these barriers to treatment of denial and low motivation to change. These might be said to fall under three broad headings:

a) the structure of the functional analysis – i.e. it may well be possible to

build up a comprehensive analysis of the offender's offence behaviour from interviews, documentary evidence and other material as
to why and how the offender behaves as he does. As inconsistencies
and gaps in his story begin to emerge denial can be gradually challenged.
b) persuasion – i.e. the way in which the therapist couches the options
available to the offender can play a central role in whether, or how
fully, the offender co-operates in treatment. Put more extremely, some
offenders can sometimes be persuaded into treatment, even where
there are no external pressures such as impending court cases or
parole hearings bearing down upon them, simply by the use of
various techniques of persuasion. Most therapists tend to do this, even
if unsystematically or non-explicitly, although not all will
acknowledge this as a part of their treatment approach.
c) negotiation – i.e. the ability of the therapist to vary outcomes for the
offender within the context in which therapy occurs. Again most
therapists tend to do this, albeit sometimes unsystematically and incidentally to their treatment. Sometimes there may be attempts to link
this with the offender's co-operation in treatment. Amongst the
contingencies which the therapist may choose to highlight with the
offender are the fact that a failure to change offence behaviour may
result in continued hospitalisation or loss of family relationships.

Discussions of such issues are not threats from the therapist in that
they are already facts in the offender's life irrespective of the
therapist's actions. The therapist is simply drawing the offender's
attention to these contingencies, discussing all possibilities with him
and, ideally, offering constructive solutions which might be open to
the offender to help him both control his offending and achieve his
other legitimate aims.

Bancroft (1979) alludes to such techniques in his paper on 'the nature of
the patient–therapist relationship' in the behavioural treatment of
offenders. Other strategies have been suggested (Perkins, 1991) from the
specific area of working with sex offenders (Perkins, 1984, 1986, 1987).
Amongst those which have been most successful in engaging therapeutically with sex offenders are, under the above-mentioned categories of
persuasion and negotiation:

Persuasion

a) establish common goals with the offender: start from where the
offender is prepared to accept change, even if this means accepting a
lesser level of commitment or insight than ideal;
b) always keep the purpose of intervention in mind: guide interviews
with 'open' questions (who, what, when, where, why, how) but pin

down facts with 'closed' questions. Accept that not all facts will be elicited at once: be prepared to come back to potentially threatening topics;

c) clarify, but do not challenge the offender's beliefs too early: positively reinforce rather than punish revelations. Pick the right time to challenge offence-related thinking, i.e. once data gathering is at an advanced stage;

d) make reference to likely offence scenarios: this can help unblock offenders too anxious or ashamed to describe details, e.g. 'There are often two main reasons why people have committed your sort of offence [spell this out with examples – e.g. sexual deviance versus social inadequacy explanations]. Which do you think most applies to you?' Sometimes offenders will give clues to which might apply to them by their verbal and non-verbal responses to these descriptions;

e) the use of a casual approach to potentially threatening questions, e.g. an off-the-cuff, low-key style of questioning, perhaps whilst looking away from the offender, can sometimes work well;

f) do not persist with advice to argumentative or rationalising clients. Rather, attempt to place them in the position of making suggestions for therapy, and reinforce good suggestions;

g) make sure that the, particularly uncooperative, offender attributes as many good therapeutic ideas as possible to himself rather than to the therapist: the therapist can facilitate this by making references to, for example, 'your good idea from last week's session';

h) stress the 'togetherness' of therapy with co-operative clients: use of terms like 'we could' rather than 'you should' can help with this. However, be careful to avoid assuming personal responsibility for the offender's problems.

Negotiation

a) provide the client with information relevant to the process of becoming committed to behaviour change, e.g. types of treatment options available and the consequences of no treatment;

b) make the client aware of reinforcement contingencies operating outside the therapy situation, e.g. the likelihood of further imprisonment, loss of contact with family if offending continues;

c) capitalise on the principle of 'cognitive dissonance' (Festinger, 1957) by encouraging the client to view treatment as his choice: in this way genuine attitude change at the end of treatment is likely to be maximised;

d) capitalise on any short-term external reinforcers to treatment which might be available, e.g. improving relationships with relevant others in the institution or community.

To give but three examples by way of illustration, if we imagine a sex offender, a rapist perhaps, entering prison and being interviewed by the therapist with a view to ascertaining if the offender wishes to engage in any kind of treatment, the following scenario might unfold. The offender may claim that, although he has been convicted of rape, he is not really guilty of rape in as much as the woman in question was 'mainly to blame' and that the offence 'probably did no harm' anyway. A natural temptation in such situations might be to begin addressing these distorted perceptions/minimisation from the outset, with the consequent risk of the offender finding the early interactions punitive and thereby removing himself from therapeutic contact altogether.

An alternative strategy might be to note the distorted perceptions/ denial for later targeting within treatment, if the offender eventually agrees to this, and then to move on to a process of simply eliciting more and more information from the offender in connection with these perceptions and his offence behaviour. Typically, as increasing amounts of information are elicited, inconsistencies and contradictions begin to appear which can then be targeted for cognitive intervention. Through this process, offenders can quite often come to see that their reasoning is illogical and ultimately against their own life goals.

Turning to a second technique within this same scenario, the offender may come to a position where he accepts that some form of treatment is necessary but may find it difficult to articulate the particular aspects of his sexual interests and fantasies. Simply to keep asking the offender what these are may result in a repetition of the unhelpful response 'I can't remember' or 'They are normal'. It may be that the offender wishes to conceal details of his sexual interests because he feels this will put him in a better light for subsequent parole reports, etc.; it may be that he is too ashamed to describe his fantasies in a detailed way, believing that they are unique to him. The strategy we have termed 'likely scenarios' enables a set of likely possibilities to be described to the offender in a non-emotive way that quite often enables him to acknowledge one or other possibility. It is as if the process of acknowledging the deviation is made a little easier for him by hearing the words come first from the therapist's mouth rather than his. There is clearly the danger here of words being put into the offender's mouth and it would be important where information has been elicited in this way to corroborate the disclosure by reference to subsequent descriptions by the offender and testing his statements with other questions and comments at different times.

Thirdly, and again within the same scenario, there may be some treatment options appropriate for the particular problems elicited from the offender, but he may have some reservations about opting into these. A technique sometimes referred to as 'delayed compliance' often seems to encourage offenders to opt into particular therapeutic programmes. The essence of delayed compliance in this context is that, rather than attempting to persuade the offender into an immediate acceptance of treatment, the various options would be put to him and he would be specifically advised that there is 'no need to decide immediately'. Quite often, taking the pressure off the offender in this way results in his preparedness to opt into, rather than resist treatment.

Once an offender has embarked upon treatment, the task is to help him do what is necessary to achieve his therapy goals despite his own defences. In attempting to do this the therapist treads a difficult line between legitimate discussion with the offender and illegitimate coercion of the offender into adopting goals and carrying out procedures with which he fundamentally disagrees.

Relapse prevention

One relatively new approach to sex-offender treatment which has been developed through the work of Pithers *et al.* (1983, 1989) and Laws (1990) is that of relapse prevention, a concept introduced into the area of sex-offender treatment from work with drug and alcohol abusers. For many years, those working with alcohol and drug addiction have known the importance of identifying, in advance of treatment termination, factors within the lives of the patients which would be likely to precipitate a relapse into further drug or alcohol abuse.

Relapse-prevention work has established that such factors precipitating relapse predominantly fall into the areas of *social pressure*, i.e. other individuals in the life of the patient prompting or encouraging him/her into situations likely to be associated with relapse; *negative emotional states*, i.e. feelings of anxiety or depression which in the past may have been ameliorated by recourse to drug or alcohol abuse; and the patient him/herself moving, not necessarily in a totally active or conscious way, into *high-risk situations* in which relapse would be more likely.

All three of these factors seemed to those working with sex offenders to be potentially relevant to addressing the high levels of relapse or re-offending in this client group in the same way as had occurred with the drug and alcohol addicts. Laws and Pithers have developed these ideas into a systematic and integrated approach within a broadly cognitive-behavioural framework of assessment and treatment for sex offenders.

They have identified, for example, that sex offenders leaving treatment programmes often put themselves into risky situations through a combination of general life-style deficiencies, i.e. living within situations high on anxiety and stress but low on positive reinforcers, as well as engaging in what are termed *'apparently irrelevant decisions'*, i.e. distorted patterns of thinking which inexorably move the offender closer and closer to situations in which self-control over subsequent sex offending is reduced and offences recur.

CASE STUDY

The following case study is compiled from data on the assessment and treatment of three offenders. This is partly in order to preserve the confidentiality of the offenders and partly to illustrate the range of issues faced in assessment and treatment. This composite case is 'real' in that it includes the range and severity of problems encountered in working with sex offenders in prison and special hospital/secure units who will ultimately, in most cases, return to the community.

Peter was 33 when first admitted to special hospital for treatment without limit of time. He had a history of sexual assaults on young girls and had been subject to one probation order with a condition of psychiatric treatment, one in-patient stay in a non-secure psychiatric hospital, and one period of imprisonment with no specific treatment for his sexual offending.

Peter's 'index offence', i.e. the offence bringing him into special hospital, was the strangling of a girl aged eleven in the course of an indecent assault. His previous victims, of whom there were recorded as having been about fifteen, had ranged in age from 8 to 12 years, and for these offences he had been convicted of indecent assaults. Following the index offence, Peter had by his own account attempted suicide by hanging but there was no evidence to substantiate this.

At the time of his trial, Peter was assessed psychiatrically and diagnosed as suffering from 'psychopathic disorder'. The Mental Health Act 1983 Section 1 defines psychopathic disorder as 'a persistent disorder or disability of mind (whether or not including significant impairment of intelligence) which results in abnormally aggressive or seriously irresponsible conduct on the part of the person concerned'. A person suffering from psychopathic disorder may be detained in hospital for treatment where such treatment is likely to alleviate or prevent a deterioration in his/her condition and detention in hospital is necessary to secure treatment.

Psychopathic disorder is essentially a medico-legal classification which, if the offender is so diagnosed, is the first of three requirements for him to be admitted without limit of time to a maximum security special hospital for treatment.

The second requirement for a special-hospital admission is that the offender should represent a grave and immediate danger to the public if not detained. The third requirement is that treatment in special hospital is likely to alleviate or prevent a deterioration in the offender's condition and that detention in hospital is necessary to secure such treatment.

In meeting all three criteria, Peter was duly admitted to special hospital where his care, assessment, and treatment were the responsibility of a multi-disciplinary clinical team. Permanent members of the team are a consultant forensic psychiatrist (legally known as the responsible medical officer) together with nursing staff, social worker, clinical psychologist, occupational therapist, and teacher.

The first part of Peter's hospitalisation was concerned with assessments of his behaviour, personality, and features of his sexual-offending history, culminating in the index offence of homicide. During this period, Peter was encouraged to discuss and reflect upon his offence history with a view to agreeing with him a 'treatment plan' on which he would work with the aim of treating or controlling those aspects of his psychopathic disorder and propensity to offend such that the risk of his re-offending outside conditions of maximum security would be reduced.

As part of this process, members of the multi-disciplinary team responsible for Peter's treatment tried on a number of occasions to encourage his involvement with the clinical psychologist member of the team, but he tended to be resistant to this. When he finally agreed to participate in such sessions, he expressed the view that the death of the girl was a tragic accident and that he required no treatment specifically relating to his sexual and social functioning.

In support of this position he cited the fact that he had held down a responsible job before admission the hospital and that he had been married (for two years) prior to the index offence and that the victim had herself initiated the sexual contact between them which led on to her death. In attempting to put this position forward, Peter displayed many of the characteristics typical of sex offenders' denial and minimisation of their behaviour and motives, referred to earlier. The task in treatment would be to work through this barrier of denial in order to address and hopefully ameliorate problems in Peter's personality and sexual functioning which underlay his offending behaviour.

The *first strategy* adopted was to attempt to see matters from Peter's point of view so as to enter effectively into a negotiation with him about assessments and treatments which would follow. It seemed evident that Peter's account of himself and his circumstances reflected two themes which can often become blurred or misidentified. The first theme was an apparent attempt on his part to justify and minimise his behaviour with the intention of persuading those responsible for his detention, and ultimately his transfer, that his motives were less deviant and his dangerousness less severe than they might at first have imagined. In this respect the first theme represented a conscious strategy of distortion in order to achieve his own end of as rapid a transfer from hospital as possible.

The second theme seemed more related to Peter's own distorted belief system that his offending was somehow not particularly serious or, in some perverse way, justifiable because of problems he had himself suffered as a child and adolescent. This second theme therefore seemed to represent more of a genuinely distorted perception rather than a consciously contrived manipulation. These two themes can of course become interlinked.

In order to gain maximum insight into Peter's thinking, a *second strategy* was adopted which often seems to pay dividends in terms of gaining rapport with sex offenders. This involved going through with Peter aspects of his early life and problems he had encountered. During this series of interviews, it became clear that Peter had indeed suffered various difficulties centred around, as he described it, a close but over-controlling mother and distant and uninterested father. His accounts of these relationships remained consistent both in general terms and in terms of very specific details which were repeated consistently, sometimes months apart. His accounts of this period of his life were also charged with an apparent emotional, and believable, quality.

Over a period of several months, during both individual and group therapy, it eventually transpired that Peter had himself been a subject of sexual abuse at the hands of a trusted relative and subsequently a teacher. Peter's account of this abuse was filled with anger and distress. Moving from accounts of his own abuse to that which he subsequently inflicted upon others, his description was marked by an apparent emotional flatness in the latter case. It was almost as if his ability to generalise from the suffering he had experienced to empathy for his victims was absent. This lack of emotional responsiveness to the plight of others, or conscience, is a feature often noted amongst those diagnosed as psychopathic.

As Peter's account of his own childhood and adolescence unfolded, various features emerged which appeared to have some explanatory potential in terms of his subsequent sexual offending. Firstly, there was considerable hitherto unexpressed anger at the sexual abuse he reported having experienced together with hitherto unarticulated feelings that he, somehow as a result of this, had the right to inflict harm upon others. The relationships with his mother and father appeared to have resulted in a combination of secretiveness (in response to his mother's over-involvement) and lack of trust/emotional distance from others (in reaction to his father's lack of involvement).

At this stage in therapy, Peter was beginning to take the view that these revelations and explanations for his behaviour were probably all that were necessary to render him 'treated and cured'. Whilst he acknowledged that deviant sexual interests of a sadistic nature had developed during his childhood and adolescence, and the fact that these had indeed played a part in his sexual offending, including the index offence, he maintained that such deviant sexual interests and fantasies were no longer with him. His inconsistency and anxiety in discussing this suggested that he was attempting to conceal his current interests and feelings for fear that revelation of these would impair his transfer from maximum security. In one sense he felt that 'he had done his bit' in working through his early history.

It was at this point that a *third strategy* was introduced. This involved establishing with Peter what his goals for hospitalisation were. He stated these as tackling his personality/behaviour problems so as to reduce his risk of future offending and (more convincingly) a desire to be transferred/discharged from hospital as soon as possible. By using this second and clearly (for Peter) more important objective, it was possible to work with him on agreeing a set of assessments which would be necessary in order to address the question of his current level of disorder and dangerousness. It was during these discussions that the issue of direct (psychophysiological) assessment of his sexual interests was raised.

Peter exhibited considerable anxiety during these discussions, reflecting, it was felt, concern that such an assessment might identify deviant sexual interests/arousal patterns which he had hitherto denied. His questioning about the procedure and possible outcomes tended to confirm this as well as highlighting a perception often expressed by sexual offenders at the time of such assessments. This perception is that by denying deviant sexual interests and refusing to participate in assessment of these, the patient is somehow making things better for himself as far as proving himself to be 'non-dangerous' or 'cured' is concerned. The alternative view is, of course, that those responsible for decision making about the patient's safety and transfer would not be convinced by such assertions and refusals to be assessed and indeed would be more persuaded by the patient's agreement to participate in assessment and tackle any problems which are thereby identified.

This second line of thought is one which, although initially rejected by patients, nevertheless sometimes holds sway after discussion within therapy, and this in fact was the case with Peter. He duly participated in psychophysiological assessment of his sexual interests. In this procedure the patient either views or listens to sections of stimulus material depicting three types of scenario – consenting sexual activity, rape, and aggression against a female devoid of sexual content. Twelve sequences are used, four of each category. The patient is asked either simply to let his sexual reactions occur ('arouse' condition) or to attempt to suppress his sexual reactions whilst still attending to the stimulus material ('suppress' condition).

Figure 8.3 illustrates Peter's sexual responses during this assessment. He responded less to consenting material than to either rape or aggression in the 'arouse' condition, suggesting a preference for aggressive rather than consenting scenarios. When asked to suppress his responding, he was able to do this, by approximately 50 per cent for both the consent and rape material but hardly at all for the aggression material.

This profile is typical of sadistic offenders we have assessed and forms the baseline against which future changes need to be assessed in the area of sexual interests.

After this assessment had been completed, Peter acknowledged without further prompting, or indeed reference to his previous denial, that he indeed still experienced sexual arousal to thoughts of harming or strangling young females. He reported that masturbation to such images were still quite common, although, he maintained, less than when he had originally entered the hospital. Fantasies were often centred around imagery from television programmes which would be elaborated in Peter's mind to include the sadistic elements.

Treatment with Peter is still under way, focusing on possible modification/control of his deviant sexual interests, further work on helping him to conceptualise accurately his previous offending pattern and to appraise his risks in new situations accurately, and finally to work on relapse-prevention strategies relevant to situations in which he might find himself in the future. It is still too early to say how far these interventions will bring about sufficient change within Peter to result in transfer from maximum security.

WORKER SUPPORT

Emotional reactions to working with sex offenders – anger, anxiety, etc. – can occur with workers in all disciplines and regardless of length of service. Sometimes these reactions occur in response to particular types of offence or at times when the worker is reminded by the offender or the offence of some particular personal experience. To expect workers to be totally devoid of emotion in hearing or reading about sexual offences

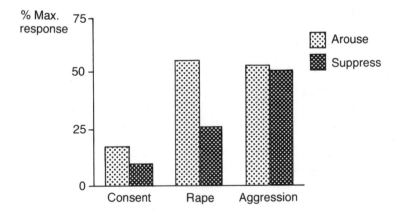

Figure 8.3 Penile plethysmograph (PPG) responses to consenting sex, rape and non-sexual aggression stimuli

would be unreasonable and not necessarily a good thing. Equally, for a worker to be rendered unable to relate to sex offenders because of emotional reactions would be problematic given our assessment and therapeutic roles.

The ability to relate constructively to offenders who have committed particularly distasteful acts may be rendered even more difficult if the offenders present unsympathetically – hostile, arrogant, self-justifying, etc. – and the worker may need to adopt particular coping strategies. Anyone working with sex offenders will need to have access to emotional support. Among the methods raised by participants in courses on working with sex offenders run by the author are:

a) regular peer group meetings within the office to air and share feelings about the work;
b) access to specialist supervision/consultancy dealing with specific treatment techniques, psychotherapeutic issues, etc.;
c) joining multi-disciplinary 'special interest' groups on, for example, child sexual abuse, working with rapists, etc., with colleagues from other relevant agencies; and
d) developing a 'charter' or practice guidelines for working with sex offenders, e.g. 'don't see sex offenders just before going home', 'build in time for technical research/reading and emotional unburdening with colleagues', etc.

CONCLUSIONS

Most comprehensive treatment programmes for sex offenders are now broadly cognitive-behavioural in orientation, addressing the full range of problems presented by the offender as outlined earlier, but with an equal recognition of the importance of dealing with unresolved factors within the sex offender's developmental history, including brutalisation or sexual abuse which the offender may himself have suffered.

Despite some claims that focusing on the offender's history is counter-productive in that it provides a lot of excuses for his behaviour, it remains the fact that anyone who has experienced physical or sexual abuse during childhood, as many sex offenders have, does not simply get over these experiences without counselling and supportive therapy. Engaging in such work with sex offenders where this is necessary has the added advantage of establishing rapport with the offender and eliciting child-hood factors which may have some bearing on the development of his present offending, both of which can facilitate working with the offenders on their contemporary patterns of offending.

There is clearly a need for more research in this area in order to explore the efficacy of different approaches to work with sex offenders in the realm of sexuality. However, Furby *et al.* (1989) in their review of forty-two studies of sex-offender recidivism, which included some treatment programmes for sex offenders, pointed to a disappointing prevalence of methodological inadequacies in most studies. In their conclusions, Furby *et al.* felt it apposite to quote Quinsey's earlier comments in reviewing work with rapists that 'The differences in recidivism across these studies is truly remarkable; clearly by selectively contemplating the various studies, one can conclude anything one wants'. Although this disappointing conclusion is clearly supported by Furby's findings, the fact remains that not all treatment programmes or evaluation studies are the same and some clearly stand out as more comprehensive, appropriately focused, and better evaluated than others. Marshall, Laws and Barbaree's (1990) programme is a good example. Here offenders received a broad-based cognitive-behavioural package of interventions tailored to their individual needs and were followed up for four years. Although reconviction rates for the treated group increased from 5.5 per cent to 25 per cent between the two-year and four-year follow-up periods, the corresponding reconviction rates for a comparable group of non-treated offenders rose from 12.5 per cent to 64 per cent.

Returning to the earlier stated proposition that treatment for sex offenders must aim to reduce victimisation, evidence on balance suggests that, although treatment effects are weak, long-term, broad-based therapy can work. It is better to treat than not to treat sex offenders. Well-run, broad-based treatment programmes (covering the range of needs with which sex offenders present) might reasonably be expected to halve reconviction rates. Yet, whilst the sexual offending itself will occupy a central position in any treatment, it is also essential that wider issues relating to sexuality form part of the agenda. There is currently a surge of interest in the treatment of sex offenders not only in hospitals but also in prisons and the community, and this is being supported by the agencies primarily involved. The importance of multi-disciplinary and multi-agency collaboration is also being increasingly recognized and a number of major treatment initiatives are being developed.

Key issues now will centre around the question of how successfully the different disciplines and agencies can co-ordinate their activities to ensure:

a) that the full range of causes of the sex offender's behaviour are identified and treated (as in appropriate combinations of dynamic and behavioural psychotherapy);
b) that likely future risk factors are identified and addressed in the settings to which offenders will pass after maximum security (as in relapse-prevention therapy); and
c) that adequate evaluation research can be built into this work.

REFERENCES

Abel, G.G., Barlow, D.H., and Blanchard, E.B. (1973) 'Developing heterosexual arousal by altering masturbatory fantasies: a controlled study', paper presented at the Association for Advancement of Behaviour Therapy, Miami, December 1973.

Abel, G.G., Mittelman, M.S., and Becker, J.V. (1985) 'Sexual offenders: results of assessment and recommendations for treatment', in M.H. Ben-Aron, S.J. Huckle, and C.D. Webster (eds) *Clinical Criminology: The Assessment and Treatment of Criminal Behaviour*, Toronto: M & M Graphic, pp. 191–205.

Abel, G.G., Becker, J.V., Mittelman, M., Cunningham-Rathner, N., Rouleau, J.L., and Murphy, W.D. (1987) *Self-Reported Sex Crimes of Non-Incarcerated Paraphiliacs* (Final Report No. MH-33678) Washington, DC: Public Health Service.

Bancroft, J. (1979) 'The nature of the patient–therapist relationship', in G.B. Trasler and D.P. Farrington (eds) *Behaviour Modification with Offenders: A Criminological Symposium*, Occasional papers No. 5, Cambridge: Institute of Criminology.

Baxter, D.J., Barbaree, H.E., and Marshall, W.L. (1986) 'Sexual responses to consenting and forced sex in a large sample of rapists and nonrapists', *Behaviour Research and Therapy* 24: 513–20.

Brownmiller, S. (1975) *Against Our Will: Men, Women, and Rape*. New York: Simon & Schuster.

Burgess, A.W., Hartman, C., Ressler, R.K., Douglas, J.E., and McCormack, A. (1986) 'Sexual homicide: a motivational model', *Journal of Interpersonal Violence* 1(3): 251–72.

Cautela, J. (1967) 'Covert sensitization', *Psychological Reports* 20: 459–68.

Cohen, M.L., Garofolo, R., Boucher, R., and Seghorn, T., (1971) 'The psychology of rapists', in *Seminars in Psychiatry* Vol. 3: New York: Grune & Stratton, pp. 307–27.

Cole, M. (1982) 'The use of surrogate sex partners in the treatment of sex dysfunctions and allied conditions', *British Journal of Sexual Medicine* 9: 13–20.

Costell, R. and Yalom, L. (1972) 'Institutional group therapy', in H.L. Resnick and M.E. Wolfgang (eds) *Sexual Behaviour: Social, Clinical and Legal Aspects*, Boston: Little, Brown & Co.

Criminal Statistics for England and Wales (1989), London: Home Office.

Curtis, L.A. (1976) 'Rape, race and culture: some speculations in search of a theory', in M.J. Walker and S.L. Brodsky (eds) *Sexual Assault*, Lexington, MA: Lexington Books.

Elliott, M. (1985) *Preventing Child Sex Assault*, London: Vigo Press.

Feldman, M.P. (1977) *Criminal Behaviour: A Psychological Analysis*, Chichester: Wiley.

Festinger, L. (1957) *A Theory of Cognitive Dissonance*, New York: Harper & Row.

Finkelhor, D. (1984) *Child Sexual Abuse: New Theory and Research*, New York: Free Press.

Finkelhor, D. (1986) *A Sourcebook on Child Sexual Abuse*, Beverly Hills, CA: Sage.

Furby, L., Weinrott, M.R., and Blackshaw, L. (1989) 'Sex offender recidivism: a review', *Psychological Bulletin* 155(1): 3–30.

George, L.K. and Winfield-Laird, I. (1986) 'Sexual assault: prevalence and mental health consequences', final report submitted to the National Institute of Mental Health.

Groth, A.N. and Birnbaum, H.T. (1979) *Men who Rape: The Psychology of the Offender*, New York: Plenum Press.

Grounds, A.T., Quayle, M.T., France, J., Brett, T., Cox, M., and Hamilton, J.R. (1987) 'A unit for "psychopathic disorder" patients in Broadmoor Hospital', *Medicine, Science and Law* 27(1), 21–31.

Hartman, V. (1965a) 'Notes on group psychotherapy with paedophiles', *Canadian Psychiatric Association Journal* 10: 283–8.

Hartman, V. (1965b) 'Group psychotherapy with sexually deviant offenders (paedophiles) – the peer group as an instrument of mutual control', *Criminal Law Quarterly* 7: 464–79.

Herman, J.L. (1990) 'Sex offenders: a feminist perspective', in W.L. Marshall, D.R. Laws, and H.E. Barbaree (eds) *Handbook of Sexual Assault*, London: Plenum Press, pp. 177–194.

Howard League Working Party (1985) *Unlawful Sex*, Oxford: Pergamon.

Jehu, D. (1991) 'Clinical work with adults who were sexually abused in childhood', in C. R. Hollin and K. Howells (eds) *Clinical Approaches to Sex Offenders and Their Victims*, Chichester: Wiley.

Knight, R.A. and Prentky, R.A. (1987) *Motivational Components in a Taxonomy for Rapists: A Validation Analysis*. Unpublished paper.

Koss, M. (1990) 'The women's mental health research agenda: violence against women', *American Psychologist* 45(3): 374–80.

Koss, M.P. and Oros, C.J. (1980) 'Sexual experiences survey: investigating sexual aggression and victimization', *Journal of Consulting and Clinical Psychology* 50: 455–7.

Koss, M.P., Gidycz, C.A., and Wisniewski, N. (1988) 'The scope of rape: incidence and prevalence of sexual aggression and victimization in a national sample of higher educational students', *Journal of Consulting and Clinical Psychology* 55: 162–70.

Kutchinsky, B. (1971) 'Towards an explanation of the decrease in registered sex crimes in Copenhagen', *Technical Report of the Commission on Obscenity and Pornography: Erotica and Behaviour*, Vol. 8, Washington, DC: US Government Printing Office.

Laws, D.R. (1990) *Relapse Prevention with Sex Offenders*, London: Guilford Press.

Lazarus, A.A. (1976) *Multi-modal Behaviour Therapy*, New York: Springer.

Leyton, E. (1983) 'A social profile of sexual mass murderers', in T. Fleming and L.A. Visano (eds) *Deviant Designations: Crime, Law and Deviance in Canada*, Toronto: Butterworth.

Lipton, D.N., McDonel, E.C., and McFall, R.M. (1987) 'Heterosocial perception in rapists', *Journal of Consulting and Clinical Psychology* 55: 17–21.

MacCulloch, M.J., Snowden, P.R., Wood, P.J.W., and Mills, H.E. (1983) 'Sadistic fantasy, sadistic behaviour and offending', *British Journal of Psychiatry* 143: 20–9.

Marquis, J. (1970) 'Orgasmic reconditioning: changing sexual object choice through controlling masturbation fantasies, *Journal of Behaviour Therapy and Experimental Psychiatry* 1: 271.

Marshall, W.L. (1973) 'The modification of sexual fantasies: a combined treatment approach to the reduction of deviant sexual behaviour', *Behaviour Research and Therapy* 11: 557–64.

Marshall, W.L., Williams, S.M., and Christie, M.M. (1977) 'The treatment of rapists', in C.B. Qualls (ed.) *Perspectives on Rape*, New York: Pergamon.

Marshall, W.L., Laws, D.R., and Barbaree, H.E. (eds) (1990) *Handbook of Sexual Assault*, London: Plenum Press.

Matthis, J.L. and Collins, M. (1970) 'Mandatory group therapy for exhibitionists', *American Journal of Psychiatry* 126: 1162–7.

McGuire, R.J., Carlisle, J.M., and Young, B.G. (1965) 'Sexual deviations as conditioned behaviour, *Behaviour Research and Therapy* 2: 185–90.

Mental Health Act (1983) London: Department of Health.

Murrin, M.R. and Laws, D.R. (1990) *The Influence of Pornography on Sexual Crimes*, Department of Law and Mental Health, Florida Mental Health Institute, University of South Florida, Tampa, Florida 33612–3899.

Overholser, J.C. and Beck, S. (1986) 'Multi-method assessment of rapists, child molesters and three control groups on behavioural and psychological measures', *Journal of Consulting and Clinical Psychology* 54: 682–7.

Perkins, D.E. (1984) 'Psychological treatment of offenders in prison and the community', in T. Williams, E. Alves, and J. Shapland (eds) *Options for the Mentally Abnormal Offender*, Issues in Criminological and Legal Psychology, No. 6, Leicester: The British Psychological Society.

Perkins, D.E. (1986) 'Sex offending: a psychological approach', in C. Hollin and K. Howells (eds) *Clinical Approaches to Criminal Behaviour*, Issues in Criminological and Legal Psychology No. 9, Leicester: The British Psychological Society.

Perkins, D.E. (1987) 'A psychological treatment programme for sex offenders', in B.J. McGurk, D.M. Thornton, and M. Williams (eds) *Applying Psychology to Imprisonment: Theory and Practice*, London: HMSO.

Perkins, D.E. (1991) 'Clinical work with sex offenders in secure settings', in C.R. Hollin and K. Howells (eds) *Clinical Approaches to Sex Offenders and their Victims*, Chichester: Wiley.

Pithers, W.D., Marques, J.K., Gibat, C.C., and Marlatt, G.A. (1983) 'Relapse prevention with sexual aggressives: a self-control model of treatment and maintenance of change', in J.G. Greer and I.R. Stuart (eds) *The Sexual Aggressor: Current Perspectives on Treatment*. New York: Van Nostrand Reinhold, pp. 214–39.

Pithers, W.D., Cumming, G.F., Beal, L.S., Young, W., and Turner, R. (1989) 'Relapse prevention: a method for enhancing behavioural self-management and external supervision of the sexual aggressor', in B. Schwartz (ed.) *Sex Offenders: Issues in Treatment*, Washington, DC: National Institute of Corrections, pp. 292–310.

Prentky, R.A., Knight, R.A., and Rosenberg, R. (1987) *Validation Analyses on the MTC Taxonomy for Rapists: Disconfirmation and Reconceptualization*, paper presented at the New York Academy of Sciences Conference on Human Sexual Aggression: Current Perspectives, 7–9 January 1987.

Prentky, R.A., Burgess, A.W., Rokous, F., Lee, A., Hartman, C., Ressler, R., and Douglas, J. (1989) 'The presumptive role of fantasy in serial sexual homicide', *American Journal of Psychiatry* 146: 887–91.

Quayle, M.T. (1989) *Group Therapy for Personality Disordered Offenders*, paper presented at Annual Conference of Special Hospital Psychologists, Scarborough.

Resnick, P.A., and Markaway, B.E.G. (1991) 'Clinical treatment of adult female victims of sexual assault', in C.R. Hollin and K. Howells (eds) *Clinical Approaches to Sex Offenders and their Victims*, Chichester: Wiley, pp. 261–84.

Resnick, H.L. and Peters, J.J. (1967) 'Outpatient group therapy with convicted paedophiles', *International Journal of Group Psychotherapy* 17: 151–8.

Ressler, R.K., Burgess, A.W., and Douglas, J.E. (1988) *Sexual Homicide Patterns and Motives*, Lexington, MA: Lexington Books, pp. 137–66.

Russell, D.E.H. (1982) 'The prevalence and incidence of forcible rape and attempted rape of females', *Victimology* 7: 81–93.

Salter, A.C. (1988) *Treating Child Sexual Offenders and Victims: A Practical Guide*, Beverly Hills, CA: Sage.

Sanday, P.R. (1981) 'The socio-cultural context of rape: a cross-cultural study', *Journal of Social Issues* 37: 5–27.

Scully, D. and Marolla, J. (1985) 'Riding the bull at Gilley's: convicted rapists describe the rewards of rape', *Social Problems* 32: 251–63.

Seghorn, T. and Cohen, M. (1980) 'The psychology of the rape assailant', in W. Cerran, A.L. McGarry, and C. Petty (eds) *Modern Legal Medicine, Psychiatry, and Forensic Science*, Philadelphia: Davis, pp. 533–51.

Williams, T., Alves, E., and Shapland, J. (eds) *Options for the Mentally Abnormal Offender*, Issues in Criminological and Legal Psychology, No. 6, Leicester: The British Psychological Society.

Woodward, R. (1980) 'Brief report on the effects of a sex education course on borstal trainees', *Home Office Prison Department Psychological Services DPS Reports*, Series II(78), July 1980.

Wyre, R. (1989) Personal communication.

Chapter 9

Sex and the injecting drug user

Geraldine Mulleady

INTRODUCTION

Prior to HIV, the sexual behaviour of drug users was considered only in relation to the adverse consequences to the foetus of continued drug use during pregnancy (Tylden, 1983; Blatman, 1980; Priestly, 1973). This chapter will examine the implications that HIV infection has had for both the policies and the practice of working with drug users in relation to counselling for sexual-risk reduction. In particular, this will be addressed to injecting drug users, because, although other forms of drug and alcohol use have been shown to be associated with increased risk of unsafe sex (Stall *et al.*, 1986), it is injecting drug users who have been the main focus of attention.

For the injecting drug user (IDU), the main emphasis of risk-reduction counselling has been focused on the reduction of HIV transmission associated with sharing injecting equipment. The risk of sexual transmission of HIV (at least initially) was largely ignored. There are a number of possible explanations for this: the route of HIV transmission via shared needles and syringes is fairly straightforward, easy to understand, and carries a high risk; drug users who shared injecting equipment were clearly at higher risk by this method of HIV transmission than those who used other methods of administration – such as oral, smoking, or sniffing; the largest group of illegal drug users visible to official and treatment agencies were heroin users, many of whom injected their drugs; and, finally, heroin has been reported to reduce libido (Mirim *et al.*, 1980). Therefore, sexual transmission among IDUs was not considered to be a major cause for concern. This initial complacency was subsequently shown to be mistaken.

The alarm signals began to go off when HIV transmission statistics for North America and Europe showed that a significant number of HIV-positive children had parents where one or both was an HIV-positive drug user (Davison *et al.*, 1989). It was around this time that terms referring to IDUs as 'bridging groups' or 'potential bridges of infectivity' to the heterosexual community began to emerge (Brown *et al.*, 1987). At the same time, research into risk behaviours among IDUs has consistently indicated a reduction in syringe sharing, but no corresponding change in unsafe sexual behaviour (Mulleady and Sherr, 1989; Mulleady *et al.*, 1990), essentially mirroring the general heterosexual response to changes in sexual behaviour in the light of HIV. Thus there is an awareness about modes of HIV transmission, but behaviour has not changed as a result of this knowledge.

In 1987, the Advisory Council on the Misuse of Drugs (an expert advisory group) published recommendations on how best to approach the problem of HIV among drug users (ACMD, 1988). Among the conclusions drawn was that 'The Human Immune Deficiency Virus (HIV) is a greater threat to public and individual than drug misuse'. As a result of HIV infection among drug users, the terms 'risk reduction' and 'harm minimisation' have become everyday additions to the drug worker's language and consciousness. Risk reduction can be defined as any measure which reduces the risks of transmission of HIV. Harm minimisation is an approach to problem drug use, which aims to reduce the legal, social, and health consequences caused to both drug user and the community by their drug use. It is a model which aims to improve the drug user's quality of life and, perhaps, prolong life. The concept of harm minimisation is not a new one – in 1968 when drug dependence clinics were first established, this was the model of treatment initially adopted (Wilks, 1989). Subsequent approaches to treating problem drug users moved away from this model, but with the advent of HIV – *plus ça change, plus c'est la même chose.*

Obviously, there was a need for empirical research on both the injecting and the sexual behaviour of injecting drug users, and subsequent research has attempted to address this need. However, there is less evidence of attempts to translate this knowledge into practical guidelines for counselling drug users about sexual-behaviour change than there is for minimising the harm associated with injecting drug use. This chapter discusses some empirical findings on drug users' sexual behaviour and the implications these have for sexual-risk-reduction counselling. This is based on my work as a clinical psychologist at St Mary's Hospital Drug Dependency Unit (DDU). My experience is therefore predominantly with injecting drug users where heroin is the main drug of choice (although polydrug use is the norm). As well as client work, I will also draw on four pieces of research work that have been carried out at St Mary's DDU and syringe exchange between 1985 and 1990, which are reported more fully elsewhere (Mulleady and Sherr, 1989; Mulleady *et al.*, 1990).

DEMOGRAPHICS

The demographic descriptions of the clients included in each of the four studies are very similar, as Table 9.1 shows. The main drugs used by all groups were opiates – heroin and methadone. The studies were cross-sectional rather than longitudinal, therefore the variation in the different routes of administration reflects the situations clients were then in.[1]

Similarly, whether data were collected on HIV antibody status depended on the particular emphasis of each of the studies; 19 per cent of clients in the 1986 study were HIV positive, and 18 per cent of the 1989/90 sample.[2] Equivalent information is not available for the clients in the 1985 and 1988 survey.

SEXUAL BEHAVIOUR OF INJECTING DRUG USERS

As a result of the reported low levels of sexual activity among regular heroin users, we considered it important to establish whether or not this was in fact the case. We found that a significant percentage were not sexually active, giving support to the evidence for lowered libido. But, equally, a significant proportion were regularly sexually active

Reported levels of sexual activity indicate that a significant proportion of clients were regularly sexually active (see Table 9.2).

In terms of choice of sexual partner, women IDUs are significantly

Table 9.1 Demographics of clients

	1985	*1986*	*1988*	*1989–90*
N	119	74	62	141
Men	64%	66%	61%	69%
Women	36%	34%	39%	31%
Age range	18–45	18–52	16–42	20–46
Mean range	28.3	27.1	29.6	32
Routes of drug administration (%)				
Intravenous	85	38	50	72
Intramuscular	10	2	2	8
Subcutaneous	3	2	0	10
Oral	28	48	26	98
Inhalation	31	6	23	76

Note: Many clients were using more than one method of administration.

Table 9.2 Sexual activity in previous month

Sexual activity in previous month	% of clients			
	1985	*1986*	*1988*	*1989–90*
None	40	29	28	41
1 or 2 per month	26	27	27	19
1 or 2 per week	16	17	17	19
3 or more times per week	15	25	25	13
Once daily or more	3	2	2	8

more likely to have a partner who injects than a male IDU (x^2 = 18.67, d.f. = 1, p<0.001 for the 1985 data). According to France *et al.* (1988), male IDUs often choose women sexual partners who are not drug users. Very little is known about these women in terms of empirical research. If an IDU is in a sexual relationship with a non-user then they are more likely to have regular sex than if the partner is also a user (x^2 = 7.85, d.f. = 1, p<0.01 for 1985 data), with a potentially greater risk of possible HIV exposure if safer sex is not practised. Most drug services do not involve the non-drug-using partner in treatment unless, for example, their participation is necessary for family therapy or relationship work; if this is not the case, then the non-using partner will receive no specific risk-reduction advice or help. This group will be mainly women. If they are to receive appropriate risk-reduction advice then efforts will need to be made to contact them. One approach is to offer practical assistance, e.g. a drug agency where they could receive welfare advice, creche facilities, general medical care, well women and family planning clinics, etc. Obviously this carries significant service, policy, and resource implications for the drug agency which chooses to follow this route.

SEXUAL PROBLEMS

Table 9.3 Sexual problems

	% sexual problems	
	1985	*1989–90*
Lack of interest	70	76
Impotence	2	6
Anorgasmia	6	4
Premature ejaculation	2	–
Not specified	8	–
Delayed ejaculation	–	12
Passivity/powerlessness	–	2

The most commonly reported sexual problem is lack of interest in sexual activity. This can lead to relationship problems where a non-drug-using partner wants a higher frequency of sexual activity than the drug-using partner desires. There is also the contradiction inherent between low levels of interest in sex and significant levels of sexual activity. Drug use will tend to be high on the IDUs list of priorities – obtaining the money for drugs, getting hold of the drugs they want, in the quantities they require. Although the IDU may engage in sexual activity, it is often not a particularly important part of their lives (unless they are trying to have a child). This factor can be particularly pertinent in relationships where both partners use drugs, where drugs are the main thing that the couple have in common. The drug user may also be in a stable relationship and therefore not consider that safer sex is an issue for them (even though there may be sexual contacts or incidents of syringe sharing outside the relationship). Furthermore, quite a large proportion of IDUs may already have had an HIV test and thus no longer feel that HIV is an issue for them. Many drug workers report that the IDU is frequently unreceptive to safer-sex counselling. Any of these factors could mitigate against the adoption of safer-sex practices.

Further evidence of the low priority ascribed to sexual activity is provided by information collected on 'how troubled clients are by their sexual problems'. Clearly, although the majority volunteer lack of interest as a sexual problem, most of them indicate that they are not especially troubled by this – 52 per cent of the 1985 sample and 60 per cent of the 1989/90 sample responded that they were 'Not at all bothered' by their sexual problem/s; only 8 per cent and 4 per cent respectively indicated that they were 'Extremely bothered'.

CONTRACEPTIVE ISSUES

Contraceptive choice and use is of both theoretical and clinical importance, given the emphasis on safer sex for those at any risk of HIV infection. Over the five years covered by these surveys there have been no significant changes in the type of contraception used, hormonal methods being the most common method, and condom use has only increased slightly. There is some evidence that there have been slight increases in condom use with casual partners, but not with regular partners.

Table 9.4 shows some form of contraception was used in all sexual encounters by about half of the sexually active sample. Forty-one per cent of men report never using any form of contraception although in over a third of these cases (18 per cent of the sexually active respondents) this was because an attempt was being made to conceive. This indicates high risks of sexual transmission for many of these individuals, as safer-sex practices are not being adhered to.

Table 9.4 Contraceptive use of the sexually active

	Men		Women	
	N	%	N	%
Frequency of contraceptive use				
Always use contraception	36	49	13	39
Sometimes use contraception	8	11	3	9
Never use contraception (not wanting to conceive)	17	23	12	36
Never use contraception (trying to conceive)	13	18	5	15
Form of contraception used				
Pill/depo provera	12	27	10	63
IUD	6	14	1	6
Condom	25	57	4	25
Diaphragm	1	2	0	0
Sterilisation	0	0	1	6

In this context it is interesting to note the different interpretations of the term 'safer sex'. In 1990, 68 per cent of clients defined it as condom use for all partners, 21 per cent believed it involved selective use of condoms for casual or drug-using partners, and 11 per cent believed it involved 'no casual sex'. These varying beliefs obviously exert an influence on behaviour, and reduce or increase likelihood of risk. Equally the selection criteria that the individual exercises for choice of sexual partner – including factors such as drug use, reputation, appearance, length of acquaintance – will determine whether or not they will use a condom.

A further factor which will influence the likelihood of safer sex is perceived risk of acquiring HIV. In the 1990 group, 19 per cent either knew or believed themselves to be at moderate or high risk, 62 per cent believed their risk to be very low or non-existent. A further influence may be that 48 per cent of the 1990 sample reported that they were in relationships of three months' duration or longer. The majority described these as 'close coupled', i.e. a relationship with little or no outside sexual contact. If people believe themselves to be in monogamous relationships, where both partners have the same HIV status, then the perceived need for safer sex will be reduced.

Women may experience particular problems associated with their drug use. Menstrual disruption is very common among regular heroin users (81 per cent in 1985, 85 per cent in 1990). Most frequently amenorrhoea is the result. Obviously, this condition will influence the perceived importance of contraception for women. As a result of absence of menses, many women believe that they are at little or no risk of becoming pregnant. In 1990, 58 per cent believed they were unlikely or extremely unlikely to become pregnant through unprotected sex. In reality, fertility may be only slightly impaired and, as a result of this, so-called 'unplanned' pregnancies are common.

Women have been advised that if they want to avoid pregnancy, then they should use a back-up form of contraception. Low perceived risk of HIV will reduce the likelihood of condom use, low percieved fertility will have a similar effect on the likelihood that this contraceptive advice will be followed.

COUNSELLING AND TRAINING ISSUES

Where counselling about safer sex is concerned, the drug worker is in a difficult position. They are familiar with counselling about drug use and associated problems, and when discussing such issues are also fulfilling the client's expectation of what will take place when they attend an agency for help with their drug problem. Very few drug workers are trained in the fields of relationship or sexual therapy, and consequently they feel either uncomfortable in this new role or ill equipped to cope with the potential problems that may arise once this subject is addressed, such as having to cope with the distress that may emerge in disclosure of a history of sexual abuse. Some drug workers still hold the view that 'a little knowledge is a dangerous thing' and perhaps safer-sex counselling is best left to workers who specialise in this field. However, as drug workers have a responsibility to enable clients to reduce their risks of HIV then it is essential that they attempt to talk to their clients about their sexual behaviour; there is usually no one other than the drug worker who is able to take on this work with their clients. In order for this to be possible, appropriate training is necessary. Yet, as Cranfield (1990) observed in his survey of HIV and drugs training that the issue of safer sex was the one that provoked most embarrassment and the greatest degree of resistance from trainees, this obviously needs to be handled with skill and sensitivity.

Training on issues of sexuality requires a skills-based approach to learning which is situation specific. The social context of sexual interaction needs to be taken into account. In context with drug users, sex often involves people who may well have very differing views on what they want/do not want to do, and what takes place will be affected by the substances ingested either before or during the activity, how long they have known the person, the quality of the relationship, and power imbalances between the couple. Many of these issues are clearly relevant to discussions of sexuality with any client group but the influence of drugs on sexual behaviour and on expectations will complicate the dynamics of the interaction.

In order to be effective, training should ideally be a component of each agency's in-service training programme and be on an ongoing basis. If 'in-house' trainers are available, i.e. as a unit or as a local resource, then there is greater opportunity for a proactive approach to the content of training, rather than one which is reactive – operating only once a problem has emerged. It is essential for the drug worker to be enabled both to explore their attitudes and to practise skills. For, whilst we hear a great deal about drug users' reluctance to talk to workers about their sexual behaviour, until workers are enabled to feel comfortable talking to each other and to the client about these sensitive subjects, then the client will be reluctant to talk to the worker about sex (Cranfield, 1990).

Yet the discussion of sexuality with the drug-using client is not always welcomed. Staff frequently encounter sexist comments and behaviour from clients that they may find personally offensive. A constructive proactive educational process will ensure that clients cannot easily use sexism as a defence (or weapon), it can be worked with and negative attitudes examined. Difficulties may also be encountered in introducing the subject of safer sex to clients known to the drug worker for years who may misinterpret the discussion as an invitation for physical intimacy. Many workers also find it more difficult to counsel opposite-sex clients, especially with those unused to this subject being discussed in a drug agency setting. The discussion of sexuality with someone of different culture, race, or sexual preference may also present problems: all examples of questions and problems that have become increasingly apparent and that require the worker to develop specific skills in their client work, skills that go beyond attitudinal change and consciousness raising which is frequently the limit of sexuality and sexual-health training courses.

However, even with adequate training there is often a lack of clear-cut answers to questions about safer sex, for example the safety of oral sex. Information is often conflicting and answers to the questions are not always available in textbooks; ignorance about these issues is difficult for the worker to admit. The worker needs to be able to defuse potentially very uncomfortable situations, such as what to say if the client asks 'do you use condoms?'. This situation may be threatening to the worker because many of us have not faced up to the need for safer sex in our own lives, or, if we have, still find it an emotive subject. It confronts us with our own hypocrisy. There is also the question of how far training should go for the drug worker, with uncertainty over issues such as whether it is appropriate for them to deal with the client's sexual problems using generic sex therapy techniques. It is difficult to ascertain whether the training of staff makes any difference to whether or not the IDU practises safer sex, a question which is being addressed in a training evaluation study currently under way at St Mary's DDU and syringe exchange.

The absence of empirical research in this area makes it difficult for concrete conclusions to be drawn at the moment. However effective education may be, behaviour changes can lapse over time. If the client decides to use safer sex there is no guarantee that this will be for all of their current relationships or for all relationships in the future, so counselling about safer sex needs to be ongoing. Frequently clients respond, 'I'm not having sex so it doesn't apply to me', especially just after a diagnosis of being HIV positive. Invariably, this situation changes as people do adjust and become active again so the counselling needs to be appropriate to the current circumstances of the person seen. Planning for the future with an individual who lives for the present is not easy, but should not be abandoned as hopeless.

The role of prescribing

Where methadone is prescribed to the IDU, this frequently becomes the focus for the client and negotiations around the prescription can dominate the counselling sessions. This can be depressing for the worker who may feel their skills as a counsellor are diminished by a client group which comes to see them only in order to obtain their prescription. In many cases workers put in considerable effort for what can be very small changes. This can be very frustrating for the worker, unless they are encouraged to have a liberal view of what constitutes progress with a client. There can also be a risk of the IDU trying to please the worker by telling them what they think the worker wants to hear – even though this does not reflect the reality of the user's situation. This can ultimately lead to an enhanced sense of failure and isolation for the client.

Assessment

In many drug agencies, there is at least the opportunity to see the client in private in a one-to-one situation. There is usually the basic understanding that some questions will be asked to which the client will respond, and perhaps ask some questions of their own. This luxury is not afforded to all drug workers who work in a wide variety of settings where lack of opportunity and sometimes issues of confidentiality preclude a basic assessment. In fact, for most drug workers, formal therapeutic interventions are the exception rather than the rule. 'Counselling' in many drug agency settings more frequently takes the form of supportive talk and the provision of practical help such as a prescription or help with welfare entitlements or legal problems. However, this practical help can form the basis for a trusting relationship between the worker and the drug user from which more sensitive therapeutic issues can be examined.

A major difficulty in a drug agency setting is that the client has not (usually) come to see you for help with a sexual problem. Therefore the worker has to be able to gauge the situation and decide on the appropriate intervention. Sometimes sex will be a completely closed issue and the client will not engage in discussion. This taxes the worker's ingenuity. Due to the IDUs apparent lack of interest in sexual activity, the worker may have to adopt an indirect approach in order to address the issue, e.g. using contraception and sexual health as a starting point. It is here that joint work with, say, a midwife or family-planning worker can provide the opportunity for discussion of safer sex with the client.

Early on the worker needs to establish the client's preparedness to discuss sex and be sensitive to cultural issues which may influence this. It is also important to establish a common language of sexual terms. For example, one drug worker was worried that the IDUs might find it offensive to be asked if they were involved in prostitution. To avoid this he asked the IDU if she 'worked'; if she answered 'yes' he was still none the wiser as to whether or not this was as a sex worker. Drug workers sometimes feel that they need to be *au fait* with the language of street cred in order not to appear naive to the IDU but this is less important than engaging in real communication with the client.

Where assessment is possible, the quality and motivation behind the client's sexual activity are important to discuss as each partner may have a different view of these. The counselling process needs to take account of the fact that two individuals (at least) are involved in the sexual behaviour. If the client does not enjoy sex, but their partner wants sex, then the client may want to get sex over and done with as quickly as possible. There is no point in having a stockpile of 'really useful phrases' for negotiating safer sex if you are going to get your head kicked in as soon as you mention it to your partner.

In some circumstances, the worker may not be likely to see the client again, and in this situation, if the client is halfway out of the door, then the question 'would you like to take some condoms with you?' may be the most practical approach to take. However, most of us do not work in this 'barber shop' scenario and frequently see clients again. Our ingenuity in making safer sex meaningful for the client is continuously challenged.

One method of containing the worker's anxiety about sexuality is by simple information giving. But, although this is an important component of HIV counselling, if it is done in the absence of an accurate, sensitive assessment of the client's situation, then it can lead to feelings of alienation and merely serve to raise the client's anxiety and enhance feelings of low self-esteem. If possible, it is useful to avoid the information giving until the necessary details are obtained from the client to put that information into a realistic framework for them. A mediating variable linked to reduction of risk is the extent to which individuals expect that preventive behaviour will produce a positive outcome and perceive themselves as capable of enacting preventive practices (Eldred and Washington, 1975; Christiansen and Goldman, 1983). Adoption of safer sex requires that the person perceives themselves to be at risk from HIV (Marlatt and Ronsenow, 1980), and since many IDUs do not perceive themselves to be at risk of HIV from sexual behaviour, the worker's task is made increasingly difficult (Mulleady et al., 1990).

POST-ASSESSMENT

The following is a discussion of some of the counselling issues that can emerge following the initial assessment.

Contraception and safer sex

In response to regular methadone use, menstruation can recommence. Women can suffer from painful and irregular periods at this time. This probably also coincides with an increase in fertility. Once a woman starts a methadone programme, this factor needs to be taken into consideration. Pregnancy may seem a very remote possibility to her, particularly if she has never used contraception before and managed to avoid pregnancy. Contraceptive choices are still fairly limited and all carry inherent advantages and disadvantages. Overall, regular use of contraception among IDUs is low. Any advice given must be tailored to the life-style of the individual, i.e. what is practical and feasible, and also take into account the context in which it will be used – what is the necessary and likely level of co-operation from their partner and the type of relationship the couple are in? The clients should be enabled to make an informed decision; however, sometimes the 'choices' are made in less than ideal circumstances. For example, Sue was due for an operation for termination of pregnancy and was asked just before the operation if she wanted to have a coil fitted. She said yes and then changed her mind, but, in her anxiety before the operation, forgot to say this. She has the coil in place now and has not bothered to get it removed. It could be argued that this decision was not reached on a fully informed examination of the options.

Clearly more research is necessary to clarify the effect of various contraceptive methods on the health of HIV-positive women. The information so far is sketchy. Not suprisingly, with respect to HIV most work has been carried out on the condom which has a dual role both as a contraceptive and a barrier against transfer of body fluids. The fact that the condom is a barrier can be an advantage for people working as sex workers, as it provides both a physical and psychological barrier between them and their customers. But it makes it more difficult for sex workers to use condoms in their personal relationships because they are associated with their 'punters' and this cheapens the quality of their personal relationships. As one client put it, her partner would feel she was 'rejecting his sperm' (Cupitt *et al.*, 1992).

In a study of 211 IDUs in New York, condom use was found to be independently associated with greater personal acceptance of condoms and greater partner receptivity. Partner receptivity is a factor that is not given sufficient emphasis if the worker focuses solely on the woman's role in contraceptive use (Magura *et al.*, 1990). There have been suggestions that condoms could be marketed for women on feminine hygiene shelves, with the emphasis on protection from cervical cancers or provided when women attend well woman clinics for check-ups and smear tests. The female condom (worn inside the vagina) has recently become commercially available, yet using it is unlikely to avoid the need for negotiation with a prospective partner, even though it may be an alternative to the difficulties around negotiating condom use. If the woman is to take the lead in suggesting safer sex or initiating contraceptive use, then she must feel confident about asserting her needs. In order to do this she will require a healthy level of self-esteem and be able to assert the importance of caring for herself. A chronic problem facing many drug users is their low levels of self-esteem, even more so among women who use drugs. It is for this reason that some workers maintain that an effective barrier method that the women can use without the necessity for negotiation or interruption of sexual activity is the most practical way forward. It seems that we are willing to go to extraordinary lengths to ensure that the burden of contraceptive use and safer sex still remains with the woman, presumably because this seems less daunting than encouraging responsibility between both partners.

Women's health

Studies on female drug users are rare (Rosenbaum, 1979); research on the sexual behaviour of women IDUs has concentrated on fertility patterns, i.e. management of the pregnant drug user, rather than on their sexuality, or on the care of the drug-using woman. Behavioural research on the relationship between sex and drug use has concentrated on the male subculture, hence the paucity of data on the relationship between female drug use and decision making.

For reasons that are not fully understood, women in the USA and other Western nations are more likely to contract HIV from men than to transmit the virus to them through sexual contact (MMWR, 1989; Wiley and Herschkom, 1989). Women with HIV have been found to have a higher incidence of abnormal cervical cells (Byrne *et al.*, 1989). It has not yet been shown if this leads to symptomatic cervical cancer in HIV-positive women, although there is some evidence that pre-malignant lesions worsen and respond poorly to treatment (Bradbeer and Heyderman,

1989). It is important for all women, but for HIV-positive women especially, to have regular smear tests. Lack of medical care, lack of concern for their own health, and poor attendance can lead to more serious consequences for the drug-using woman. For example, Cathy found she had seriously abnormal cervical cells only when her pregnancy was discovered. She decided she wanted to risk having the baby because of the possibility of hysterectomy should the results of her cone biopsy show malignancy. She was advised against this decision, and had her pregnancy terminated. The results of the biopsy indicated that she did not require the hysterectomy. The termination was an outcome that might have been avoided had she received appropriate advice and regular cervical screening.

Pregnancy

For a drug-using woman with low self-esteem having a child can seem like the one worthwhile thing she can do. The desire to have a baby can vary between the overt 'we're trying to get pregnant' and 'if it happened I'd quite like it'. In others the desire for a child is a desperate need. Having children (provided you are able to take care of them physically, emotionally, and materially) is something that is respected in our society. For this reason, desire for a child is a major influence on willingness to consider safer sex. Information about pregnancy and HIV can be one of the most difficult areas on which to counsel, owing to the emotive nature of the subject and the ever-changing statistics on transmission risk to the child. There is also the problem that clients have 'hearing' information when it is not the advice that they want, e.g. Sophie, an HIV-positive IDU, protested angrily on hearing the latest statistics 'that I just did not want her to have a baby, no one did'. It emerged that she had been to at least four different professionals for information, none of whom had said she should not have children, but all of whom simply gave her the up-to-date information on transmission. She had wanted someone to tell her there was no risk, she could not find this and therefore interpreted us as trying to put her off.

For HIV-positive couples who have fertility problems, it can be difficult if not impossible for them to get assistance with this problem. Indeed, some doctors have concluded that it is unethical to provide fertility treatments to HIV-positive couples. Bashore *et al.* (1981) found that pregnant heroin users were younger than non-addicted pregnant women and more likely to be separated or divorced from their partner. In contrast to the reality of their lives, most drug-dependent women hold very conservative views of women as wives and mothers (Williams, 1985). The contrast between what they believe a good parent is and what they are able to do makes IDUs extremely vulnerable to low self-esteem and guilt. Problems can begin to emerge within the first year and especially when the baby starts to run around and become more demanding.

Prostitution (sex working)

Much has been written about sex workers and the potential they have to transmit HIV, particularly drug-using sex workers. For example, it has been suggested that drug-using sex workers will be less likely to use condoms with their customers. It also is suggested that the drug-using sex worker will be more vulnerable to customer demands, that the need for money for drugs will override the desire for safer sex if they are offered more money for not using a condom. In some areas of the UK it has been observed that competition for clients may lead drug-using sex workers to take greater risks for customers and may interfere with prudent patterns of work, e.g. going off in a car alone with two or three men (Rosenberg and Weiner, 1988). However, this contrasts with reports of regular condom use among drug-using sex workers in other studies (Perkins, 1985; Carmen and Moody, 1985).

In the 1990 St Mary's study, all the women working as sex workers carried condoms, and most of them expressed anxiety about these due to police harassment. Research evidence in this area is patchy and frequently contradictory. In three separate surveys among intravenous drug abusers, sex working was not an independent risk factor for HIV (Padian, 1988; Tirelli *et al.*, 1986; Dan *et al.*, 1987). Needle-sharing practices in different locations will influence the level of HIV in the community of those engaged in sex working. The problem for many of the studies is access to adequate numbers of drug-using women who work as sex workers. Data on male sex workers is even more scant; there are virtually no adequate empirical data on male sex workers.

There appears to be a group of women and men drug users who may intermittently engage in sex working as a source of funding for drugs. As a result of the intermittent nature of this activity, they may be more likely to take risks (not only in terms of HIV transmission) and less likely to care for their sexual health – they may not perceive themselves to be professional sex workers. The risks for the 'occasional freelancer' are very difficult to assess.

Many drug-using sex workers will also have sexual partners who are drug users themselves. Therefore, there is a dual risk of infection via shared injecting equipment and sexual transmission. They are less likely to use condoms with their regular sexual partners.

According to Padian (1988), research amongst women engaged in sex work has indicated a distinct trend towards not using condoms with their regular sexual partners, or indeed some long-term regular clients, due to their qualitatively different relationships. Therefore, with people involved in sex work, a different approach to safer sex will be required in order that condoms are not used to distinguish customers from lovers. Love and trust do not foster condom use. The relationship between drug use and sex working is complex. For many, sex working may be the sole support for their own and their partner's drug habit, so that economic pressures to continue working are significant. However, in the 1990 study conducted at St Mary's (Mulleady *et al.*, 1990), sex working accounted for only 8 per cent of the funding for drugs; shoplifting and employment (mostly casual labour) constituting the two major sources (27 per cent and 21 per cent respectively). In the 1985 study (Mulleady and Sherr, 1989), fifteen clients (20 per cent) reported at some time having sex for drugs or money (a broad definition of sex working). In the 1990 sample, 31 per cent of clients reported that they had at some time engaged in sex working as a source of funding for their drugs. However, only 11 per cent reported currently working. What is worrying is that over half (55 per cent) of those who worked professionally had been offered more money by their customers for not using condoms.

There is anecdotal evidence that women who are recruited into sex working with a drug habit or women who acquire a drug habit after becoming sex workers may have a somewhat shorter career than those who do not use drugs. Equally the nature of the work may expose the sex worker to pressure to use drugs. One IDU working for a high-class escort agency was offered cocaine at most of the 'parties' she went to. Her customers, who used cocaine themselves, often actively encouraged her drug use to enhance the sexual experience. One woman, Sophie, who worked for an escort agency took drugs in order to cope with her work, taking it just before she went out to work. Her income was declining as she got older and she worried because she had not managed to save her earnings. As to finding a partner – 'most decent blokes would mind about my past, and if they said it didn't matter, I wouldn't respect them any-way'. Yet the sex worker often has limited economic options if she wants to stop working. They are also at a far greater risk of arrest because of having both an illegal drug habit and engaging in sex working as a source of income.

Prison

The illegal activities which drug users engage in in order to fund their drug habits such as shoplifting, burglary, etc., may well lead to terms in prison. The majority of clients have some previous legal history and many have spent time in prison (70 per cent of 1990 sample). Prison is an environment that can present further risks of HIV exposure. Many clients continue to use drugs in prison (90 per cent of 1990 sample), most of which are non-prescribed (43 per cent heroin, 38 per cent cannabis).

Although the main method of drug administration reported was smoking (54 per cent), 28 per cent injected and 54 per cent of these individuals shared syringes half of the time or more frequently. Fourteen per cent of the 1990 sample had sex whilst in prison, only one person reporting condom use. According to Dolan *et al.* (1990), for these reasons IDUs may be at even higher risk of HIV exposure whilst in prison than in the community. For the drug worker, trying to prepare the client for possible future exposure risks in this situation is an almost pointless task in the absence of realistic service provision in prisons.

Sexual abuse and assault

Many clients in the 1990 study report having been physically or sexually abused: 41 per cent of the 1990 group reported that they had at some time been sexually assaulted. Over half of these were assaults on women in the last five years, suggesting that women drug users may be more vulnerable to sexual assault in their adult lives, possibly as a result of the life-style associated with their drug use. One woman, Jan, reported that she had been gang raped after leaving her dealer's flat in the early hours of the morning as she wandered through a large housing estate alone. Unfortunately, the association with drugs means that this type of attack is extremely unlikely to be reported to the police, and so the crime remains invisible on official statistics.

HIV has been reported as transmitted by rape (Murphy *et al.*, 1989), and it has been suggested that, due to the physical trauma involved, risk of transmission may be greater under circumstances of rape. Thus HIV antibody testing should be offered to a person who has been raped at intervals of three and six months after the assault. The possible role of early AZT treatment to prevent seroconversion in victims of rape has yet to be clarified. Psychological support should also be available during this period and as long afterwards as the individual requires it (Bradbeer, 1990). However, if the crime is not reported, this may not happen.

Childhood sexual and physical abuse is also commonly reported by clients. When she was a teenager, Sue's father would wait for her to come home at night and try to catch her climbing back in through the window. When he caught her he closed the window on her arm and broke it in two places. IDUs also report childhood sexual abuse occurring when they were staying in children's homes.

These histories of abuse are often revealed when talking about sex with the client – even in the early assessment phase. For many it is the possibility of stirring up these painful memories for the client that inhibits some workers from introducing the subject of sex. One implication of this is that, if a worker is going to discuss sexual behaviour with their clients, they will need to be competent to cope with the situation should such sensitive and emotive information be disclosed. This is not to suggest that the worker should be able to do in-depth counselling for those suffering from sexual trauma. What it does mean is that they should have clear lines of referral to therapists who specialise in this work if they feel this is required. A further implication of the effect of sexual abuse on the individual is the devastating effect it can have on the person's self-esteem. If an IDU has to take the lead in contraception or condom use, then they will need to feel confident about themselves and the need to care for their own bodies. A history of sexual abuse is unlikely to facilitate this attitude.

HIV-discordant couples

This term applies where one partner of a couple is HIV antibody positive and the other negative. Where HIV-discordant couples do not practise safer sex, delayed seroconversion in the negative partner can facilitate their belief that it 'will not happen to me', particularly in the absence of illness or physical evidence in the HIV-positive partner. Comments like 'well if that's the case, why am I still negative?' or 'I don't think the virus is going to go any further' are not unusual. In many couples, not practising safer sex can be seen as a way of declaring your regard for your positive partner. For example, Tina and Pat were a couple who had known each other for many years and who had restarted their relationship. Tina was HIV positive. They were not having safer sex although Pat was fully aware of her HIV status: 'He says he doesn't mind.' Clearly the consequences were far removed, and neither of them felt the need to prevent the vague and non-evident HIV. This reaction is more common when the HIV-positive partner is asymptomatic, presumably because AIDS is still a remote possibility in the future and the denial process can operate more effectively. In many cases, even when the couple adopt safer sex initially, as the relationship develops they may forget about their past and issues of trust and intimacy can take precedence over the need for safer sex. Whatever the couple's response to HIV, both partners face the consequences either directly or indirectly, and, even when safer sex is practised by the couple, it can present its own problems. One HIV-positive man commented, 'I don't know why we both bother [to have sex], I get up immediately, tie a knot in the condom, go to the bathroom and make sure it flushed down the toilet. It's all so clinical, I don't think my wife enjoys sex any more, and all it does for me is remind me about the virus.'

The other common reaction is where the negative partner becomes fearful of having sex, even though they are practising safer sex. Cathy expressed profound relief that her HIV-positive partner did not want sex. 'I try to hide it, but I'm sure he knows how frightened I am. We take all the precautions that we can, but I just can't help being afraid. ' Cathy also encouraged her partner not to reduce his methadone dosage in the hope that the drug would curtail his desire for sex. A further implication of this is that if the sexual relationship breaks down, people may not try to sort this out because of the relief they feel that they no longer have to have sex. In an example of this, Claire was quite content to stay with her partner although he had told her that he wanted the relationship to finish. She could cope better with a platonic relationship, and she had no other accommodation to go to. Yet at the same time it was clearly damaging to her self-esteem that he had rejected her.

Equally, waiting for illnesses to occur or continuously watching out for them can put a terrible strain on the relationship. The negative partner also has to cope with fear and sometimes anger about their partner's HIV status; which is accentuated if there are children involved, as there are fears about how the family will cope, if and when their partner dies.

The other aspect of relationship problems are the many difficulties experienced by those clients not in a relationship – recently diagnosed HIV-positive clients complain of having serious problems in meeting suitable partners. According to John, 'even if I did meet someone, what would I say to them? I'm hardly a catch am I?' A number of clients in this position have seen support groups as their only means of meeting a partner, someone in the same position as themselves, with whom they can avoid difficult explanations of their antibody status. The client can have greater expectations of the support group than its ostensible function.

CONCLUSION

Perhaps more than in any other area of clinical work, the quality of the client–worker contact in drug work is influenced by the range and intensity of practical services provided by the drug agency. This will also influence the worker's perception of whether or not it is appropriate to discuss sexuality in their work setting.

Where the opportunity arises for therapeutic intervention, the worker can draw on a variety of approaches, e.g. cognitive methods, sex therapy, relationship counselling, skills training, and group work. Techniques such as role play and modelling can be especially useful as they encourage the IDU to put themselves in the position of 'the other person' and enable them to develop and practise interpersonal communication skills. Group work which encourages the development of communication skills in the negotiation of safer sex is an important development in this field and merits further evaluation of its effectiveness (Schilling et al., 1991). Peer support groups (although difficult to sustain with drug users due to erratic attendance) can be extremely influential in encouraging the practice of safer sex and safer drug use.

There is nothing particularly new about the therapeutic techniques used to deal with the counselling issues mentioned in this chapter, it is the context that is unusual. The level and intensity of the intervention will depend on a multitude of factors – the function and setting of the drug agency, the background and training of the drug worker, the client's motivation for the contact, their cultural background, the time span for the contact, etc. Drug workers need to be innovative in the way they use their chosen intervention techniques with the client.

Furthermore, many health and other professionals, for example, health advisers and probation officers, come into contact with drug users in the course of their work. In order that they feel equipped to respond appropriately to the drug user, it is essential that drug counselling and awareness is given greater prominence in their training. In order to sustain the worker it is my belief that there are two basic requirements – an integrated on-going training programme that can be proactive in content rather than reactive and, secondly, the regular provision of clinical supervision and support.

As a result of research carried out following the epidemic of HIV, we have a greater understanding of drug users' injecting and sexual behaviour, as well as a more extensive range of services, for example, syringe exchanges. There is a need for continued empirical research on drug users' behaviour, but equally we require implementation and evaluation of innovative therapeutic approaches. Applied research can be more difficult both to undertake and interpret as it involves interventions with both staff and clients in what may be a 'complicated' work setting. However, despite the difficulties it is a worthwhile endeavour since it can provide the drug worker with an increased repertoire of therapeutic methods in a field where their skills of persistence and ingenuity are likely to be tested to the limit.

NOTES

1 Data from the 1985 sample reflect the route of administration used by clients before commencing a methadone treatment programme. Clients in the 1986 study were already in receipt of prescriptions for methadone which explains their higher reporting of oral use. The higher percentages using oral/inhalation routes in 1989–90 reflect prescribed methadone and the fact that a more detailed drug history was taken, revealing high levels of alcohol and cannabis use.

2 In the 1990 study, 110 of the 141 clients had sought a test and, of these, twenty reported themselves to be HIV positive (18 per cent), but true figures may be higher, as a number of untested clients (8 per cent) believed themselves to be HIV positive due to risk behaviours they had or were currently engaged in, i.e. sexual relationship with HIV-positive partner or syringe sharing with someone they knew to be HIV positive.

REFERENCES

Advisory Council on the Misuse of Drugs (1988) *AIDS and Drug Misuse*, Part 1, London: HMSO.

Bashore, R.A., Ketchum, J.S., Staisch, K.J. *et al.* (1981) 'Heroin addiction and pregnancy – interdepartmental clinical conference', *Western Journal of Medicine* 134: 506–14.

Blatman, S. (1980) *Methadone Effects on Pregnancy and the Newborn*, unpublished, Dartmouth Medical School, USA.

Bradbeer, C. (1990) 'Human immunodeficiency virus and its relationship to women', *International Journal of Sexually Transmitted Diseases and AIDS* 1: 233–8.

Bradbeer, C.S. and Heyderman, E. (1989) 'The risk of progression of cervical dysplasia in women with HIV', Vth International Conference on AIDS, Montreal, Abstract MBP58.

Brown, L.S., Murphy, D.L., and Priman, B.J. (1987) 'Sex partners of intravenous drug abusers: implications for the next spread of the AIDS epidemic', paper presented at the 49th Annual Scientific Meeting of the Problems of Drug Dependence, Philadelphia, Pennsylvania, 14–18 June.

Byrne, M.A., Taylor-Robinson, D., Munday, P.E., and Harris, J.R. (1989) 'The common occurrence of human papiloma virus infection and intraepithelial neoplasia in women infected by HIV', *AIDS* 3: 379–82.

Carmen, A. and Moody, H. (1985) *Working Women: The Subterranean World of Street Prostitution*, New York: Harper and Row.

Christiansen, B.A. and Goldman, M.S. (1983) 'Alcohol related expectancies versus demographic/background variables in the prediction of adolescent drinking', *Journal of Consulting and Clinical Psychology* 51: 245–57.

Cranfield, S. (1990) 'Safer sex education with drug users', in P.M. Fleming (ed.) *Harm Reduction: Drugs and HIV/AIDS*, Wessex Regional Health Authority.

Cranfield, S. and Dixon, A. (1990) *Drugs Training, HIV and AIDs in the 1990's: A Guide for Training Professionals*, London: Health Education Authority.

Cupitt, C., Mulleady, G., Phillips, K. and White, D. (1992) 'Barriers to safer sex: why condom availability doesn't lead to safer sex', *Druglink* 7(2): 13.

Dan, M., Rock, M., and Bar-Shani, S. (1987) 'HIV antibodies in drug addicted prostitutes', *Journal of the American Medical Association* 257: 1047.

Davison, C.F., Hudson, C.N., Ades, A.E., and Peckham, C.S. (1989) 'Antenatal testing for human immunodeficiency virus', *Lancet*, 16 Dec.: 1442–4.

Dolan, K., Donaghue, M.C., and Stimson, G.V. (1990) 'Drug injecting and syringe sharing in custody and in the community – an exploratory survey of HIV risk behaviour', *The Howard Journal of Criminal Justice* 29(3): 177–86.

Eldred, C.A. and Washington, M.N. (1975) 'Female heroin addicts in a city treatment programme: the forgotton minority', *Psychiatry* 38: 75–85.

France, A.J., Skidmore, C.A., Robertson, J.R., Brettle, R.P., Roberts, J.J.K., Burns, S.M., Foster, C.A., Inglis, J.M., Galloway, W.B.F., and Davison, S.J. (1988) 'Heterosexual spread of immunodeficiency virus in Edinburgh', *British Medical Journal* 296: 526–9.

Magura, S., Shapiro, J.L., Siddiqi, Q., and Lipton, D.S. (1990) 'Variables influencing condom use among intravenous drug users', *American Journal of Public Health* 80(10): 82–4.

Marlatt, G.A. and Ronsenow, D. (1980) 'Cognitive processes in alcohol use: expectancy and the balanced placebo design', in N. Melloy (ed.) *Advances in Substances Abuse: Behavioural and Biological Research*, JAI Press, pp. 115–36.

Mirim, S.M., Meyer, R.E., Mendelson, J., and Ellingboe, J. (1980) 'Opiate use and sexual dysfunction', *American Journal of Psychiatry* 137: 909–15.

Morbidity and Mortality Weekly Report (1989) 'Update: heterosexual transmission of AIDS and HIV infection – United States', MMWR, 38, pp. 423–34.

Mulleady, G. and Sherr, L. (1989) 'Lifestyle factors for drug users in relation to risks for HIV', AIDS Care 1(1): 45–50.

Mulleady, G., White, D., Phillips, K. and Cupitt, C. (1990) 'Reducing sexual transmission of HIV for injecting drug users: the challenge for counselling', Counselling Psychology Quarterly 3(4): 325–41.

Murphy, S., Kitchen, V., Harris, J.R.W., and Forster, S.M. (1989) 'Rape and subsequent seroconversion to HIV', British Medical Journal 299: 718–19.

Padian, N.S. (1988) 'Prostitute women and AIDS: epidemiology', AIDS 2: 413–22.

Perkins, R. (1985) 'AIDS and prostitution', British Medical Journal 143: 426.

Priestly, B.C. (1973) 'Drug addiction and the newborn', Developmental Medicine and Child Neurology 15: 200.

Rosenbaum, M. (1979) 'Becoming addicted: the woman addict', Contemporary Drug Problems 8: 141–6.

Rosenberg, M.J. and Weiner, J.M. (1988) 'Prostitutes and AIDS: a health department priority?', American Journal of Public Health 78: 418–23.

Schilling, R.F., Eo-bassel, N., Schinke, S.P., Gordon, K., and Nicols, S. (1991) 'Reducing sexual transmission of AIDS. Skills building with recovering female drug users', Public Health Reports.

Stall, R., Mc Kusick, L., Wiley, J., Coates, T., and Ostrow, D. (1986) 'Alcohol and drug use during sexual activity and compliance with safe sex guidelines for AIDS: The AIDS behavioral research project', Health Education Quarterly 13: 359–71.

Tirelli, V., Vaccheri, E., Sorio, R., Carbone, A., and Monfardini, S. (1986) 'HTLV III antibodies in drug addicted prostitutes used by U.S. soldiers in Italy', Journal of the American Medical Association 357: 1047.

Tylden, E. (1983) 'Care of the pregnant addict', MIMS Magazine June: 61–3.

Wiley, J.A. and Herschkom, S.J. (1989) 'Heterogeneity in the probability of HIV transmission per sexual contact: the case of male to female transmission in penile–vaginal intercourse', Statistics in Medicine 8: 93–102.

Wilks, J. (1989) 'Drug treatment and prescribing practice: what can be learned from the past?', in G. Bennett. (ed.) Treating Drug Abusers, London: Routledge, pp. 137–54

Williams, A. (1985) 'When the client is pregnant: information for counsellors', Journal of Substance Misuse Treatment 2: 27–34.

Chapter 10

Sex, love, and relationships
Issues and problems for gay men in the AIDS era

Heather George

INTRODUCTION

Psycho-social interventions for people with AIDS arose in response to direct need (Miller, Weber, and Green, 1986). The deficiencies in solely adopting a biomedical model of care and the desirability of providing psychological support for people experiencing any serious illness have long been recognised (Davis and Fallowfield, 1991). Yet, for individuals facing the uncertainties of a new disease, AIDS, psychological care was even more essential. One major area wherein support and intervention was clearly needed was in the realm of sexuality. In 1985, at St Mary's Hospital, Paddington, I started working with people affected by AIDS. There were huge demands for therapeutic interventions with high numbers of distressed people and for dissemination of firsthand experience to other workers via training and lecturing: work which was emotionally intense and urgent, as has subsequently been acknowledged (Mearns, 1990). From my initial encounters with people with HIV, I had adopted the general principles of cognitive therapy (Ellis, 1962; Beck, 1976; Meichenbaum, 1977) and the 'new sex therapies' (Masters and Johnson, 1970; Kaplan, 1974). This chapter describes how these principles have been applied to a client group which emerged in the mid-1980s – those non-heterosexual men for whom AIDS precipitated psycho-sexual problems or created an avenue for therapy via the establishment of AIDS services. In addition, the concept of 'sexual myths', viz. false ideas and expectations about love and sex (Zilbergeld, 1980), is discussed and examined in terms of how this may be used in clinical practice to help individuals clarify the nature of their problems, provide comfort for their distress, and encourage increases in confidence and self-esteem.

The chapter is something of a self-indulgence, in being based very largely on my own clinical experience. However, the paucity of theories, techniques, or research findings which could be applied to the sexual problems of gay and bisexual men and the absence of any work on how AIDS affected sexual and relationship difficulties (since, of course, AIDS created a new context) presented me with the task of developing a workable approach. The reality of the work within a London teaching hospital, where high case loads and long working hours are part of the ethos of the institution, involved adopting a reflexive approach to therapy, responding with any techniques and skills which seemed effective. The emphasis was on outcome (relief of distress). Any analysis or theorising about the therapeutic process had to be *post hoc*. I found similar work pressures when, in 1989, I moved to provide a specialist AIDS/HIV clinical psychology service in Brighton. Reflection on themes which occurred in clinical sessions and discussion with colleagues in the HIV/AIDS field led me to identify a number of ideas or beliefs about sex and relationships. These 'myths' I came to use in subsequent sessions to help gay and bisexual men make sense of their experience, and to form part of the framework for my interventions with them. Four common themes are presented here, with case studies to illustrate how these relate to the general approach I have developed over the years in AIDS work. They parallel directly the myths or beliefs held by heterosexuals, and the general framework is the one I have applied in work with all patients.[1]

This chapter therefore comprises:

1. A description of the development of a common-sense, workable model of care which arose out of the need to respond to people seeking help from AIDS services.
2. An outline of how this model is applicable to work with gay and bisexual men.
3. A brief review of the literature on therapy with gay and bisexual men.
4. A discussion of the current issues which gay and bisexual men may bring to therapy.
5. Accounts of four themes frequently encountered in clinical practice, with case histories to illustrate how these may be used within the general model of work with non-heterosexual men, and conclusions.

ORIGINS AND DEVELOPMENT OF A GENERAL APPROACH TO PSYCHOLOGICAL CARE IN AIDS WORK

During my training for clinical psychology in the early 1980s, I recall my attempts to reconcile textbook accounts of various therapeutic approaches with what was possible in practice. Whilst on placement at London hospitals I was able to gain some practical experience of the 'new sex therapies' developed in the 1970s, and the cognitive-behavioural approach to psycho-sexual problems (Jehu, 1979) favoured by my supervisors. Far from being embarrassed by dealing with people's sexual experiences, preferences, and feelings, I was relieved to find a therapeutic framework which equipped me with effective techniques yet allowed freedom for creativity to produce individual interventions; therapy was fitted to the patient, rather than the reverse. Patients attending sessions seemed equally comfortable, and almost without exception found the outcome of interventions successful in feeling that they had been helped. At last, I had found an area of work and a therapeutic framework where the gap between theory and practice was minimal.

In addition, the basic philosophy was congruent with my own feelings about how people function, the extent to which therapy is able to help with their problems, and the appropriate demeanour to adopt as therapist. Although, for example, psychoanalytic theories are much richer in accounting for the complexities of people's experiences and problems than cognitive or behavioural ones, I feel that people are not complex in quite that way, and only a limited number of patients seem able to use psychoanalytic formulations and interpretations, particularly with respect to sexual dysfunction problems. In reality, workers in the 'caring professions' find that people's lives are certainly complicated; but I have found that the most that our interventions would seem able to do is to help clients cope or manage, and to help them feel sufficiently comfortable and confident so that they are able to deal with their past and current experience without extreme anxiety, misery, or self-doubt. Patients present to us for 'expert' help with their problems and our training allows us to make suggestions about how their difficulties have developed, provide them with information from research, and encourage them to use techniques and methods which may prove useful. Except in rare situations where patients' behaviour would be viewed as harmful to themselves, to other people, or to myself, I have seen my role as encouraging them to change as they feel appropriate, not 'develop' along particular theoretical lines, as acknowledging what may be unusual rather than 'abnormal' about their experiences, and as employing terms and methodologies which present alternative ways of seeing or doing things rather than labelling their views and behaviours pejoratively.

These lines of thought were to prove useful in responding to the needs of people who sought help from AIDS services. For a variety of reasons, the atmosphere in AIDS work tends to be more open, more straightforward, and generally 'warmer' than in other fields of clinical psychology (Mearns, 1990). Professional boundaries are essential, but a professional facade or 'superior' therapist stance would not be acceptable to users of AIDS services. The basic concepts and components of cognitive therapy (as discussed by Baker, Chapter 5, this volume) and the psycho-educational model of sex therapy (Cole, 1988) are congruent with the style which has been successfully adopted by myself and others working in the field (see Table 10.1). Furthermore, the approach and style may be used to form the basis for therapy with the significant numbers of gay and bisexual men who present with sexual and relationships problems via AIDS services.

Table 10.1 Therapeutic approach and clinical style

- Features of psychological interventions: psychological approach based on coping with 'problems of living' (e.g. anxiety, depression, obsessions and compulsions, phobias, sexual and relationships problems, adjustment reactions, including bereavement) as distinct from the traditional psychiatric model of mental illness.
- Length of sessions: 50–60 minutes, or up to 90 minutes for couples attending together.
- Frequency of sessions: scheduled appointments from several times a week to follow-up appointments at three or six months, 'crisis intervention' appointments by arrangement.
- Note keeping: background data (age, sex, referral source, presenting problem, sexual orientation, location) kept for statistical purposes; notes taken during session (with patient's permission) as a record of therapy, kept under lock and key; letters typed by secretarial staff also bound by rules of confidentiality.
- Therapeutic model: problem-solving, structured, broadly based cognitive approach based on coping with problems; alternative ways of dealing with problems explicitly suggested by therapist; 'homework' assignments and themes of sessions negotiated between therapist and patient.
- End of therapy: negotiated when therapist/client feel sessions are no longer helpful, when presenting problem is no longer a difficulty, or when referral to another agency is more appropriate.

THE ROLE OF GUM: FROM AIDS COUNSELLING TO PSYCHO-SEXUAL THERAPY FOR GAY MEN

With the advent of AIDS came the development of counselling and psychology services within departments of genito-urinary medicine (GUM) (O'Rourke, 1989). Staff working in GUM departments, legally bound by the Venereal Diseases Acts (NHS VD Regulations, 1974) to keep confidential any information given by patients and any notes giving details of patients' sexual histories, have always been accustomed to seeing people who would be reluctant or unwilling to present to their GPs with worries about their sexual health. Staff would routinely see people who suffered sexual guilt because of having engaged in acts or behaviours contrary to their own sexual mores (e.g. having had an extra-marital affair, a casual sexual contact, or used the services of a prostitute); or patients who felt their life-styles would incite disapproval from others (e.g. unmarried women with several sexual partners or men who had sex with men); and those who simply felt that their sex lives were too private and personal to discuss with a family doctor. Many GUM department doctors, nurses, and health advisers became extremely skilled at dealing with the emotional aspects of these sensitive areas of people's lives. However, the availability of tests for detecting antibodies to HIV ('AIDS tests') and the concomitant necessity explicitly to provide pre- and post-test counselling within GUM departments resulted in an even greater awareness of psychological issues related to sexuality.[2]

From the HIV-testing and care agencies came the impetus to identify and establish therapeutic interventions for complex psycho-sexual and emotional problems which occur both for people infected with HIV and for others where AIDS touches their lives in some less obvious way. The availability of AIDS counselling and psychology services through GUM departments was an important historical step for the development of psycho-sexual work with gay and bisexual men. Via GUM, psychologists and therapists are bound by the same confidentiality regulations as the other staff and are not accessed by referral from family doctors (the very use of this term to replace GPs may alienate gay and bisexual men). It is clear that men who have sex with men are among the people who use the AIDS services to gain access to confidential support for psycho-sexual problems where the issue of HIV is not necessarily of great importance for them. Although AIDS is, of course, an issue for almost all gay and bisexual men (principally because in public awareness it is linked with men who have sex with men), the sexual and relationship problems for which they seek therapeutic help via the HIV services may or may not be directly linked to HIV.

Hence the development of AIDS/HIV services generated a growing awareness of the need to provide therapeutic interventions which are informed about and supportive of the life-styles of gay and bisexual men. Only a few decades ago, the dominant therapeutic paradigms defined life-styles of non-heterosexual men as pathological, either because of unresolved childhood conflicts which resulted in immature adjustment in adult life (classical psychoanalysis) or due to faulty learning which could be 'corrected' (classical behaviour therapy). This chapter uses the case histories of men referred from GUM clinics over the past six years to demonstrate how – via recognition of gay life-styles and the particular problems they may create, accurate knowledge about homosexuality, and confrontation of the issue of homophobia – techniques developed primarily or exclusively from work with heterosexual populations may be developed and employed in a 'gay affirmative' approach.

HISTORICAL PERSPECTIVE

Prior to the 1970s, homosexuality, if considered at all, was seen as a disorder. In 1973, homosexuality was deleted from the diagnostic and statistic manual (DSM) of the American Psychiatric Association. However, it is clear from the behaviour of therapists and other care workers, and from the reports of gay men themselves, that a corresponding shift in professional attitudes did not take place. Awareness of gay life-styles and discussion of homosexuality were almost universally absent from professional training or, where they occurred, continued to be framed within models of abnormality, perversion, or immaturity. The very jargon and terms used in traditional therapeutic approaches, such as 'marital' and 'family' therapy, implicitly excluded gay people. Much theoretical reasoning and therapeutic practice, if not 'blaming' individuals, sought to identify the 'disease' in the system or their upbringing which resulted in them being homosexual. Gay men and lesbians were presented as victims of biology or social forces.

As recently as 1976, Davison drew attention to the continuing therapeutic practices designed to change the sexual behaviour of gay men, commenting that there was almost no work at that time aimed at helping therapists 'change their prejudicial biases'. Throughout the 1970s debate continued over whether gay men seeking 'conversion' to heterosexuality should be provided with techniques to help them do this, and some therapists continued to prescribe such 'treatment' to gay men who presented with any sexual problem, regardless of their own interest in changing their sexual orientation. Aversion therapies and psychotherapies aimed at providing insight into 'sexual deviance' or 'immature adjustment' remain realities in the minds of many gay people, and serve as a reminder for them to be cautious in approaching the conventional helping agencies for psychological support.

During the 1980s there was evidence of some general discussion of issues relevant to psychological therapy with gay men and lesbians (e.g. MacKinnon and Miller, 1985; Stein, 1988) but, paradoxically, it was the fact that gay men were identified as a 'risk group' for HIV infection in Western societies, a fact that generated increased fear, prejudice, and hostility, that led to the widespread examination of the needs and problems of gay people (Altman, 1988) and concerns about homophobia among health-care professionals (Douglas *et al.*, 1985; Wallack, 1989; Croteau and Morgan, 1989).

Since the mid-1980s, governments and health-care workers of the Western world have woken up to the reality of AIDS in the huge numbers of published articles specifically examining the emotional impact of AIDS on gay men and the type of supportive work which may help with the issues raised by HIV (e.g. Casper, 1986). There has also been an increase in publications on sexual and relationship work where HIV is discussed as an issue which may lead to gay and bisexual men having problems and seeking therapy (e.g. Hart, 1984; Gordon, 1988; Yaffe and Fenwick, 1988; Ussher, 1991). This body of work – and this chapter – are based on the following assumptions.

1. The need for psychological therapy which addresses the issues and problems which may arise in gay life-styles.
2. A recognition of the fact that gay people do not form a homogeneous client group, but require individual assessment and appropriate therapy just as for heterosexual patients.
3. The recognition of the need to modify established forms of intervention for gay people who seek therapy.

In the remainder of this chapter, concepts and components developed from psycho-sexual therapy with heterosexual couples and single straight people are re-worked to address issues relevant to gay and bisexual men in the AIDS era.

SEX, LOVE, AND RELATIONSHIPS: THEMES EMERGING FROM INTERVENTIONS WITH MEN WHO PRESENT FOR AIDS COUNSELLING

Encouraging safer sexual practices in order to decrease risks of HIV transmission has become central in literature about AIDS and HIV, in training of people involved in pre- and post-test counselling and other care of people with AIDS, and in research into sexual behaviour. In studies of gay men, there has been recognition of how perceived risks of exposure to the virus may vary with the degree of emotional involvement and length of relationships with partners (Fitzpatrick *et al.*, 1990) and of how sexual encounters are structured by notions such as ejaculation being the end marker of a particular sexual encounter (Davies, 1989).

Little attention has been given to general beliefs about sex and relationships, yet in my own clinical work these frequently underlie the worries of non-heterosexual men who present for AIDS counselling (George, 1988, 1989, 1990).

During the mid-1980s, sexual dysfunctional difficulties such as erectile problems and premature ejaculation were commonly identified as important by gay and bisexual men, and I used interventions to address these problems (programmes along classical 'new sex therapy' lines, such as modified sensate focus assignments and other techniques developed for heterosexuals – see Cooper (1988) for a full description). However, in more recent years I found an increase in the number of gay and bisexual men who saw a dysfunctional problem as secondary to more complex difficulties with sexuality and relationships. Conventional sexual assignments continue to be requested and found acceptable by many patients, but there has been a shift towards a focus on their beliefs about sex and relationships, and consequently more emphasis in therapy on substitution of more 'realistic' ideas about casual and long-term involvement with others. This change was illustrated by an examination of the case notes of eighty gay or bisexual men attending psychology sessions during 1989 to 1991, which revealed that over 50 per cent identified relationship difficulties as the presenting problem, compared with 20 per cent of a sample of 105 men who attended during 1986 to 1988.

In relationship work, I have found it helpful to use interventions based largely on cognitive-behavioural approaches to 'marital' problems, using techniques originally developed almost exclusively with heterosexual couples and single straight people (Zilbergeld, 1980; Beck, 1989; Nowinski, 1989; Crowe and Ridley, 1990). Within this framework, didactic elements such as providing information and giving instructions may be used with debate and discussions in sessions which focus on people's assumptions about themselves and others. Negative self-evaluations and unrealistic expectations about sex and love are examined and reformulated to foster more positive experiences and decrease the likelihood of disappointment in relationships and more casual encounters with others. The aim of interventions is not to replace optimism with pessimism, leaving individuals without hope, but to help people to identify realistic expectations and feel comfortable with themselves, their relationships and their life-styles.

Initial sessions comprise a fairly conventional 'whole person' psychology assessment carried out by interview with an individual or couple and including issues of particular relevance to AIDS (see Table 10.2). A provisional formulation of the problem is provided, and the process of intervention proceeds as follows:

- Formulation of problems and coping difficulties
- Identification of beliefs about sex and relationships
- Examination of how beliefs relate to problems
- Discussion and exploration of the basis of beliefs in reality, via accounts from the patient or couple of current or past experiences
- Creation of realistic beliefs to enhance self-esteem and coping
- 'Reality testing' the new beliefs by reflection and relation to experience.

In practice, evaluation and intervention occur in parallel, and no work has such a clear-cut form, and nor should it – these interventions are effective only within the caring therapeutic relationship necessary for emotional support. Change in people's feelings, thoughts, behaviours, and self-concepts takes time. Good rapport with the therapist is essential. Hence in my work if any individuals or couples find it difficult to discuss their problems, for example, if they find it hard to work with a female therapist because they feel more comfortable with a gay male, I attempt to meet their requests by referring them to another worker. However, most of the gay and bisexual men have expressed only concern about receiving professional and empathic support and very few have been bothered about my gender (in fact, some have preferred seeing a woman).

Table 10.2 Assessment interviews: issues relevant to AIDS

Current emotional problems

Development of problems

Health status with respect to HIV (i.e. untested and symptom free; untested with symptoms of HIV infection; tested and found negative; positive and symptom free; positive with symptoms of HIV-related illness, including diagnosis of AIDS)

Knowledge of HIV/AIDS (source of information; beliefs about transmission, safer sex, course and management of illness, and ideas about treatments, including counselling and therapy)

Past emotional problems (episodes and dates; past therapy and outcome; past coping and resources)

Past and current physical problems – HIV-related and non-HIV-related (experience of illness and any hospital admissions; attitudes towards health, illness, hospitals, and care received)

Current general health (energy/fatigue level; sleep, rest, and relaxation; appetite and weight change)

Experience of illness and death of others (who was affected, their diagnoses, the outcome and dates of their illnesses; others known with HIV/AIDS and outcomes; coping with illness and death of others)

Sexual orientation and experience (current, intended, and preferred activities; any regular partners or sexual contacts; personal rating of importance of sex; current and past loss of libido or other dysfunctional problems)

Partner (if any – quality and nature of relationship; partner's age, health status; partner's knowledge of problems; contact with partner's friends and family)

Family (parents, siblings, extended family, dependants, and quality of these relationships; degree of contact with them; their knowledge of HIV problems)

Social network (close and other friends, and degree of contact with them; social and lone activities or interests; religious beliefs and supports; contact with any HIV-related agencies)

Work and income (current and past work or study; personal rating of importance of work; financial status)

Home (resident alone or with others; owner or tenant; how long there and satisfaction with accommodation; distance from social support; distance from HIV services)

Current thoughts (about self, situation, future; distressing or frightening ideas; suicide)

Current mood (fluctuations; best and worst times of day; level of enjoyment)

How patient spends time (before and since problem; last week and month; immediate and longer-term intentions)

Expectations of therapy

Conventional psycho-sexual and relationship approaches can form useful frameworks in therapy with gay and bisexual men, but they must be re-worked and expanded to include issues such as homophobia which are central to gay life-styles, as described below.

The effects of myths and stereotypes on gay relationships

As discussed by Nicolson, Chapter 3, and Ussher, Chapter 1, for hetero-sexuals, there are conventional life-styles and gender roles in relation-ships, plus a 'phallocentric' notion of sex where success is measured by penetration (vaginal intercourse). These do, of course, lead to problems for straight men and women (see Baker, Chapter 5), particularly for those who do not comply by adopting a 'normal' role (e.g. the stigma felt by some single, childless women) and because expectations such as sexual loyalty are frequently not matched by reality (extra-marital affairs are extremely common), or in the case of the physically disabled, as is illustrated by Williams, Chapter 7.

However, there is security in 'knowing the rules' and having clear roles with which to identify (or reject). For gay people these do not exist. Clear life-styles are hard to establish in a society which is hostile to non-heterosexuals, and rules for relationships have to be created and negotiated. A myth commonly held by straight people is that homosexual relationships mirror heterosexual ones, with one partner taking on the more dominant 'masculine' role and the other the 'submissive female'. Such roles have very occasionally been described in clinical sessions by gay couples, but these are rare. Yet the absence of clear roles is not necessarily liberating. Gay men have described the difficulties they have establishing and maintaining relationships, since they have to 'guess' what is expected of them by a partner, and there are no structures, markers, or 'rewards' from society (such as wedding celebrations when a couple get together) supporting the relationship as for heterosexual couples. They more frequently question why they stay in a relationship than straight people, for whom commitment and long-term involvement are more likely to be expected by a partner and the rest of society.

Another common stereotype is that gay men are 'sexually rampant', always ready for sex, and all having very high numbers of partners. Although surveys of the sexual behaviour of samples of gay and bisexual men generally show that the upper limit of numbers of partners is higher than for straight men (Fitzpatrick et al. (1990) report the number of partners in one year for a group of gay men ranged from zero to 248), and there is a greater tolerance and degree of honesty about sexual contact outside an established relationship (i.e. more 'open' relationships), it does not follow that all or even the majority of gay men have very high numbers of sexual contacts or very frequent sex. It does mean that sexual expression for gay men may range from close-coupled monogamy (sexual contact with one long-term partner only) to purely recreational sex with many men. Having such a range from which to 'choose' a sexual life-style is not always easy. For some gay men, having a high level of recreational sex has political as well as personal significance, as a symbol of pride in the gay movement, whilst for others sex must be part of a longer-term relationship. What frequently appears to happen is that gay and bisexual men feel torn between what they perceive as the norm for gay life-styles and the ideal of heterosexual society; these perceptions tend to be based on stereotypes of the sexually obsessed single gay man and the idealised romantic love of the heterosexual marriage. Hetero-sexual values – including those about the nature of homosexuality – are, of course, the more pervasive and may be internalised by non-heterosexual men in a self-punishing, homophobic way. When this happens it is impossible for a gay or bisexual man to feel pride and high self-esteem, since the (albeit unrealistic) romantic marriage is not available to him because of his (also untrue) 'promiscuous nature'.

The influence of the stereotypes and 'myths' about the lives of gay and bisexual men which are dominant in Western culture became apparent from the beliefs and expectations they expressed during clinical sessions. Five themes emerged so commonly that I began to introduce them in discussions with patients as examples of beliefs which undermine the security and esteem of many non-heterosexual men. These are outlined below, with examples from my own clinical work to illustrate how a focus on these beliefs may form the basis of therapeutic interventions which are affirmative and supportive of gay and bisexual life-styles.

THEME 1: A HIDDEN OR SINGLE LIFE-STYLE MEANS PERSONAL FAILURE

Men who have sex with men have to face the issue of whether to tell others of their sexual preference. Discrimination certainly still exists to-wards gay and bisexual men and, although, of course, if they all disclosed their sexual orientation this might lead to greater social acceptance of homosexuality, many find themselves in situations where hostility and ostracism would be the likely outcomes. Some gay groups advocate 'coming out' as the only solution, but unfortunately, until non-heterosexual life-styles are widely accepted in society, the quality of some individuals' lives would be sacrificed for the common good – a laudable gesture, but unbearably painful for most. Perhaps the one universal feature of adjustment is the need to come out to the self, i.e. for non-heterosexual men to acknowledge their attraction to their own sex. One obstacle to doing so is internalised homophobia – if a man views homosexual contact as deviant, inferior, or abnormal he may attempt to preserve heterosexual identity in order to maintain a 'normal' self- concept rather than suffer a loss of esteem by accepting that he is attracted to men. Furthermore, if he has internalised the heterosexual 'norm' of the long-term monogamous relationship as the only valid life-style, and he does not live in this way, or would have to divorce his wife to establish regular contact with men, he may regard himself as a failure in this respect also.

In therapy with non-heterosexual men who are ashamed or ambivalent about their sexual orientation or about their single gay life-style, the beliefs which are frequently challenged are that:

1. Belief 1: Men who have sex with men are abnormal. Challenge 1: This may be challenged by substituting the view of homosexuality as one of a number of acceptable sexual preferences which form the 'normal' dimensions of sexuality.
2. Belief 2: The only valid way to live is within a long-term one-to-one monogamous relationship. Challenge 2: It is questionable whether this life-style inevitably leads to happiness and other life-styles which may be fulfilling, satisfactory, or at least adequate can be suggested.

The accounts of two men – Len and John – are given below to illustrate how beliefs about a 'closet' life-style and about personal inadequacy can be modified to elicit thoughts and actions which build rather than destroy self-esteem.

Case study 1: Len, a 'closet gay'

Len was an unmarried 61-year-old man. His sexual activities for the previous fifteen years had comprised mutual masturbation only, all very casual and brief contacts which lasted only a few minutes and occurred in public places (lavatories, heathland, parks). He had become very distressed and tearful when describing these incidents, and it was apparent that he felt very ashamed of them. He explained that he had received treatment from a psychiatrist in his distant past to 'cure his condition'.

Len was an articulate man with a gentle and self-deprecatory manner. At the time of referral he lived with his mother. His father had died when Len was thirty, and since then he had remained in very close contact with his mother, frequently acting as her companion at family and social functions. He had a sister who lived nearby, but as she was married and because he had always been so close to their mother, he had been the one to take over her care as she became increasingly dependent. In order to do so he had retired early from his career, and sacrificed the majority of his interests (playing the piano, concert and theatre going, writing poetry) since he was able to go out only if his sister stayed with their mother. He managed to attend psychology sessions only by combining them with an extended shopping trip.

Len had first become aware of sexual feelings towards men when he was doing his National Service. There had been a degree of sexual contact between the men, which he had found exciting, but it was never discussed nor acknowledged as anything to do with relationships or 'normal' sex – most of the other men had wives or girlfriends, and there were never conversations about men having sex with men, only jokes about 'queers' and 'Nancy boys'. Len quickly discovered how to access sexual contact with men, but that this was something which took place furtively and with minimal conversation. He felt inadequate because he had no sexual interest in women, and would therefore be unable to have a close relationship via marriage.

He had considered marriage to a close woman friend, Kay, during his thirties. As he had been unable to show any sexual interest, he explained that he had 'other tendencies', which Kay had accepted. She remained a good friend, continuing to see Len after marrying another man. To other friends and relatives, Len's sexual orientation had always remained 'hidden'.

Initial sessions consisted of giving Len 'permission' to discuss his sexual experiences freely and acknowledging the problems of his current situation, caring for an elderly mother. He seemed relieved to be able to express his guilt and shame over his sexual activities, and was quite surprised to find that I was to make no attempt to change his sexual orientation either at that point or in future sessions. He felt guilty not only because of failing to reveal his 'true self' to his family and friends, but also as he was aware that many younger gay men were able to live quite openly, and he felt in some way disloyal to them.

We discussed how, prior to the 1960s, the majority of gay men were able to express their sexuality only by extremely casual, brief, and secret contact, and I suggested that Len's behaviour had been normal and adaptive rather than shameful, a means of coping with the real hostility and misunderstanding that still exists among the public. We also examined how, for Len, sex and affection were split, the former being associated with what he experienced as negative feelings (lustful excitement; fear of being apprehended and charged by the police; and guilt and shame over a secret part of his life) and the latter with positive ones (appreciation and love from colleagues, friends, and family). Hence his sexuality he had defined as bad, and his self-esteem was poor. Several sessions centred on general building of self-esteem, eliciting from Len 'evidence' of good parts of his life, in which he could feel pride and satisfaction (loving care for his mother; well-established and close relationships with family and friends; a successful career; artistic talents) and reformulating aspects which he saw as bad (redefining his sexual contacts as exciting, albeit short term and difficult; gay sex as healthy and normal, and for some as an expression of a long-term relationship; gay relationships as acceptable, whether short or long term).

At the time Len had attended nine sessions, his mother died. He had never expressed any bitterness or regret over having had his life disrupted by providing full-time care for her over almost three years, but he did need to adjust to a life without her and without paid employment, which he found difficult. We also looked at how she had died with Len never having told her he was gay, but that this information was private rather than hidden by deception.

In twelve further sessions Len began to create more positive beliefs about himself and homosexuality, and to develop a life-style where he felt he was not a fraud nor unfaithful to other gay men who felt able to disclose their sexuality to everyone. He became involved as a voluntary helper at a hospital, initially on general wards and later at a unit for people with AIDS, where he found he was able to mix with other gay people and be completely accepted as gay himself by them and straight people alike. His confidence boosted by this experience, and by reminding him that the one person he had told in the past (Kay) had not rejected him, Len was able to tell several old friends and his sister that he was gay, and was much relieved to find that most had always felt this to be the case. He continued to have brief sexual contact with gay men in public places, and to be worried about the possibility of being arrested, but he had hopes of establishing more regular and private sex via his new network of gay friends. However, he was realistic about how he might never want a partner to share all aspects of his life, and felt he would have no sense of inferiority or inadequacy if he lived his entire life as a single gay man.

Len's story is a good illustration of how internalised homophobia and beliefs about either the necessity to live completely openly as gay or be heterosexual and married may be challenged so that he was able to feel comfortable about his past and present life-style. The difficulties of 'coming out' need to be acknowledged, and a distinction made between what people prefer to keep 'private' rather than 'hidden'. Casual sexual contact may redefined as a pleasure and an acceptable part of a single life-style; celibacy is also 'normal' when contact with short-term partners is difficult. These alternative interpretations about gay life-styles were unlikely to be discussed among Len's social circle; in therapy they became available.

Case study 2: John, bisexuality as 'the worst of both worlds'

John was a 29-year-old man who presented with extreme worries about having been infected with HIV. He reported that his anxiety was so great that he had contemplated suicide. He found it impossible to concentrate at work as a sales executive. He had been to his GP, describing worries about his general health with pressures at work and depression following the break-up with his girlfriend, and had been prescribed antidepressant medication and signed off from work for a month.

John told me that he was bisexual, which he described as 'the worst of both worlds' since he did not feel accepted in either the gay world or straight society. In his early twenties he had sexual relationships with both men and women before living with a girlfriend, Paula, for four years. Paula had moved out of the flat they had shared about eighteen months earlier, but they had remained good friends. Since Paula had left, John had been going to gay clubs and pubs. He had been attracted to a few of the men there. On three occasions he had sex (mutual masturbation) with new partners whom he had met on the same night. Two months previously he had been surprised to meet at the club a man, Phil, who was a married friend of John's parents. They had started talking and Phil had remarked that he was probably going to get a divorce, because it was impossible to stay living with one woman 'as a bisexual man'. Some weeks later, John had felt extremely uncomfortable when his parents told him that Phil had called and they were upset to find that he and his wife were separating. He started to worry about whether his parents would learn that he was bisexual from Phil. In addition, he started to have ruminations about what precisely had happened during his sexual encounters with men from the gay club; these thoughts had plagued him since reading an article in a newspaper which suggested that HIV was much more easily transmitted than had been formerly thought.

John showed the usual pattern of difficulties for someone with an AIDS phobia, and during the first eight sessions the focus was on implementing a structured programme to decrease his obsessive thoughts.[3] Sexual and relationship difficulties commonly underlie fears about AIDS, and John was surprised at my suggestion that we discuss his thoughts and feelings about love, sex, and relationships from the first session. He told me one of his beliefs was that once a man had experience of sexual contact with men and women he would never be satisfied with one or other. Having said this, he reported having been monogamous with Paula without major problems or strong desires to have sex with men until they decided to split up. John liked the idea of family life with children, or at least the situation of living with one long-term partner, male or female. His impression of the gay scene was that a few couples did stay together, but most partnerships did not last. Phil's comments about leaving his wife finally led John to conclude that there is something in the nature of men who have sex with men that means they are incapable of having long-term relationships and, since he was bisexual, this meant that he would always fail to establish a relationship.

John was very rigid in this and other ideas about bisexuality, and it was difficult to encourage him to see things in a different way. He eventually did concede that a four-year relationship with Paula did constitute some degree of 'success' in his terms, but it proved much harder to get him to examine:

a) whether bisexual men were doomed to unhappiness because of some inherent failure to bond with others;
b) whether this bonding in heterosexuals was as ideal as he believed; and
c) whether a long-term one-to-one relationship was necessary to be a fulfilled adult, or even universally desirable or possible given the chances of meeting someone with whom to live so harmoniously.

With many sessions looking at these points, and asking John to 'reality test' his own ideas about heterosexual couples by considering the marriages of friends, he did concede that he had an idealised idea of long-term relationships, and began to consider whether being in a couple was the only acceptable life-style. He saw bisexual men as a more hetero-geneous group and, whilst acknowledging the problems – such as re-jection by some gay and some straight people, felt he could be more open minded about how his life might be in future, whether it involved several male or female partners or a long-term relationship with a man or a woman or even being single and celibate. He was also able to consider whom he should tell about his bisexuality and decide whether this was relevant. He decided not to tell his parents, who were elderly, strictly religious, and very conventional, or his colleagues, with whom he had good business relationships and little social contact, but he did tell his sister, to whom he had always been close. Paula had always known of his past sexual contact with men, and he was able to tell her that he had resumed sexual contact with men, but felt open minded about whether he would establish a long-term involvement with a male or female partner. John's AIDS phobia diminished, and he was even able to discuss with Paula how the advent of AIDS had complicated all sexual relationships – gay, straight, or bisexual.

Like Len, John felt bad about his sexuality and about leading a 'double life' by failing to tell everyone about his sexual orientation: self-hate developed from internalising society's negative view of men who have sex with men, from what he saw as deceiving other people, and from failing to establish a long-term relationship with someone of either sex. Each needed to 'come out' to himself, to feel secure and positive about his sexual orientation, and to find ways of coping with sex and relationships in his particular situation. For both, AIDS had precipitated a crisis which led to them presenting for help – Len had become aware of how many gay men were able to 'come out' through the increase in media coverage of homosexuality and HIV, and had a slight worry about AIDS because of having had sex with men, and John feared actual infection with HIV because of his general life-style and particular sexual encounters. Actual risk of HIV infection was negligible for Len and John, but each had difficulties which pre-dated the advent of HIV and caused them much distress. It is interesting to speculate whether either would have presented for therapy had AIDS services not existed. I suspect not.

THEME 2: THE LURE OF ROMANCE AND THE NEED TO LOOK FOR MR RIGHT

The theme of romance, as an emotional, fulfilling love affair which satisfies all needs, commonly underlies the relationship difficulties of gay and bisexual men. I had encountered the notion of the idealised loving couple as the source of distress among heterosexuals – men and women within established relationships who expected far too much from their partners (believing they should spend all their time together or that their partners should be able to 'know' their needs without discussion), and those who were single and looked forward to life with a partner which would solve all other problems ('love conquering all': financial, work, health, and family difficulties) or attributed all their difficulties to their single status. When I first started working with large numbers of gay clients I was surprised by how similar beliefs were held by many non-heterosexual men. The accounts of Doug and James which follow describe how beliefs about romance were explored within therapy for two gay men in different situations. The core beliefs and 'reality-tested' alternatives of these men are that:

1. Belief 1: 'Initial chemistry' (strong mutual attraction) is indicative of true and lasting love. Challenge 1: Alternatively, this may be a 'honeymoon' period or a time of physically satisfying recreational sex and friendship.
2. Belief 2: Security and confidence result from a long-term relationship. Challenge 2: This may be true, but a love affair is not the sole source of security – work, money, health, family, friends, and other factors are involved in self-assurance.
3. Belief 3: Engaging in intimate sexual acts heralds serious emotional involvement with a partner. Challenge 3: Some people may feel particularly close to partners with whom they have had particular sexual experiences, but there is no universal agreement about what is 'intimate' or about intimate behaviours leading to long-term relationships.

Case study 3: Doug, an 'incurable romantic'

Doug was a 48-year-old man who was referred because of depression following the breakdown of two affairs. He spent a great deal of session time describing how good life had been with Alan, with whom he had lived for ten years. Their respective families knew and generally approved of their relationship, and they had been a well-known and popular couple in the village where they lived. The sexual side of the relationship had become routine and rather unexciting, and they accepted that each had occasional sex with other partners ('an open marriage'). When Alan made a closer emotional attachment to another partner, Doug felt rejected and bitter. The end of the relationship had obviously been as traumatic as any heterosexual divorce.

In the following three years, Doug made strenuous efforts to establish a new relationship, regularly going to gay clubs and saunas, and placing personal advertisements in the gay press. As he looked considerably younger than his age Doug believed that he could still attract attention on the gay scene, and had been optimistic about meeting a new long-term partner. Although quite shocked about how little attention some men paid to HIV, he found sexual contact quite easy to establish, and, since he was usually the older partner, was assertive about minimising risks of infection. He described having had enjoyable sex with a good number of men since leaving Alan ('at least fifty partners'), but was extremely disappointed that most encounters were for only one or a few nights. He would always make it clear where he could be contacted, and plan a next 'date', and he said he was 'devastated' when anyone failed to call or meet as arranged. When this happened, he tended to stay away from the gay scene for a while, instead spending time with family and friends, most of whom were heterosexual, or diverting his energy into work. At work and with some friends Doug kept his sexual orientation private. He said he had no difficulty in doing this, feeling it wise in a career where people had conventional and parochial attitudes. After a few weeks away from the gay scene he would return, again hoping to meet a long-term partner.

Overall, Doug felt he coped well and believed he had sorted out his priorities and needs in a very mature way. He was shocked when he felt depressed after an attachment to a new man, Ray, had ended. When they first met, Doug described a special 'chemistry' between them. Ray had stayed the night and following weekend with Doug, and in the next few months they spent most of their free time together, meeting each other's family and friends and spending few nights apart. They had identical tattoos made on their forearms as concrete markers of the strength of the relationship. Doug had felt sure this was 'the real thing'; he remarked that he felt they had fallen in love just as had happened with Alan so many years before. He described sex with Ray as 'wonderful', and was astonished when Ray did not agree to moving into Doug's flat on a permanent basis. They had argued over this, and Ray had felt it best to end the relationship.

As soon as Doug stopped seeing Ray he felt that he had gone into a deep depression. He had difficulties getting to sleep, ate very little, lost a stone in weight over four weeks, and began to smoke very heavily. His concentration at work was poor, and he started to take days off sick. He complained of having no interest in sex or other men – he felt that only Ray could meet his needs and no one could take his place.

The first few psychology sessions allowed Doug a forum to express his mixed feelings for Ray. He felt extremely disappointed in Ray, but still had strong positive feelings for him. I likened this to the state of bereavement, and encouraged Doug to seek support of his old friends and pleasure in former interests, just as a bereaved person would need to start building a new life whilst still feeling strong attachment to the past. I suggested that Ray's departure probably rekindled some of the feelings Doug had felt after ending the relationship with Alan, and also had a more fundamental effect in rendering Doug 'incomplete', since he seemed to have a very strong belief in the close-coupled state as the best and most natural. He expressed a need for emotional and physical closeness, saying that he felt that he would be unable to feel interested in sex or to achieve erections until he met someone with similar needs. I pointed out that this need not be the case, since he had been able to have satisfactory sex with several men after his affair with Alan ended, and that for many people it is the excitement of a new partner which leads to arousal. In addition, I said that perhaps his time with Ray had only constituted a 'honeymoon' which had possibly ended because Doug had been too hasty in asking Ray to make a long-term commitment. Doug conceded that it was the novelty of sex which was exciting for many people – and even for himself in the past – but he flatly refused to see his four months with Ray as a honeymoon period, claiming that the chemistry between them must have indicated more than this.

Gradually Doug's depression lifted and he began to gain self-confidence. He returned to the gay scene, saying he was cautious but that his interest in sex was returning. I asked him about masturbation, but he felt this a poor substitute for sex with a partner. Doug's mood and libido certainly seemed to improve, but he still had a very firm belief in 'single' life being much inferior to being in an affair.

Within weeks he had met another man, Graham, with whom, he felt, there was 'something special'. Graham had also had a long-term relationship in the past, and was keen to settle down again. He and Doug exchanged rings, and spent most of their time at Graham's house. My reminding Doug of how similarly things had started with Ray was not well received. Within six months this relationship had also ended. Doug initially attributed this to them both having become involved 'on the rebound'. However, after some further sessions examining Doug's beliefs about the natural state being within a couple and about how this was the only fulfilling way to live, he came to see that he idealised the heterosexual married state and had an unrealistic view of how 'chemistry' (strong initial physical attraction) constituted a sign of later compatibility and long-term commitment. He accepted that, just because this had been the case in his one long affair with Alan, it need not be the way in which all relationships developed. By discussing these ideas with friends – some of whom were involved with partners where there had been little or no immediate physical attraction – and considering how others lived happily without a partner, Doug felt better about his current way of life and relieved of the burden of finding a new partner as the only way to future happiness.

The details of Doug's story illustrate well how unrealistic expectations about romance may lead to depression and distress in a mature man who in other ways functions very well. He was quite sure of his gay identity, feeling at ease on the gay scene and with close friends and relatives who knew his sexual orientation, and comfortable with keeping aspects of his life private where he felt it pragmatic to do so. However, Doug had strongly internalised the idealised heterosexual notion of a partnership which is 'perfect' from the first encounter, and will bring meaning and depth to existence, rendering a single person 'whole'. Pain from loss or lack was inevitable when he believed that all strong physical attraction indicated emotional 'chemistry', and that happiness was available only as a partner in a close couple.

Case 4: James, seeking the perfect partner

The fear of being alone, and the idea that a single life-style is somehow indicative of personal inadequacy, is very common and may fuel a person's attempts to find the perfect partner.

James was a 30-year-old gay man who had a highly successful career in advertising. He was extremely worried about having HIV and avoided having a blood test because he was convinced that he would be suicidal if antibody positive, but he repeatedly presented at the GUM clinic for counselling about risks of infection. He was referred for psychology sessions because his anxieties were so great that at times they disrupted his work and social life, and counselling about risks of infection did not lead to any lasting reassurance or behaviour change. Typically, there would be a period of days every few months when he was so worried that he was unable even to leave his flat. Over time, his fears would subside – having telephoned AIDS helplines and HIV clinics for reassurance – and he would feel able to face things again. For James, there was a very clear pattern to his distress. Unlike John's (case 2, above), James's worries did not spiral into chains of obsessive thoughts and compulsive behaviours which exacerbated his fears into an AIDS phobia. Instead, he appeared to be genuinely confident that he would not take risks in future, or that if he had anal intercourse this would be with only one partner within a lasting affair.

Identification of beliefs about sex and love during initial psychology sessions showed how James perceived his behaviour as consistent with his intentions. He enjoyed going to gay clubs and saunas, and described a feeling of elation when he met a new man. He was always quite aware of what he did sexually with others. He was knowledgeable about HIV and knew how to avoid or minimise risks of infection, but he also had a belief that anal intercourse was the most intimate of sexual acts, and further that in intimate relationships concerns about infection were unimportant (the idea of 'love me, love my virus'). Hence, when James met a new partner and had high expectations of the relationship lasting, he would abandon any plans to limit sexual behaviours to safer ones or to limit his emotional involvement to enjoying the encounter at the time.

James repeatedly anticipated a lasting affair if he perceived any positive response from another man. When these short-term encounters ended, he became depressed and then agitated and fearful, as he considered his risk of HIV infection. He not only anticipated appalling illness and death, but also a life which would be inevitably lonely and unfulfilled, since he felt he would be unacceptable to a partner. When fears about HIV abated a little, he felt even more compelled to establish a relationship, and in an attempt to do this and to cheer himself after several days of being alone at home, James would return to the gay scene. Over time, this cycle of thoughts had become even more insidious; in the desperate belief that 'any relationship is better than none', James interpreted even the slightest sexual interest from another man as a potential affair.

Clearly, James was leading a dangerous life-style in terms of both physical and psychological health. Some session time was spent examining his erroneous beliefs about living with HIV and encouraging him to consider the life-styles and coping of friends and acquaintances who had HIV. He acknowledged that HIV was no longer the harbinger of a lonely and terrible existence leading rapidly to a painful death – although two friends had died with AIDS three years earlier, he had several who were leading lives that were full and little changed by HIV, and others who had started new relationships with partners who knew their health status. Later sessions focused on his assumptions about life as a 'couple' and single life-styles. He had lived with a partner for two years, but all other affairs had lasted a maximum of a few months. When asked to consider this two-year relationship, he allowed that, apart from HIV worries, he had been happier since living alone. In fact, of his friends, more were unattached and happy than in good relationships – several couples he knew only stayed together to avoid the effort of starting a new routine in their lives.

After attending sessions for fourteen months, James was much calmer and had broken the chain of thoughts and behaviour which resulted in extreme distress. He remained untested for HIV, but assumed that he was infected. He had less of a dread of HIV-related illness, and intended to attend a specialist clinic if he developed any physical symptoms in future.

The fear of being alone and the idea that a single life-style is somehow indicative of personal inadequacy are very common in both gay and straight people. For James, this fuelled a desperate search for the perfect partner. Despite having been accepted as gay by family, friends, and colleagues when he 'came out' at the age of 22, James felt that true confidence and security were available only from a lasting relationship within which penetrative sex denoted intimacy – an internalisation of the notion that 'phallocentric' sex is required and demanded when there is emotional bonding. James concluded that he felt anal intercourse to be an important part of his gay identity, but he no longer expected that it would lead to a serious affair nor regarded a relationship as the ultimate goal in life.

THEME 3: PERFORMANCE VERSUS ROMANCE – SEX MUST BE SPLIT FROM LOVE

For some men, sex is entirely associated with recreation and has nothing to do with emotional involvement. This may lead to difficulties when they meet a partner for whom sex and love are essentially bound together, or when they desire a long-term relationship but never establish anything further than a very casual encounter. For one gay couple, Tim and Geoff, each held very different ideas about the relationship between love and sex. For Steve, a single gay man, high expectations about sexual excitement and performance seemed to preclude long-term relationships. The main beliefs examined and challenged for these three men are that:

1. Belief 1: Sexual excitement results from novelty. Challenge 1: For some people, sex with a new partner is exciting in itself, but arousal can also result from a regular partner who knows our sexual tastes and preferences.
2. Belief 2: Good sex follows from a good emotional relationship. Challenge 2: Understanding between partners may aid communication, and good communication is a basis for giving and receiving sexual pleasure, but a strong and loving relationship does not guarantee a good sex life.
3. Belief 3: Sex with the same partner becomes dull. Challenge 3: It is normal for sexual interest in a regular partner to fluctuate over time; some couples consciously avoid routine, whilst others decide that an 'open' relationship is a realistic alternative.

Case 5: Tim and Geoff, incompatibility from the sex/love split

Tim, a 46-year-old man with HIV, met Geoff, 38 and also HIV antibody positive, on a gay pride march. They found that they had much in common, being active in different parts of the country in the gay rights movement and in support groups for people with HIV, as well as sharing an interest in art and design. Tim, who came from a wealthy background, had given up paid work except for nominal roles on various company boards and committees, and devoted most of his time to gay and HIV issues. Geoff continued to work, but although very busy felt lonely at home in his large house where he lived alone. After investigating the possibilities for continuing his HIV work from Geoff's home town, Tim moved in with him.

In general, Tim and Geoff lived very happily together. They found that they enjoyed home life, whether by themselves or when friends called; they shared an enthusiasm for developing self-help activities for people with HIV; and had a number of independent interests which allowed a fair degree of time alone. Each felt very warmly for the other, had considered how the future might be if either or both were ill, and, made a commitment to the other. One area in which they differed was in their views of love and sex. For Geoff, sex had never been very satisfactory unless he knew his partner well, and in the past he had lived with a partner in a largely sexually monogamous way. Tim had lived with men, but always in 'open' relationships. For him, sexual arousal was associated with novelty, immediate sexual attraction, and entertainment, and he 'cruised' gay clubs and public areas with the intention of finding new sexual contacts. This discrepancy in sexual style caused enormous problems for the couple; they began to have many arguments, and as they were aware of the psychology service available at the GUM department for people with HIV, referred themselves for couples therapy.

Sessions followed the conventional pattern for 'marital' work in terms of allowing Tim and Geoff some respective time alone, and then a period together with me at the end of each session; however, I did not work with a co-therapist as in some approaches to couples work.

Tim and Geoff were an articulate, very insightful couple who had little or no difficulty in expressing their feelings about their problem. Tim described how he enjoyed physical affection from Geoff, but how he had begun to feel quite repelled by any advances Geoff made because he knew there would be an expectation of sexual contact in which he had no interest. Geoff felt that Tim was thoroughly unreasonable in continuing to link sex with socialising, and felt rejected and hurt by Tim's reactions to his desire for sex and physical closeness. He found it ridiculous that they were in such strong agreement about which sexual acts they preferred – both enjoyed mutual masturbation and oral sex more than anal intercourse, so neither had found safer sex a problem – yet they had such different views about casual sex. A first aim of therapy was to find some short-term compromise to avoid the situation spiralling into anger and frustration which would threaten the relationship. The couple agreed to a 'ban' on any overtly sexual act, and to re-establish physical contact by limiting it to kissing and caressing.

In subsequent sessions we examined Tim's and Geoff's ideas about sex and love, and the underlying beliefs about what sex meant to each. For Tim, sex did not require deep positive emotions towards a partner, only physical attraction; he believed an advantage of a gay life-style to be the honesty and openness about sexual arousal which he had experienced in previous affairs, where sex may have been the basis for starting the relationship but where excitement rapidly waned. However, at times he did question whether he had some fear of intimacy which manifested itself in being unable to commit himself physically in a long-term relationship. Geoff rarely enjoyed sex with a casual partner, and in latter years had had sex only within established relationships. His beliefs directly parallel the heterosexual ideal where sex and love are always bound together, where sex would follow 'naturally' from loving feelings, and any problems with sex indicated some lack of affection. Thus both Tim and Geoff interpreted their current situation as indicative of some personal inadequacy – for Tim, some deficiency in the ability to be intimate, and for Geoff, a lack of physical attractiveness or a personality problem which must underlie Tim's rejection. I suggested that, given the situation led each to feel a threat to self-esteem, it was unsurprising that defensiveness and argument resulted, which in turn made them feel that their relationship was no good and must end.

It was important for Tim and Geoff to reflect on how their ideas about sex had become tastes which had developed from their previous experiences, and that neither held a 'faulty' or 'incorrect' view about sex and love. We looked at how they had each internalised the dominant idea of sexual intimacy as a function of emotional intimacy and maturity – although Tim was aware that this was not the case for him, he felt that perhaps it 'should' be. We discussed how, for both heterosexual and gay couples, sex was not necessarily problem-free if strong emotional ties existed, but that good communication and trust were associated with finding some resolution to any difficulties. Encouraged by this and reassured by their respective expression of commitment and affection for the other, Tim and Geoff gradually introduced mutual masturbation into their physical contact. Although it took some time for Tim to become aroused, and Geoff was disappointed that Tim's erections were not stronger and more frequent, this level of contact did provide some satisfaction for them both.

Further session time was devoted to creating more realistic general beliefs about the future of their relationship. In sum, these addressed that in long-term relationships sex is generally 'adequate' rather than extremely exciting (as Tim had hoped) or intense (as Geoff had expected), hence they aimed for 'good enough' sexual contact and not some idealised performance. They also came to regard sex as only one aspect of their relationship. Tim began to enjoy sex with Geoff as something positive but different in quality from recreational sex with others, and Geoff stopped feeling so rejected and threatened by Tim's casual sexual encounters. The couple stayed together for two further years, until Geoff died from HIV-related illness.

Case 6: Steve, a recluse as a result of recreational sex

Steve was 31 when he started to worry about his future. He was very well informed about HIV and generally kept to safer-sex activities, but since he had taken some risks and had HIV-positive friends who felt reassured by regular support and follow-up by the HIV clinic, he believed he should be tested. Upon finding that he was negative, he did not experience the elation he expected, and he was referred after post-test counselling because of his depressed mood.

Steve lived alone, but generally spent very little time at home. He had a small circle of gay and straight friends, a successful career in teaching, and during evenings and weekends would frequently go to gay clubs and bars. In the past he had enjoyed casual sex; some encounters in his twenties had led to non-sexual friendships, but in later years he had accepted contacts with new men as unlikely to be for more than one evening of physical satisfaction. For over a year though, he had felt increasingly unhappy about these evenings. He was bored with the people at his regular clubs, and by the routine which would follow if someone showed interest in him. He had begun to go to 'cottages' (public lavatories) for sex, where he felt that at least he met men who were not part of the usual scene. If anyone asked to see him again he found himself making excuses to avoid another meeting, and he felt that this was because whenever he had met a partner over several months in the past he had found sex much less exciting. He was worried that he would never make any relationships and would spend his later life alone and lonely.

During his twenties Steve had felt quite happy leading a single life. However, more of his friends seemed to be 'pairing off', and since three friends had been ill with HIV infection he had become increasingly aware of his life passing, of his own ageing, and of 'time running out'. He felt a compulsion to find a regular partner, yet could not conceive of having sex with the same person over time. He also found he was spending more time alone at his flat, and that he actually preferred some evenings at home – reading, listening to music, or watching television – to going out to meet new people. Steve had great fears of never finding a long-term affair, and so becoming a recluse.

For Steve, sex was essentially recreational. However, since he had never experienced sex as part of a long-term relationship, he expected it to remain the same in quality as when two people first met. Whenever sex had been routine, dull, or failed to lead to ejaculation, Steve had stopped seeing a partner or, when he was younger, made it clear that sex would stop and friendship would take over. His beliefs were that a prospective partner should always 'turn him on'; that 'good performance' (achieving erections and orgasms) is essential; and that any decrease in sexual interest in a particular person signals inevitable decline in sexual satisfaction. Basically, Steve felt that sex should always be good, according to his criteria. He was puzzled about how heterosexual or gay couples managed to maintain good sex for longer than a few weeks. Furthermore, although he believed that friends, family, and colleagues tended to perceive him as a warm person, he did not associate sex with affection, and he had never experienced feeling increasing sexual attraction for someone as a result of being emotionally close.

We discussed how these beliefs had developed. Quite simply, Steve's direct experience was based on sex as performance and affection as friendship. However, theoretically at least, Steve assumed that love and sex go together – he expected sexual excitement, novelty, and interest never to wane nor to recover again over time in a long-term relationship. By considering the relationships of his friends he could see that these expectations were unrealistic. He also saw that, despite the emphasis on the heterosexual 'norm' of sexual fidelity within marriage, a range of life-styles was available for his later life – that a 'closed' relationship might develop, where sex and love did coexist, or he might find an open relationship better, or he might continue to live alone. After nine sessions he was more open minded about his future, less worried about a need to find a permanent partner, and had begun to socialise more but saw his solitary interests as merely a change in his tastes rather than heralding isolation and loneliness.

THEME 4: FORBIDDEN REALISM: PRESSURE TO ESTABLISH RELATIONSHIPS

For some people, it is not their own beliefs but the influence of others' ideas which leads to distress. Pressure to find a new partner when a relationship ends may be very high. When a partner dies from HIV-related illness, becoming involved with somebody else may seem to be a good solution, to avoid loneliness, re-establish sexual contact, and give new meaning to life. However, a new relationship is unlikely to remove the pain of the loss, and a new partner may seem a very poor substitute for the dead person who may be idealised in memory as well as realistically remembered as the most important person in the surviving partner's life. To grieve a dead partner may seem poignant and morbid, particularly when the grieving person has HIV or AIDS himself, but perhaps this disturbs the sensibilities of others rather than the mourner, who feels his adjustment is appropriate and necessary. Carl and Andy, described below, were brought together by having in common bereavement of a partner; whilst Dean's situation was that he remained single after the death of his partner, despite concern and pressure from others about spending too much time alone. The beliefs and alternative interpretations used in therapy with these three men were that:

1. Belief 1: Any relationship must be better than none. Challenge 1: In fact being alone is almost certainly preferable to a poor or distressing relationship.
2. Belief 2: To want to live alone and remain celibate is a sign of depression. Challenge 2: Living alone and without sex is just one of a range of normal life-styles, and is particularly common for bereaved people.

Case 7: Carl, content after 'the relationship of a lifetime'

Carl's partner Barry died having been ill with AIDS for two years. They had lived together for eight years, each having had occasional sex with other partners, but with a commitment to their relationship and home life. Carl had HIV infection, but remained fairly well. When Barry died, Carl felt that he had lost the most important relationship of his life, but overall he felt pleased to have known Barry and to have had the life they shared. He expected to live alone in their home until he became more ill himself, when he planned to move nearer to his parents, to whom he was very close. Carl's friends dismissed these plans as morbid for someone of his age, saying that at 33 he was bound to meet another partner. They introduced him to Andy, whose partner had also died with HIV infection.

Carl and Andy got on well. They had experiences in common, having both cared for a partner with AIDS, and they enjoyed each other's company. Friends suggested that they lived together, particularly as Carl had given up work when he looked after Barry, Andy did part-time work because of fatigue associated with HIV infection, and each found it difficult to manage on a reduced income. Andy moved into the flat which Carl and Barry had shared. Almost immediately, Carl found Andy's presence irritating – he had adjusted to having time and space to himself – and after seven months things had become so bad that the couple had arguments which usually led to physical violence. They were referred for relationship therapy.

In individual and joint psychology sessions, Carl and Andy expressed their disappointment over the outcome of their living together. They had both felt that finding each other had been the solution to their problems. They acknowledged that they were comforted by the sexual and emotional content of the relationship, but that living together had been a mistake. Carl knew that he idealised his life with Barry, but by virtue of the length of time of the involvement alone, knew that a few months with Andy could not compare with the years of happiness with Barry. Carl and Andy were annoyed that friends still maintained that they should live together and that any relationship must be better than living alone, but they both felt that they needed to live independently.

Despite major practical problems, Andy moved to separate accommodation. He and Carl continued to meet and to have occasional sexual contact, but they felt that an essentially single life, with a friendship which included occasional sex, was far preferable to remaining a couple. Each was then allowed his private grief and adjustment to the death of a partner.

Case 8: Dean, satisfied with celibacy

Dean, a 26-year-old West Indian, had a similar experience. After his partner Dave died with AIDS, Dean rarely went to the clubs and bars where they had been well known as a local couple, even though they had never lived together. Dean felt that he needed to spend time alone or with his family. His mother, who had never understood how men could love or be sexually attracted to each other, and believed men to be 'naturally promiscuous', requiring high numbers of female sexual partners, hoped that Dave's death would lead to Dean's 'conversion' to heterosexuality. Dean described her as having 'typically West Indian' attitudes to men, and wanted time to talk with her about his sexuality, the effects of Dave's death, and the possibility of his own death from AIDS. His sisters were understanding and supportive, and he felt that he was becoming closer to his mother, and that he would be cared for by his family when his illness progressed. His friends, however, were very worried; they felt that a celibate life with little socialising was no existence for a young gay man. They continually encouraged him to accompany them to nightclubs and parties, and the three gay men with whom Dean shared a house would never allow him to spend more than a few hours alone in his room. They believed he must be depressed, and it had been at their suggestion Dean had referred himself for psychological support.

I found Dean quietly responsive. He seemed appropriately sad for someone adjusting to life without a close partner. He was realistic about his future – he had begun to develop chronic symptoms of HIV infection such as weight loss and fatigue, and because his energy level demanded that he rested in the day and slept for at least ten hours at night, he had no desire to go to clubs or parties. Dean did feel he was influenced by his friends' and even his mother's beliefs about a man needing sexual contact, but only in so far as he was beginning to believe he was abnormal for feeling satisfied with his current life-style. He became more assertive in expressing his preference for time with his family, and gradually his friends accepted that Dean was well aware of his own needs, rather than identifying these for him. Dean attended eight sessions, largely for bereavement therapy, before dying at home with his mother and sisters.

CONCLUSION

The therapeutic interventions I have used with gay and bisexual men were developed from the cognitive approach most widely applied to work with heterosexuals, outlined by Baker in Chapter 5 of this volume. Although I have found themes which commonly occur with gay men – four of which are identified in the sections above – these are used here to illustrate the application of largely cognitive techniques in a 'gay affirmative' manner. Essentially, the interventions are no different from those with any client – assessment of problems is followed by therapy which helps individuals to function without feeling overwhelmed by emotions or events, builds self-esteem, and increases the likelihood of coping in their particular situation. However, the themes do show that the expectation to be entirely happy and fulfilled via a sexual relationship is both pervasive and persuasive in society, for straight and non-heterosexual people. Many people seem to feel a burden of responsibility to be happy (in a one-to-one relationship) and successful (in sex), and hold notions which are bound to lead to disappointment and dissatisfaction, such as:

- love and sex are always bound together: good love must lead to good sex, and vice versa, and hence any problem with one denotes a problem with the other;
- romantic love and sex provide the most fulfilling human experiences; therefore it is abnormal to feel strongly about non-romantic attachments or behaviours other than sex which can only be poor substitutes or 'stop gaps' to fill the interim until 'true' love and sex are found;
- love conquers all; so the search to find 'the real thing' is worthwhile, since a partner should solve all life problems;
- sex is the ultimate pleasure, far surpassing all others, and if it fails to be this way, there must be something wrong with the acts, the feelings, or the adjustment of the individual or the partner;
- a relationship or affair should meet all our needs, and, when this fails to be the case, the search for a more adequate partner is necessary.

The distinctive aspect of work with gay and bisexual men is the necessity to be aware of notions about the inherent 'goodness' of long-term hetero-sexual relationships and 'inferiority' of men who have sex with men, which may be internalised by the therapist and the patient. If therapists and clients work to rid themselves of homophobia (and, in fact, lose the fear of anyone with an alternative life-style – such as that of the single, childless, multi-partnered, or celibate – of being inferior to the idealised, phallocentric, heterosexual 'norm') conventional psychological ap-proaches can certainly be successfully applied to men who have sex with men (and to other marginalised client groups).

NOTES

1 Throughout this chapter, the terms 'patient(s)' and 'client(s)' are used inter-changeably to denote person(s) attending services.
2 People attending for HIV testing present for a variety of reasons. Some experi-ence physical symptoms which they believe to be related to HIV infection. Others have engaged in acts which they believe would expose them to the virus, or have nagging doubts and worries about having been infected – not by any particular behaviour but because of their life-style – and these thoughts play on their minds to the point of obsessions, disrupting their everyday functioning. Those who decide to take the test and are found positive usually continue to attend for several sessions of counselling from a health adviser or HIV counsellor. People who are particularly distressed when found negative or positive, or when they first present to discuss testing, are referred for more intensive psychological interventions, and many GUM clinics have developed close links with clinical psychologists to meet this need. As a minimum, counselling services have been provided in GUM departments to help people cope with the expected issues and possible crises which arise when they first present for HIV testing (pre-test counselling) and when, if they decide to take the test, they return for the negative or positive test result (post-test coun-selling). A full description of the development of pre- and post-test counselling services is given in Miller, Green, and McCreaner (1986) and Bond (1991).
3 Characteristics of AIDS-phobic and 'worried-well' people have been well defined and interventions tend to follow cognitive-behavioural approaches to obsessive-compulsive disorders (Green and George, 1988; Hedge et al., 1988; Miller et al., 1988; Hedge and Acton, 1989).

REFERENCES

Altman, D. (1988) 'Legitimation through disaster: AIDS and the gay movement', in E. Fee and D.M. Fox (eds) AIDS: The Burdens of History, University of California Press.
Beck, A.T. (1976) Cognitive Therapy and the Emotional Disorders, New York: Inter-national Universities Press
Beck, A.T. (1989) Love is Never Enough, Harmondsworth: Penguin.
Bond, T. (1991) HIV Counselling: Report on National Survey and Consultation 1990, Rugby: British Association for Counselling.

Casper, E. (1986) 'AIDS: a psychosocial perspective', in D.A. Feldman and T.M. Johnson (eds) *The Social Dimensions of AIDS*, New York: Praeger.

Cole, M. (1988) 'Sex therapy for individuals', in M. Cole and W. Dryden (eds) *Sex Therapy in Britain*, Milton Keynes: Open University Press.

Cooper, G.F. (1988) 'The psychological methods of sex therapy', in M. Cole and W. Dryden (eds) *Sex Therapy in Britain*, Milton Keynes: Open University Press.

Croteau, J.M. and Morgan, S. (1989) 'Combatting homophobia in AIDS education', *Journal of Counselling and Development* 68: 86–91.

Crowe, M. and Ridley, J. (1990) *Therapy with Couples*, Oxford: Blackwell.

Davies, P. (1989) 'Some notes on the structure of homosexual acts', in P. Aggleton, G. Hart, and P. Davies (eds) *AIDS: Social Representations, Social Practices*, London: Falmer Press.

Davis, H. and Fallowfield, L. (1991) *Counselling and Communication in Health Care*, Chichester: Wiley.

Davison, G.C. (1976) 'Homosexuality: the ethical challenge', *Journal of Consulting and Clinical Psychology* 44: 157–62.

Douglas, C.J., Kalman, C.M., and Kalman, T.P. (1985) 'Homophobia among physicians and nurses: an empirical study', *Hospital and Community Psychiatry* 36: 1309–11.

Ellis, A. (1962) *Reason and Emotion in Psychotherapy*, New York: Lyle Stuart.

Fitzpatrick, R., McLean, J., Boulton, M., Hart, G., and Dawson, J. (1990) 'Variation in sexual behaviour in gay men', in P. Aggleton, P. Davies, and G. Hart (eds) *AIDS: Individual, Cultural and Policy Dimensions*, London: Falmer Press.

George, H. (1988) 'Sexual problems among people referred for AIDS counselling', paper given at British Psychological Society Annual Conference, St Andrews, March.

George, H. (1989) 'AIDS counselling: psychological problems in sexual and marital relationships', paper given at Association of Sexual and Marital Therapists Conference, Birmingham, September.

George, H. (1990) 'Sexual and relationships problems among people affected by AIDS: three case studies', *Counselling Psychology Quarterly* 3: 389–99.

Gordon, P. (1988) 'Sex therapy with gay men', in M. Cole and W. Dryden (eds) *Sex Therapy in Britain*, Milton Keynes: Open University Press.

Green, J. and George, H. (1988) 'Characteristics and treatment of highly distressed worried well', paper given at the IVth International Conference on AIDS, Stockholm, June.

Hart, J. (1984) *So You Think You're Attracted to the Same Sex?'*, Harmondsworth: Penguin.

Hedge, B. and Acton, T. (1989) 'Specific cognitive-behavioural interventions in a genito-urinary medicine clinic', paper given at the International Conference on Health Psychology, Cardiff, September.

Hedge, B., Acton, T., and Miller, D. (1988) 'The worried well: a cognitive-behavioural approach', paper given at the IVth International Conference on AIDS, Stockholm, June.

Jehu, D. (1979) *Sexual Dysfunction*, Chichester: Wiley.

Kaplan, H.S. (1974) *The New Sex Therapy*, New York: Brunner/Mazel.

MacKinnon, L. and Miller, D. (1985) 'The sexual component in family therapy: a feminist critique', in *Feminist Perspectives on Social Work and Human Sexuality*, New York: Haworth Press.

Masters, W.H. and Johnson, V.E. (1970) *Human Sexual Inadequacy*, Boston: Little, Brown & Co.

Mearns, C. (1990) 'Starting work in HIV and AIDS', *Clinical Psychology Forum* 28: 21–5.

Meichenbaum, D.H. (1977) *Cognitive-Behaviour Modification*, New York: Plenum Press.

Miller, D., Green, J., and McCreaner, A. (1986) 'Organising a counselling service for problems related to acquired immune deficiency syndrome (AIDS)', *Genito-urinary Medicine* 62: 116.

Miller, D., Weber, J., and Green, J. (1986) *The Management of AIDS Patients*, London: Macmillan.

Miller, D., Acton, T., and Hedge, B. (1988) 'The worried well: their identification and management', *Journal of the Royal College of Physicians of London* 22: 158–65.

Nowinski, P. (1989) *A Lifelong Love Affair*, Wellingborough: Thorsons.

O'Rourke, M. (1989) 'Psychological service development within genito-urinary medicine', paper given at International Conference on Health Psychology, Cardiff, September.

Stein, T.S. (1988) 'Theoretical considerations in psychotherapy with gay men and lesbians', *Journal of Homosexuality* 15(2): 75–95.

Ussher, J.M. (1991) 'Family and couples therapy with gay and lesbian clients: acknowledging the forgotten minority', *Journal of Family Therapy* 13: 131–48.

Wallack, J.J. (1989) 'AIDS anxiety among health care professionals', *Hospital and Community Psychiatry* 40: 507–10.

Yaffe, M. and Fenwick, E. (1988) *Sexual Happiness for Men*, London: Dorling Kindersley.

Zilbergeld, B. (1980) *Men and Sex*, Glasgow: Fontana Collins.

Name index

Subject index